Other Books of Related Interest in the Opposing
Viewpoints Series:

CIVIL LIBERTIES

OPPOSING VIEWPOINTS®

David L. Bender & Bruno Leone, *Series Editors*

Charles P. Cozic, *Book Editor*

OPPOSING
VIEWPOINTS
SERIES®

Greenhaven Press, Inc.   PO Box 289009   San Diego, CA 92198-9009

Library of Congress Cataloging-in-Publication Data

Civil liberties : opposing viewpoints / Charles P. Cozic,
    book editor.
        p.   cm. — (Opposing viewpoints series)
    Includes bibliographical references and index.
    Summary: Presents opposing viewpoints on issues relating to
civil liberties, including privacy, freedom of the press, and
censorship.
    ISBN 1-56510-058-1 (lib. bdg. : acid-free paper) —
ISBN 1-56510-057-3 (pbk. : acid-free paper)
    1. Civil rights—United States. [1. Civil rights.] I. Cozic,
Charles P., 1957-   . II. Series: Opposing viewpoints series
(Unnumbered)
JC599.U5C549   1994
323'.0973—dc20   93-16419
                                                               CIP
                                                                AC

Copyright © 1994 by Greenhaven Press, Inc.
Printed in the U.S.A.

"Congress shall make no law . . . abridging the freedom of speech, or of the press."

First Amendment to the U.S. Constitution

The basic foundation of our democracy is the first amendment guarantee of freedom of expression. The Opposing Viewpoints Series is dedicated to the concept of this basic freedom and the idea that it is more important to practice it than to enshrine it.

Contents

Chapter 3: Should Church and State Be Separate?

Chapter 4: How Can Civil Liberties Be Protected?

Why Consider Opposing Viewpoints?

"The only way in which a human being can make some approach to knowing the whole of a subject is by hearing what can be said about it by persons of every variety of opinion and studying all modes in which it can be looked at by every character of mind. No wise man ever acquired his wisdom in any mode but this."

John Stuart Mill

In our media-intensive culture it is not difficult to find differing opinions. Thousands of newspapers and magazines and dozens of radio and television talk shows resound with differing points of view. The difficulty lies in deciding which opinion to agree with and which "experts" seem the most credible. The more inundated we become with differing opinions and claims, the more essential it is to hone critical reading and thinking skills to evaluate these ideas. Opposing Viewpoints books address this problem directly by presenting stimulating debates that can be used to enhance and teach these skills. The varied opinions contained in each book examine many different aspects of a single issue. While examining these conveniently edited opposing views, readers can develop critical thinking skills such as the ability to compare and contrast authors' credibility, facts, argumentation styles, use of persuasive techniques, and other stylistic tools. In short, the Opposing Viewpoints Series is an ideal way to attain the higher-level thinking and reading skills so essential in a culture of diverse and contradictory opinions.

In addition to providing a tool for critical thinking, Opposing Viewpoints books challenge readers to question their own strongly held opinions and assumptions. Most people form their opinions on the basis of upbringing, peer pressure, and personal, cultural, or professional bias. By reading carefully balanced opposing views, readers must directly confront new ideas as well as the opinions of those with whom they disagree. This is not to simplistically argue that everyone who reads opposing views will—or should—change his or her opinion. Instead, the series enhances readers' depth of understanding of their own views by encouraging confrontation with opposing ideas. Careful examination of others' views can lead to the readers' understanding of the logical inconsistencies in their own opinions, perspective on why they hold an opinion, and the consideration of the possibility that their opinion requires further evaluation.

Evaluating Other Opinions

To ensure that this type of examination occurs, Opposing Viewpoints books present all types of opinions. Prominent spokespeople on different sides of each issue as well as well-known professionals from many disciplines challenge the reader. An additional goal of the series is to provide a forum for other, less known, or even unpopular viewpoints. The opinion of an ordinary person who has had to make the decision to cut off life support from a terminally ill relative, for example, may be just as valuable and provide just as much insight as a medical ethicist's professional opinion. The editors have two additional purposes in including these less known views. One, the editors encourage readers to respect others' opinions—even when not enhanced by professional credibility. It is only by reading or listening to and objectively evaluating others' ideas that one can determine whether they are worthy of consideration. Two, the inclusion of such viewpoints encourages the important critical thinking skill of objectively evaluating an author's credentials and bias. This evaluation will illuminate an author's reasons for taking a particular stance on an issue and will aid in readers' evaluation of the author's ideas.

As series editors of the Opposing Viewpoints Series, it is our hope that these books will give readers a deeper understanding of the issues debated and an appreciation of the complexity of even seemingly simple issues when good and honest people disagree. This awareness is particularly important in a democratic society such as ours in which people enter into public debate to determine the common good. Those with whom one disagrees should not be regarded as enemies but rather as people whose views deserve careful examination and may shed light on one's own.

Thomas Jefferson once said that "difference of opinion leads to inquiry, and inquiry to truth." Jefferson, a broadly educated man, argued that "if a nation expects to be ignorant and free . . . it expects what never was and never will be." As individuals and as a nation, it is imperative that we consider the opinions of others and examine them with skill and discernment. The Opposing Viewpoints Series is intended to help readers achieve this goal.

David L. Bender & Bruno Leone,
Series Editors

Introduction

*"Free speech is worth nothing unless it includes a
full franchise to be foolish and even . . .
malicious."*

H.L. Mencken, *My Life as Author and Editor*, 1993.

*"Abuses of speech are as eligible for legislative
control as any other destructive acts."*

Joseph Sobran, *Conservative Chronicle*, June 27, 1990.

America thrives on an open exchange of ideas and opinions.
In the halls of Congress, in the mass media, and in public
protests, freedom of speech is vigorously exercised, often heat-
edly. Those exercising their right to free speech, however, sometimes offend or harm others with their actions and expressions.

Rock or rap singers, for example, have been attacked for their
explicit lyrics that graphically describe promiscuous or exploitive sex or gratuitous violence. Many Americans oppose the
negative messages that they believe encourage impressionable
young listeners to act promiscuously or to become violent.

In 1992, for example, many police officers and others became
outraged over the lyrics to "Cop Killer" a song released by the
group Body Count and its lead singer Ice-T, whose rap and rock
recordings have sold millions of copies and are popular among
adolescents and young adults. In "Cop Killer," Ice-T states: "I'm
'bout to bust some shots off. I'm 'bout to dust some cops
off. . . . Die, die, die pig, die!" Critics asserted that such lyrics
would incite listeners—especially those who perceived police as
representative of oppression and authority—to harm or kill police officers. Doug Elder, president of the Houston Police
Officers Association, predicted that "Cop Killer" would "unleash
a reign of terror on communities all across the country." Other
critics, such as the editors of the *New Republic*, argued that, although the lyrics were meant to entertain, they also had the
power to harm: "None of the bullets of American popular music, Body Count's included, is real. But symbols are real, which
is why they influence thought, which influences behavior."
These critics believe that words and images, including the lyrics
of popular songs, have the power to motivate people to act—in

this case, to act violently.

Some people, however, including many in the music industry, saw the harm not in Ice-T's lyrics, but in the attempt to censor them. These supporters (including some who found Ice-T's lyrics vile), rushed to defend the singer's free-speech rights, arguing that the consequences of censorship were much more dangerous than inflammatory words. As *Rolling Stone* senior writer Alan Light wrote, "Far worse than anything Ice-T or any other rapper has ever said is the prospect that someone else might decide what they can or can't say." Ice-T's supporters maintained that permitting one type of speech to be censored makes it easier to censor other forms of speech, thus eroding a basic civil liberty. They also reject the idea that words and images can influence actions, arguing, for example, that the vast majority of youths who see acts of violence in movies never commit similar violence.

This battle over song lyrics exemplifies the difficulty in balancing an individual's right to exercise a civil liberty—be it freedom of speech, freedom of religion, or freedom of the press—against society's right to be protected from harm. *Civil Liberties: Opposing Viewpoints* examines this dilemma and explores other civil liberties issues in the following chapters: How Should the Right to Privacy Be Defined? Should Freedom of Expression Be Restricted? How Separate Should Church and State Be? How Can Civil Liberties Be Protected?

America's system of democracy, a model for other nations, is inconceivable without individual rights. But as important as these rights are, many Americans believe that the rights of the individual are being promoted over the interests and values of society as a whole. Clearly, the two must be balanced, for, as *Commonweal* columnist John Garvey states, "The rights of the individual and the community . . . both matter so much that no one can claim a final victory. When either wins finally, something essential is crushed."

How Should the Right to Privacy Be Defined?

Chapter Preface

Although the U.S. Constitution does not mention the word "privacy" or specifically refer to such a right, the right to privacy and what it means has been debated for more than one hundred years in U.S. courts. As a young Boston lawyer in 1890, U.S. Supreme Court justice Louis D. Brandeis cowrote a landmark *Harvard Law Review* article titled "The Right to Privacy," advocating that "the right to life has come to mean the right to enjoy life—the right to be let alone." This broad definition of the right to privacy, however, has been challenged by other legal scholars.

This "right to be let alone"—to be free to make decisions, including life and death decisions, without harassment or intrusion—has acquired notable legal status since the turn of the century. One controversial privacy case was the 1973 *Roe v. Wade* decision in which the U.S. Supreme Court determined that abortion is a private decision that women must be allowed to make. Today, similar recognition is desired by Americans who believe that the "right to die"—to end pain and suffering from serious illnesses—is also included in the right to privacy.

Many Americans, however, believe that the right to privacy has been defined too broadly. They argue that actions such as abortion and euthanasia are not private decisions because they affect people other than the one making the decision—the unborn child, for example, in the case of abortion. These Americans especially oppose abortion and euthanasia as rights, believing that these practices involve the immoral taking of human life. Fordham University law professor Robert Byrn states, "Until recently the right of privacy incorporated traditional Christian values; it had a high moral content. Courts have callously redefined the right and have moralized perversions and demoralized the law."

Those on both sides of the debate agree that privacy is a valuable right. They disagree, however, on what issues this right can and should be applied to. The authors in the following chapter address the right to privacy and how it should be defined.

"The importance of privacy as a value is tied to the importance of autonomy as a fundamental end of democratic legal institutions. "

The Right to Privacy Should Be Extensive

Vincent J. Samar

Most Americans cherish their individual privacy and many laws exist to protect it. In the following viewpoint, Vincent J. Samar argues that the right to privacy is crucial to democratic institutions because it maximizes personal autonomy and the freedom to discover one's interests. Samar contends that while the right to privacy is not absolute, it should be as broad as possible without limiting autonomy. Samar is an attorney and gay-rights activist in Chicago and a visiting assistant professor of philosophy at Loyola University in Chicago.

As you read, consider the following questions:

1. Why is privacy a necessary condition for the possibility of autonomy, according to Samar?
2. In Samar's opinion, how do privacy and autonomy differ?
3. Why does the author believe that the possession of personal information could threaten privacy and autonomy?

From Vincent J. Samar, *The Right to Privacy: Gays, Lesbians, and the Constitution,* © 1991 by Temple University. Reprinted by permission of Temple University Press.

The justification of the right to privacy depends on a peculiar relationship of the four concepts of privacy, individual autonomy, democratic government, and other fundamental ends. The feature that distinguishes democratic government from other forms of government is that individual autonomy is one of its fundamental ends. Therefore, under a democratic government, the protection of certain acts is justified in order to foster individual autonomy.

Perhaps it will be objected that although autonomy might be a hoped for result from democracy, since democracy may be justified in many other ways (as productive of happiness or peace or as an application of sovereignty), it is by no means necessary that autonomy be produced. Consequently, it may very well be that democracy does not produce autonomy.

Two Sides of Autonomy

This objection assumes, however, that autonomy (like privacy) is necessarily a form of negative freedom or freedom from certain kinds of interferences. But this is not true. As will be made clear below, autonomy in the context of Western democratic institutions has elements of both positive and negative freedom. The positive side of autonomy is related to the very quality Western democracy is supposed to promote, namely, self-rule. In contrast, the negative side is related to self-rule by making the conditions for it possible. The difference between the two is that while the positive freedom is logically connected to self-rule, the negative freedom operates by a causal connection. Hence, it cannot be said on either score that democracy does not produce autonomy.

Still, the protection afforded autonomy is not absolute, because democratic government is a species of government in general, which means that it has to fulfill all other fundamental ends of government, such as providing an economic system for the exchange of goods and services. Consequently, the permissible extent to which protection will be afforded autonomous acts is the maximum consistent with the promotion of other fundamental ends of government. Privacy is the criterion to determine which autonomous acts government can or can not proscribe. In this sense, privacy is not the same as autonomy because there are many acts that people can perform autonomously that are not private and that government can, therefore, proscribe. Privacy does reduce to autonomy, however, in the sense that those acts that government will protect are privacy acts with respect to the citizens at large. . . .

Related to private acts is the idea of a private state of affairs. The connection to autonomy, which again is causal, is made by providing a place or situation where private acts can occur. For instance, the privacy of one's home is protected because the home is recognized as a place where private acts should be able to occur.

Democracies Value Privacy

From the above discussion, it follows that privacy is valued by democratic institutions for two reasons. First, it is a sort of boundary marker setting out the area wherein an individual's actions are thought (at least in the first instance) to affect only that individual. Second, it is a means for making possible private actions. In these ways, privacy allows for the possibility of autonomy by delimiting those human actions, information, and states of affairs that prima facie should not be interfered with. In this sense, then, privacy is connected to democratic institutions, namely, in making the object for which the institutions are valued (i.e., autonomy of the individual) possible. Thus, the importance of privacy as a value is tied to the importance of autonomy as a fundamental end of democratic legal institutions. Just how important a value privacy is will be made clear below.

Protecting Personal Information and Decisions

To many people, privacy means the right to be left alone—for example, to walk or drive *in public* without being stopped by police. But it also signifies the right to do things in private—that is, without the presence of others. An extension of this aspect of privacy is the desire to keep information about oneself from other people—whether it is illegal activity, delicate medical conditions, family history, or school grades. Finally, the courts have used the term to cover the power to make key personal decisions on one's own.

Eric Neisser, *Recapturing the Spirit*, 1991.

Here it might be questioned whether one needs to protect private information or private states of affairs at all. It might be argued that autonomy can be protected merely by prohibiting interferences (that is, physical attacks or invasions or obstructions) of one's self or one's actions. Privacy, in the sense that it applies to information, does not limit interference only with one's self or one's actions. It also, and one is tempted to say, most characteristically, limits observation of one's self or one's actions. While it is clear how interference limits privacy, it is not so clear how observation or the possession of personal information does. For example, is one's autonomy limited by a Peeping Tom who watches one in the shower? Well, one might,

19

because of shyness, stop taking showers, and that would be a limit to autonomy. But what would be the cause of this limit? Arguably, the cause is shyness (not the observer); one would be more autonomous by overcoming the shyness and concern about being watched. From this, it follows that a government that wants to foster maximal autonomy might best proceed by not catering to shyness with a privacy right, and the same would hold true to unpopular (but legal) actions one might shy away from doing because of fear of adverse public opinion. Indeed, the point becomes stronger if we assume there are laws prohibiting the physical invasion of body or property that directly block people's autonomous actions.

Recall, however, previous arguments. First, to maximize autonomy, we need to protect private acts. This is logically required once we treat autonomy as a value. Second, to protect private acts, we need to protect certain information and states of affairs. This is causally required depending on the society in which one lives. The question is, does protecting certain information and states of affairs contradict maximizing autonomy? Not necessarily, depending on the way people actually view themselves in society. If people will in fact be inhibited if certain information becomes known or certain states of affairs are not protected, then not to protect these things would be to inhibit autonomy. . . .

The Value of Privacy

Now that we have established the connection between the value of privacy and autonomy, the question arises: What is the degree of protection of the privacy norm? Here it is important to recall that privacy is valued because autonomy is valued, and privacy is conceived either as part of autonomy or (at least in this world) as a necessary precondition for autonomy. Furthermore, given that democratic institutions are established to effect certain ends, to the extent that autonomy is valued as an end of such institutions, privacy must be similarly valued.

Indeed, this is the key to answering the question, namely, that there are only two circumstances in which privacy must be sacrificed in a democracy. The first occurs when a competing right is in conflict with the right to privacy and the circumstances are such that autonomy is better served by protecting the competing right. The second occurs when the government seeks to protect an interest that is more compelling than privacy to the preservation of autonomy in general. Still, privacy provides the default position if the government is unable to establish its compelling interest. Otherwise, privacy regulates the degree of the state's intrusion to the minimum necessary to satisfy the state's compelling interest. . . .

Like Richard Mohr, I feel that privacy is an implicit constitutional right. Unlike Mohr, however, I consider political morality in that I conceive of privacy in relation to autonomy, democracy, and other fundamental ends of government and not just in relationship to explicit constitutional guarantees. In this regard, I produce a justification for privacy that grounds private acts in a broad principle of autonomy a priori and private information and states of affairs in the very structure of democratic government a posteriori. That this bears resemblance to the United States is incidental, for as I have argued above, privacy should be part of any democratic society that had autonomy as one of its fundamental ends.

"The generalization of the right of privacy . . . is destructive of the very values it is designed to uphold. "

The Right to Privacy Should Be Limited

Morton A. Kaplan

A broad right to privacy harms institutions such as the family because this right defies valuable social sanctions against immoral behavior, Morton A. Kaplan argues in the following viewpoint. Kaplan maintains, for example, that dangerous acts such as drug abuse or promiscuity are often committed under the protection of the right to privacy. Kaplan states that this right sanctions immoral acts as acceptable and threatens the foundation of society. Kaplan is the editor and publisher of the *World & I*, a monthly publication covering current events, science, and the arts.

As you read, consider the following questions:

1. Why does society view the right to privacy as positive, in Kaplan's opinion?
2. Why does Kaplan disagree with the right to do anything that does not harm others?
3. According to the author, how does a lack of constraints on behavior erode one's sense of identity?

From Morton A. Kaplan, "The Right to Be Left Alone Is a Right to Be No One." This article appeared in the September 1990 issue and is reprinted with permission from *The World & I*, a publication of the Washington Times Corporation, © 1990.

The "right to be left alone" is counterproductive as a generalized doctrine, a fault that can be attributed to its abstract treatment of freedom of choice. It fails to come to terms with the complex interrelationships between self and society that make the concept of individual choice meaningful. Hence, rather than supporting, it undermines, and in extremis would dissolve, that individual autonomy and human freedom it attempts to serve. In effect, it would serve no one, for the self—the subject of ethical discourse—that freedom serves would be minimized.

Right to Privacy Can Be Destructive

The doctrine of the "right to be left alone" is dangerously seductive because we tend to restrict our attention to the many instances of freedom of choice that enhance human life in our society. There are clear and convincing reasons to support the "right to be left alone" within some limits, and those limits are less restrictive in a pluralistic society such as ours than in a more culturally homogeneous society.

The rules that governed a more parochial America—for instance, the criminal adultery law under which a Wisconsin married woman was recently convicted—cannot be imposed without social warfare on contemporary Americans. Because such rules remain important to such important institutions as the family, we must rely on social sanctions to preserve institutional strength. However, we threaten these and other vital institutions gravely if we transform the "right to be left alone" into a generalized constitutional doctrine.

The doctrine that we should be free to do those things that do not harm others, put forth by John Stuart Mill, fails to do justice to how identifications and conceptions of self develop within societies. And it misunderstands how the human mind works in solving problems. Because Mill misunderstood these processes, he also failed to understand that the generalization of the right of privacy—in his terms, the right to do anything that does not harm others—is destructive of the very values it is designed to uphold.

In making my argument, I shall neglect some obvious cases of harm to others that arise under the doctrine. Excessive drinking or smoking, the taking of mind-altering drugs, and homosexual anal sex, for instance, impose huge costs on society in terms of medical costs and lost productivity. But these huge financial costs—possibly more than sufficient to balance the budget or pay for important capital programs—pale into insignificance when weighed against other costs that are imposed. . . .

Harmful Activities

It is highly likely that many of the asocial and antisocial activities of the current period—including drugs and widespread dishonesty—are caused in part by the philosophy that underlies the concept of a generalized right of privacy. And when standards erode to this point, the very conception of the absence of, or even the capability to conceive of, direct harm to others will be seriously diminished.

For instance, at what point does consensual sadism weaken the barriers against nonconsensual sadism? Are pictures of bullwhips in anuses or adults urinating into each other's mouths, as in the Mapplethorpe exhibit, really harmless? Even if these activities occur behind private walls, the effects might become significant if it becomes widely known that they occur and are permissible. This is even more true if they win awards and are regarded highly. If one wanted to break down the minds of other individuals, would not a barrage of material of this type, or knowledge about it, be effective? What does it say of a society that so many of the elite defend or even stage such exhibits?

Moreover, continued experimentation of this kind is likely to break down the personalities that engage in these actions. The Marquis de Sade, apart from the harm he did to others, did harm to his own personality. He transformed it in dysfunctional ways by exercising his "freedom" of choice. . . .

A Right to Invade Privacy

"Privacy" is a broad, abstract and ambiguous concept which can easily be shrunken in meaning but which can also, on the other hand, easily be interpreted as a constitutional ban against many things other than searches and seizures. . . . For these reasons I get nowhere in this case by talk about a constitutional "right of privacy" as an emanation from one or more constitutional provisions. I like my privacy as well as the next one, but I am nevertheless compelled to admit that government has a right to invade it unless prohibited by some specific constitutional provision.

Hugo Black, dissenting in *Griswold v. Connecticut*, 1965.

It is undemocratic for the Supreme Court to recognize a new right of privacy while it still lacks predominant and sustained support, let alone while it remains a minority point of view. Even if the justices of the Supreme Court had the qualities of Plato's guardians—and it is painfully obvious that they lack the requisite social and political knowledge and philosophical skills—it would be a mistake for the Court to play this role. Even Plato's philosopher kings would succumb to the heady wine of power and, like autocrats, would lose their own bearing. Because no rules would guide their decisions, other than the rule to produce the best results, they would be driven to extreme and idiosyncratic invention by the lack of context for their judgments.

It is immoral to accelerate these dangerous tendencies by "legitimating" them—and this is particularly the case when the legitimation is in the form of a general principle—by, in effect, proclaiming the philosophy of flower children as the law of the land. Instead, the emphasis of the Court should be on slowing down precipitate legislative change. . . .

From a moral standpoint, we do owe respect to the opinions of others. But that respect is limited by our mutual obligation to observe boundaries that have a reasonable relationship to the needs of the society and of the individuals in it.

Individual and Society

As one who likes to do things my own way, I am sympathetic to the concept of being "left alone." In the best society internal inhibition would be the chief means for regulating individual conduct. I surely do not wish to see individuals reduced to creatures of either state or society in which conformity to generalized mediocrity becomes the rule.

But we also need to recognize that voluntary inhibitions often are insufficient. The concept of the individual is meaningless in the absence of society. The self and its identifications are the product of transactions with others. Hence, it is not possible or desirable entirely to eliminate external sanctioning.

Individual and society are symbiotic. I am a professor, but not a nineteenth-century German professor. I do not expect my students to stand when I enter the room and I want them to challenge my opinions. Introduce my other roles as husband, editor, and so forth, and you have begun to understand who and what I am. In my understanding of my own self, which is always subject to reevaluation as I discover it in new situations and when faced by new types of choices, I find my own grounds for autonomous choice.

Were I to be forced out of my role into a strange society, I would have to remake and refind myself. Force me out of a system of meaningful constraints and I would begin to lose the sense of identity without which the freedom to choose is meaningless. I would become a rudderless ship adjusting to momentary pressures, without a sense of the pattern of life I wish to lead. It is this most terrible condition, even worse than death, that the concentration camp imposed on its victims. Will we impose it on ourselves in willful surrender to one-sided doctrine?

No society can prevent harm to its members that results either from individual or collective action. Most tax laws, for instance, will do immense harm to some because no general statements, no matter how carefully written, can take into account all possible contingencies. No matter how great the care we take to avoid such consequences, almost invariably a tax law will drive some individuals out of a business or a job that represents a lifetime of accomplishment and that is essential to their self-identity. Life is filled with tragic dilemmas that we can attempt to ameliorate but that we cannot entirely avoid.

Because this is so, what we owe each other is obedience to procedures that manifest care for the equities and values that are involved. It is this kind of care that reinforces values and identifications and that protects our freedoms. These are the values that would be threatened if the program of "the right to be left alone" were carried out extensively.

Ask not whom it would threaten, for it would threaten each of us in our ability to be who and what we are. Sinclair Lewis once wrote a book entitled *It Can't Happen Here* in which fascism came to America in the guise of antifascism. The formula "the right to be left alone" contains a greater threat to individuality and the freedom to choose than fascism or communism ever posed. If carried to term, it would threaten the dissolution of the organized self, and it would do so without providing a big brother against whom we could build internalized defenses of the kind that broke out into manifest activity in Eastern Europe and the Soviet Union.

"Abortion, contraception, privacy, these are fundamental freedoms that should be off limits to lawmakers."

The Right to Privacy Includes Abortion

Faye Wattleton

Faye Wattleton, host of a cable television talk show, served as president of the family planning organization Planned Parenthood for more than fifteen years. In the following viewpoint, Wattleton argues that abortion is a fundamental right and private choice that women must be allowed to make without government interference. Wattleton asserts that reproductive freedom, including access to abortion and contraception, is inherent in the right to privacy.

As you read, consider the following questions:

1. How has government invaded women's privacy regarding reproductive freedom, according to Wattleton?
2. In Wattleton's opinion, how do parental consent abortion laws invade teenagers' privacy?
3. Why should issues involving women's reproduction never be on voting ballots, according to the author?

From Faye Wattleton's speech to the employees of Esprit de Corps, a San Francisco sportswear merchandiser, December 11, 1990. Reprinted by permission of Planned Parenthood.

Whatever our age or circumstances, we all make sexual decisions—and we cherish the freedom to make those decisions privately, without meddling or coercion.

The freedom to chart our reproductive destinies is a more recent acquisition than you might think. As late as 1965, contraception was still illegal in most of the U.S. Before then, biology was still destiny. Women were economically deprived and socially dependent. And men suffered too, saddled with children they could not feed or clothe.

In this day and age, control over our reproduction is a given. Women and men can plan our futures because we can plan our child-bearing. This dramatic advance is just one of the many steps forward our nation has made in recent decades, including enormous progress in human rights, women's rights, civil rights, children's rights.

A Dark Future

But today we look down the road toward the future and we see warning signs: "Danger ahead!" The danger isn't limited to our reproductive liberty, either; we see threats to our very progress as a democratic, pluralistic society. A tyrannical minority is determined to reverse the changes that were achieved in my generation. They want to tell us which forms of speech are censored, which books we may read, which music and art we may enjoy, even which God to pray to. Armed with Puritanical moralism, they have set out to control everything they view as obscene.

This crackdown on free expression will have a cataclysmic impact on our fundamental rights. This is not the America I know and love!

Around the world, nations are steering toward greater freedom for all citizens, holding our constitutional ideals as their compass—while here at home, we fight not to lose ideals. Is this the America we want to see as we end the 20th century?

The framers of our Constitution established the ideal of fundamental freedoms, freedoms that would endure in an ever-changing society, freedoms far removed from the reach of politicians. The Bill of Rights plainly states that "the enumeration [in] the Constitution of certain rights shall not be construed to deny or disparage others retained by the people." In plain talk, that is, the framers didn't want to spell out every one of our liberties. They didn't want to limit our freedoms to their day and age, with no room for expansion!

Given how different life was in those days, I'm glad! Let's remember that Washington and Jefferson owned slaves! Their wives didn't vote!

With few exceptions, rights have been expanded for the disenfranchised: women, minorities, children, the disabled. Americans

28

have come to take it for granted that our right to decide when and if to reproduce is as fundamental as our right to free speech or to assemble in this room! Nine out of 10 Americans believe that right is constitutionally guaranteed. For years, since the *Roe v. Wade* decision, we've counted on constitutional protection for our right to control our fertility.

But today, we are fighting to hold onto these most basic freedoms. The Reagan-dominated Supreme Court has thrown these rights into chaos.

First, women's access to abortion was restricted in the case called *Webster*, in July 1989. A year later, the court handed down the *Ohio* and *Hodgson* rulings, which allowed states to require parental notification for teens seeking abortions. All three rulings have created more restrictive standards by which all abortion laws will be judged. And though they target the most vulnerable women, the young and the poor, these rulings threaten all women.

The Most Important Right of Privacy

If the right of privacy means anything, it is the right of the *individual*, married or not, to be free from government intrusion into matters so fundamentally affecting a person as the decision whether to bear or beget a child.

William Brennan, quoted in the *Village Voice*, April 7, 1992.

I want to focus briefly on the teen cases, and the dangerous idea of legislating family communication. Parents should be involved in teens' important decisions, and their sexual decisions are no exception. I can personally identify with this. My daughter Felicia and I always discuss sexuality issues openly, only these days, *I'm* the one asking most of the questions! But compulsory communication is no joke. Besides, it doesn't work. It only disrupts families, forces young women to lie, and destroys young lives.

Instead of legislating family behavior, we should spend more time and resources on helping families communicate better. Laws should be aimed at giving our young people greater opportunities, not on treating them like property. If Felicia ever became pregnant and felt she couldn't involve me, I'd be hurt and saddened. But she's lived with me for 15 years. She knows me a little better than government regulators. If she couldn't come to me, the last thing I'd want is the government coming to her!

The government has no business telling any of us what to do with our private lives or our family lives! Teen or adult, rich or

29

poor, black, brown, or white, any female able to become pregnant must be able to prevent pregnancy and to choose whether or not to end pregnancy. The government should stay out of it.

No human right is more basic than our right to reproductive freedom. And no human right is so gravely threatened. The late Supreme Court Justice Louis Brandeis once wrote that "the greatest dangers to liberty lurk in insidious encroachment by men of zeal—well-meaning, but without understanding." When it comes to the anti-choice extremists, that description may be overly charitable!

Control of Women

This isn't really a struggle over abortion. It's over controlling women and controlling our sexuality. Otherwise, why would the extremists be intent on eliminating sexuality education and contraception? . . .

It's frightening that the end of the 20th century so closely resembles the beginning. Seventy-five years ago, the founders of the family planning movement had to battle repressive crusades begun in the 19th century, crusades like that of Anthony Comstock, the one-man vice squad who, in 1873, persuaded Congress to label birth control "obscene." In the first year the Comstock statute was in effect, Comstock himself confiscated 200,000 pictures and photos, 100,000 books, 5,000 decks of playing cards, 30,000 boxes of aphrodisiacs, and more than 60,000 of what were then referred to as "rubber articles."

Today, 120 years after his heyday, Comstock is back to haunt us, in the form of Jesse Helms! In 18 years in the Senate, Mr. Helms has tried to erode personal privacy almost as the Comstock statute did in 92 years!

The Supreme Court encouraged busybodies like Senator Helms. When it handed down the *Webster* case, the court invited state legislators to make our private decisions for us. The court declared that it doesn't trust women with our own choices.

But legislators soon found themselves facing an angry American majority, who want the government off the backs and out of the wombs of women! And in case some politicians were still missing the point, pro-choice America spelled it out for them on election day. Across the country, we remembered who our friends are! We remembered to promote our values by voting our values, the universal values of diversity, pluralism, and independence.

However proud we are of our election day victories, reproductive issues should never make it to the ballot box in the first place. Abortion, contraception, privacy, these are fundamental freedoms that should be off limits to lawmakers. And we, the pro-choice majority, have the power to turn this debate around, to remove it from the political arena. We must renew our determination to fight for permanent protection for our freedoms, whatever it takes, for as long as it takes. . . .

Time for Activism

So I urge you, become activists on behalf of reproductive freedom, for yourselves, for your loved ones, and for the millions of less fortunate women and men who have no one else to speak on their behalf.

Now is the time to improve family communication about sexuality. Start with your family! Now is the time to call for comprehensive sexuality education in the schools, to help teach young people how to live healthy, responsible lives. Now is the time to improve access to contraception for those who need it most, the young and poor. Now is the time to insist on expanded research for better birth control. The National Academy of Sciences reports that the U.S. lags decades behind other nations in this area, with fewer options available, and no concerted commitment to develop new ones.

Now is the time to demand that our government leaders stay out of our private matters. We must not rest until they recognize that the right to make personal reproductive decisions is fundamental, inalienable, and non-negotiable. It is not contingent on age or circumstances or geography. It is not a "single issue." And it is not open to partisan debate!

America's lawmakers must stop meddling in the lives of women and families. Surely they have more important things to do, like housing the homeless, feeding the hungry, and educating the ignorant. Like showing concern and compassion for the children already born. And like waging war on the root causes of abortion, unintended pregnancy. Reproductive freedom is in crisis. But realistic solutions are within our reach, if we all work together.

"The right to privacy is not a higher or greater right than the right to life."

The Right to Privacy Does Not Include Abortion

R.C. Sproul

In the following viewpoint, R.C. Sproul argues that the right to privacy does not exist in the U.S. Constitution, and even if such a right was mentioned, it would not outweigh the right to life. Consequently, Sproul maintains, abortion is not protected by privacy because the fetus' right to life exceeds the woman's right to privacy. Sproul, a minister and theologian, is chairman of Ligonier Ministries, a Christian organization in Lake Mary, Florida, that produces teaching materials for bible study and Sunday school groups.

As you read, consider the following questions:

1. How have courts included abortion under the right to privacy, according to Sproul?
2. According to the author, how is the fetus essentially distinct from a woman's body?
3. In Sproul's opinion, why should the rights of other family members be considered?

From R.C. Sproul, *Abortion*, © 1990 by R.C. Sproul. Reprinted with permission of NavPress.

One of the most frequent arguments heard in favor of legal abortion is that a woman has a right to her own body. What does this mean?

The current debate is not over whether or not a woman in the United States has the legal right to her own body with respect to abortion. Since *Roe v. Wade* she has that right. But *should* she have that right?

The Right to Privacy

The closest the Constitution comes to affirming a woman's right to her own body is an implied "right to privacy." *Roe v. Wade* utilized the Ninth and Fourteenth Amendments to make this claim. Among abortion adherents there is a strong sentiment that abortion legislation improperly intrudes into the privacy rights of persons and families. In simple language, they plead that it is none of the state's business whether a woman terminates her pregnancy or chooses to carry it to term. The relevant portions of the United States Constitution are as follows:

Amendment IX (1791)

The enumeration in the Constitution of certain rights shall not be construed to deny or disparage others retained by the people.

Amendment XIV (1868)

Section 1. All persons born or naturalized in the United States and subject to the jurisdiction thereof, are citizens of the United States and of the State wherein they reside. No State shall make or enforce any law which shall abridge the privileges or immunities of citizens of the United States; nor shall any State deprive any person of life, liberty, or property, without due process of law; nor deny to any person within its jurisdiction the equal protection of the laws.

What is immediately evident from even a cursory reading of these two amendments to the Constitution is the obvious absence of a single explicit word about privacy rights. The right to privacy concept, on which legalized abortion is based, is not mentioned explicitly anywhere in the Constitution. Without analysis, the majority opinion in *Roe v. Wade* decided the issue by simple assertion:

This right of privacy, whether it be founded in the Fourteenth Amendment's concept of personal liberty and restrictions upon state action, as we feel it is, or, as the District Court determined, in the Ninth Amendment's reservation of rights to the people, is broad enough to encompass a woman's decision whether or not to terminate her pregnancy.

The Supreme Court should not be faulted for being jealous to protect the privacy rights of citizens from the unwarranted invasion or intrusion of the state. Few of us have a desire to live with Big Brother monitoring our every action and eavesdropping on our every word. The specter of such a society is hideous. We should be thankful we have such things as a lock for the bedroom door. But this question remains: Is there any ethical or moral justification for including the right to have an abortion under the broader category of the right to privacy?

No Absolute Right

From an ethical perspective we must raise this question: Is the right to privacy an absolute right? Does God, for example, give us the right to blaspheme Him as long as we don't do it publicly? Do I have the right to murder someone or disfigure his property as long as I do it in privacy? Obviously not. There are moral limitations to the right of privacy. How far do those limitations extend?

Once again the debate returns to the question of when life begins. If the justices of the Supreme Court were persuaded that the fetus is a living human person, it is highly unlikely that they would include destroying the fetus within the right to privacy. Surely, the right to privacy is not a higher or greater right than the right to life. If it were, I would have the moral right to take your life if you invaded my privacy.

Because I speak nationally and my Ligonier video lectures are used in thousands of churches, I have experienced a substantive loss of privacy. Though not hounded like movie stars or famous athletes, nevertheless I know what it means to have my dinner interrupted in a restaurant by someone who wants me to autograph a book. These interruptions are infrequent and mild, but real nevertheless. Any person who works in the public eye knows some sense of the loss of privacy. We rarely understand how important a right is until we lose some of it.

We can understand a celebrity's annoyance when he or she is disturbed in a public place, but we could hardly argue that in such instances the celebrity has the right to kill the fan or the news reporter. We understand that the right to life transcends the right to privacy. If a fetus is a human life, then the Supreme Court erred in granting the destruction of the fetus under the application of the right of privacy.

A Woman's Moral Rights to Her Body

Most people agree that a woman certainly does have a considerable number of rights to her own body. She has a right not to be subject to rape or malicious physical injury, for example. But is the woman's right to her own body absolute? In addition to the legal right related to abortion, does a woman have the moral right to do anything she pleases with her body? For example, can a woman use her body as a battering ram to injure others? Does she have a moral right to sell her body in prostitution? Is she free to mutilate her body, or to destroy it through suicide? These questions reveal that the issue of a woman's right to her own body is more complicated than it first appears.

Whatever moral rights a woman has to her own body must be grounded in some norm or the claim is arbitrary. From where does a moral right to one's own body with respect to abortion come? Is it given by God? That would be exceedingly difficult to prove. Does it come from some other ethical norm? If so, which one?

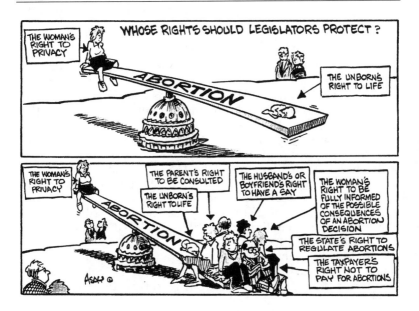

Chuck Asay, by permission of the *Colorado Springs Gazette Telegraph*.

In summary, a woman does have some rights to her own body. That she has an *absolute* right to her own body is not evident. The right to abortion, based on the right to one's own body, demands justification beyond mere assertion.

The Woman and Her Fetus

Contained within the argument concerning rights a woman has to her own body is an assumption that must be challenged: that the embryo or fetus is a part of the woman's body. The fetus is contained within the woman's body and connected to it, but that does not mean the fetus is a part of the mother's body. A more accurate description is to say that though the fetus

35

shares the same geographical location of the woman's body, the fetus is not *essentially* a part of her body. We can distinguish between the essence of the woman's body and the essence of the fetus. Given the gestation process, the fetus is neither the product essentially or organically of the mother's body alone nor is the fetus a permanent fixture of the woman's body. Left to the natural course, the unborn baby will leave the mother's body to carry out his or her own life. As such, the fetus is capable of being essentially distinct from the essence of the mother. The fetus has a brain, a heart, and fingerprints—a unique identity, which is not merely personal but is also physical. The biological structure and essence of the fetus is not exactly the same as the biological structure and essence of the mother.

A Unique Fingerprint

The startling discovery of genetic fingerprinting has added important information to this discussion. In the early 1980s, a British genecist named Alec Jeffries made a surprising discovery in the process of mapping human genes. Jeffries extracted DNA molecules from a sample of blood cells and cut them into unequal bits by adding enzymes. The fragments were put into a gel, where an electrical field caused the larger fragments to separate from the smaller ones. The DNA fragment pattern was transferred to a nylon membrane. Jeffries then added radioactively labeled pieces of DNA to act as probes. The membrane was then subjected to X-ray analysis. The X-ray film revealed vast numbers of genetic markers that exhibited an amazing degree of individual specificity.

Later experiments—both in England and in the United States—confirmed that each person, with the exception of identical twins, has a unique genetic fingerprint. In 1985, Jeffries declared,

> You would have to look for one part in a million million million million million before you would find one pair with the same genetic fingerprint, and with the world population of only five billion it can be categorically said that a genetic fingerprint is individually specific and that any pattern, excepting identical twins, does not belong to anyone on the face of this planet whoever has been or ever will be.

If any single cell of a woman's body is analyzed to find its essential biological structure, each and every cell will have the same genetic fingerprint. An analysis of the cells of the fetus will determine that each cell has the same genetic fingerprint, which is different from that of the mother. This indicates that, at the physical biological level, there is a clear line of demarcation between the body of the fetus and the body of the mother. Two distinct sets of human tissue reside in the pregnant woman's body.

36

How about the father? Does he have any rights related to the fetus? Although the father does not carry the fetus in his body, he has contributed half of the substance that is the genetic structure of the fetus. In the case of abortion, at least three persons (not to mention grandparents and other ancestors who contributed to the unique genetic structure of the fetus) have a stake in the woman's decision about "her own body."

Without a solid justification, is the argument for the right to one's own body just another way of obtaining personal preference? The least charitable interpretation is to say it is a thinly veiled tactic to earn the right to do what one wants.

I do not want to imply that selfishness is the only reason behind the argument for a woman's right to her own body. It is important, however, that those who advance this argument be careful to clarify their precise meaning. Because of the various possible interpretations and their inherent weaknesses, the argument, as it is so frequently and simply stated, is insufficient ground for justifying abortion.

"A rape victim's name should not be made public by the press without the victim's permission."

Rape Victims' Identities Are Protected by the Right to Privacy

Paul Marcus and Tara L. McMahon

Traditionally, the names of rape victims have not been disclosed. In some recent cases, however, the media has publicly identified the names of rape victims. In the following viewpoint, Paul Marcus and Tara L. McMahon argue that a rape victim's decision to remain anonymous is protected under the right to privacy and that the media and the justice system must respect this right. Marcus and McMahon contend that the need to protect a victim's identity is the essence of privacy and that this right is superior to the media's free speech right to publish facts. Marcus is a law professor at the College of William and Mary in Williamsburg, Virginia. McMahon is executive director of the Central European Institute, an organization that promotes international trade and entrepreneurship, located in Prague, in the Czech Republic.

As you read, consider the following questions:

1. How would the identification of rape victims fail to erase the stigma of rape, according to Marcus and McMahon?
2. In the authors' opinion, how could advanced technology and freedom of the press threaten the right to privacy?
3. Why do Marcus and McMahon believe that a rape victim's name is not newsworthy?

From Paul Marcus and Tara L. McMahon, "Limiting Disclosure of Rape Victims' Identities," *Southern California Law Review* 64 (May 1991): 1020- . Reprinted with permission.

When a woman is raped she experiences severe physical and emotional traumas from both the assault and the events that follow. The attack itself is a brutal and terrifying personal violation that can have a long term if not permanent impact on the victim's life. The victim also suffers the extremely difficult ordeal of disclosing the nature and specifics of the crime to law enforcement officers. If the assailant is caught, the victim will likely be asked to testify in a public trial about the crime committed against her, again subjecting her to emotional pain. Throughout this period the woman is trying to regain a sense of control and autonomy in her daily living situation. Compounding these and other difficulties, some women are being further victimized by having their identities widely disseminated by newspapers and television stations. While fortunately the phenomenon is not prevalent, if disclosure occurs prior to trial it can be one of the more cruel aspects of this traumatic experience. . . .

A Victim's Decision

Geneva Overholser, the editor of the *Des Moines Register*, suggests that by not printing the victim's name the media is subscribing to the idea that rape is not a crime of brutal violence, and she believes that this "sour blight of prejudice is best subjected to strong sunlight." But we must ask ourselves, who and what would be exposed under this strong sunlight? Revealing the identity of the victim against her wishes focuses the attention on the victim, not on those who foster prejudicial views. The goal sought by those who advocate routine disclosure of rape victims' names—erasing the stigma inflicted on victims of rape—would not be realized by publicizing their names. . . .

In response to the *Des Moines Register*'s plea for rape victims to speak out, one victim, Nancy Ziegenmeyer, did come forward to publicly reveal her identity and the terrifying, explicit details of her rape. She has been called courageous for her action and indeed she is courageous. Yet, the decision to go public was Ziegenmeyer's, not the media's. And despite the accolades she has received, she remains firm in her belief that a rape victim's name should not be made public by the press without the victim's permission. She states, "That is a decision that should be made by the victim when they're healed enough. Speaking out publicly is not for all victims." Rape is a unique crime in our society because of the stigma attached to it and the extreme psychological and physical harm caused by it. Good public policy recognizes this and gives the victim, not the media, the choice of revealing her identity. To establish such a public policy and ensure that it will withstand a constitutional challenge, one must also review the legal issues involved and determine the proper balance a policy must maintain to protect the victim's right of privacy without unduly interfering with the media's first amendment rights.

Privacy and the First Amendment

The creation of a right to privacy began in 1890 when Samuel D. Warren and Louis D. Brandeis wrote what has been referred to [by Harry Kalven] as the "most influential law review article of all." The now famous and often cited article grew out of Warren and Brandeis's belief that individuals needed to be protected from the increasing excesses of the press. They wrote:

> Recent inventions and business methods call attention to the next step which must be taken for the protection of the person, and for securing to the individual what Judge Cooley calls the right "to be let alone." Instantaneous photographs and newspaper enterprise have invaded the sacred precincts of private and domestic life; and numerous mechanical devices threaten to make good the prediction that "what is whispered in the closet shall be proclaimed from the house-tops.". . . The press is overstepping in every direction the obvious bounds of propriety and of decency. . . . [M]odern enterprise and invention have, through invasions upon [an individual's] privacy, subjected him to mental pain and distress, far greater than could be inflicted by mere bodily injury.

The propositions put forth by Warren and Brandeis generated extensive legal debate over whether existing law afforded the principle that each person had a cognizable legal interest in private life, both physical and emotional. Although the appellate court in the first state to confront the issue did not accept the Warren and Brandeis principle, a subsequent state court did recognize the existence of a distinct right to privacy in *Pasvesich v. New England Life Insurance Co.*, which became the leading case in this area. Several years after the *Pasvesich* decision, an action for privacy was included in the Restatement of Torts and today virtually all jurisdictions accept the right of privacy in one form or another.

The product of this evolution is a body of privacy law which, as defined by William Prosser, comprises the invasion of four different interests of the plaintiff. Disclosure of a sexual assault victim's identity falls under the category called "public disclosure of private facts." Scholars have not unanimously determined all the private facts about an individual that are protected under this category, but they have agreed that the law is intended to reflect the need of individuals to keep some core of their personality to themselves, outside the notice of society. The ultimate value at stake has been described as human dignity, individuality, and autonomy, but the primary point is that control of personal information about oneself is the essence of privacy. The interest a wholly private individual has in keeping her name out of the public limelight while she recovers from the personal tragedy of rape lies at the heart of this right.

Reprinted by permission of Doug Marlette and Creators Syndicate.

The constitutional right competing with the interests of the rape victim who seeks to keep her identity private is the first amendment freedom of the press to report on matters of legitimate public concern. Both the freedom of the press and the right of privacy protect interests which the Supreme Court views as "plainly rooted in the traditions and significant concerns of our society." The Court notes that "[t]he tension between the right which the First Amendment accords to a free press, on the one hand, and the protections which various statutes and common-law doctrines accord to personal privacy against the publication of truthful information, on the other," is an issue courts have frequently addressed. The mechanism the Court has developed for resolving these competing interests is a balancing test. Rather than apply a strict rule, the Court attempts to determine which party's interest is more compelling or what weights to give the competing values. The Supreme Court's use of a balancing test to resolve conflicting press and privacy interests was restated by Justice William Rehnquist in the *Daily Mail* case:

Historically, we have viewed freedom of speech and of the

41

press as indispensable to a free society and its government. But recognition of this proposition has not meant that the public interest in free speech and press always has prevailed over competing interests of the public. . . . "[t]he press is not free to publish with impunity everything and anything it desires to publish.". . . *[W]e have eschewed absolutes in favor of a more delicate calculus that carefully weighs the conflicting interests to determine which demands the greater protection under the particular circumstances presented.*

As a result of this balancing process by the courts, for most of the twentieth century our courts experienced a strong tide running in favor of the individual's right of privacy over the press's reporting interest. . . .

A Justified Restriction

In *State v. Evjue*, where the defendant published a rape victim's name in violation of a state criminal statute, the court held that the statute did not violate the constitutional freedom of the press. The court reasoned:

> [The statute] was no doubt intended to save from embarrassment and offensive publicity women who have been the subject of the kind of assault delineated in the statute, and to aid law enforcement officers to more readily obtain evidence for the prosecution of such criminal offenses. It is considered that it is a matter of common knowledge that such victims suffer far beyond anything suffered by men or women in connection with other classes of crimes. It was to prevent this and aid prosecuting officers that the legislature of this and 19 other states have enacted laws of this general character.

The court found that the publication of the identity of the female ministered to a morbid desire to connect the details of one of the most detestable crimes known to the law with the identity of the victim. Demonstrating its balancing approach, the court wrote:

> When the situation of the victim of the assault and the handicap prosecuting officers labor under in such cases is weighed against the benefit of publishing the identity of the victim in connection with the details of the crime, there can be no doubt that the slight restriction of the freedom of the press prescribed by [the statute] is fully justified.

Although the court in *Sidis v. F-R Publishing Corp.* did not rule in favor of the plaintiff because it determined the plaintiff was already a public figure, language from that case has been relied upon in subsequent cases upholding the plaintiff's right to privacy over the freedom of the press: "Revelations may be so intimate and so unwarranted in view of the victim's position as to outrage the community's notions of decency.". . . In *Nappier v. Jefferson Standard Life Insurance Co.* the court ruled against the media defendant when the defendant violated a state statute making it a misdemeanor to publish a rape victim's name. The defendant's television broadcast identified two rape victims through photos of their vehicle, which prominently displayed the name of their puppet show, "Little Jack." In holding for the plaintiff, the court reasoned:

> Aside from the personal protection of the woman involved, the object of the law, concededly is to encourage a free report of the crime by the victim. Fear of publicity might deter her from notifying police. Thus the public interest is advanced by the statute: the crime is investigated promptly and the injured person is shielded.

The above cases illustrate the significance the courts place on both the individual's interest in maintaining as private certain truthful information and the state's interests in enforcing the statutes protecting such privacy. In recent years, however, the courts have shifted away from this value assessment and their decisions have without exception sided with the press's right to publish. As Justice Byron White notes in *Florida Star*, "[T]he trend in 'modern' jurisprudence has been to eclipse an individual's right to maintain private any truthful information that the press wished to publish." With its decision in *Cox Broadcasting*, the Supreme Court appears to have charted a course which it continues to follow. . . .

Favoring Freedom of the Press

State and lower federal courts have followed the Supreme Court's current lead and consistently upheld the press's right to publish over an individual's right to privacy. In *Ayers v. Lee Enterprises* the court, citing *Cox Broadcasting*, ruled in favor of a newspaper which published a rape victim's name and address obtained from a police report. The court reached this result despite the fact that when the victim reported the crime to the police she specifically requested that her privacy be preserved and her name and address not be made public. Although the Court stated "they were understanding of [the] problems and of the reasons why the victim of a rape who reports that crime to the police with the request that her name not be made public would feel justifiably aggrieved at the release and publication of her name and address," the Court went on to hold for the newspaper because it reasoned that any information obtained from a police report is a matter of public record and thus no liability could lie for its publication.

The court in *Poteet v. Rosewell Daily Record, Inc.* dismissed an invasion of privacy claim for the truthful publication of a fourteen-year-old rape victim's name learned from a criminal complaint and published after a preliminary hearing. Again citing

Cox Broadcasting, the court said the incident was a matter of public record and therefore newsworthy. . . .

These cases, along with the most recent *Florida Star* decision, represent the radical movement of the courts toward ruling in favor of the media over individuals seeking to keep very personal aspects of their lives out of society's view. While the Supreme Court stated in *Florida Star* that it has not exhaustively considered the first amendment and privacy conflicts in cases involving government attempts to sanction the dissemination of truthful information, we believe the court's efforts to strike an appropriate balance between the rape victim's right to privacy and the public's right to know have accorded far too little weight to the victim's side of the equation. This imbalance is giving the press the freedom to delve into matters that society has always considered to constitute an impenetrable sphere of privacy. If one combines this expanded freedom with today's advanced technology and methods for obtaining and communicating information, the potential results are astounding.

The Loss of Privacy

Publication of the victim's identity intrudes upon several aspects of an individual's privacy rights resulting in humiliation and embarrassment to the victim. For example, mass public disclosure prevents the victim from freely choosing with whom and to what extent private facts will be revealed to others. The victim's interest in keeping extremely personal facts private is defeated when intimate facts are disclosed to a mass audience. Despite the victim's conscientious efforts to keep personal facts to herself, or to share them only with close relatives or friends, the victim loses control of who will known the intimate details about her.

Kim Ruckdaschel-Haley, *South Dakota Law Review*, Spring 1990.

In the late 1800's Warren and Brandeis feared the impact of inventions such as instantaneous photographs and newspapers on an individual's private life. They were concerned about private information being proclaimed from house-tops and the impact of the rise of "yellow" journalism. Could they have even imagined the media would be capable of broadcasting a victim's name on radio waves coast-to-coast or around the world in a matter of minutes; or that the private details of a person's life could be discussed at the family breakfast table while they were being portrayed on a morning television show; or that a telephone could be "tapped" and the contents of a private conversation published? The media's ability to penetrate and expose our private daily lives has far surpassed that which Warren and Brandeis sought to protect against. We believe the states must take action to curb effectively this invasion of individual privacy. We are optimistic that the final outcome of the present trend of the courts is yet to be determined. Even though the Court in *Florida Star* ruled in favor of the media, it provided a window of opportunity for correcting this current imbalance when it declined to establish a broad rule constitutionally protecting any truthful information the media wished to publish, and at the same time specifically acknowledged the possible need for sanctions for publishing a rape victim's name. We believe such sanctions are necessary and that they would not prohibit the media from sufficiently fulfilling its role of reporting to the public matters of legitimate public concern. . . .

Irrelevant Information

A rape victim's name is clearly not a piece of information relevant to the public's self-governing choices, which the Supreme Court has identified as the major underlying rationale for freedom of speech. With a rape, the value of the news item is the rape's occurrence, the location of the crime, the assailant's identifying characteristics, and the status of the assailant's apprehension. This is the type of information the public needs in order to evaluate the services provided by government, such as whether the community has appropriate safety measures in the crime area, whether the police force is performing its job effectively, or whether existing emergency procedures are adequate. Reporting the victim's name does nothing more than feed the public's curiosity. . . .

Simple Standards of Decency

Interestingly, in the time span between *Cox Broadcasting* and *Florida Star*, one member of the Supreme Court changed his views regarding the concerns of rape victims versus the burden such a disclosure rule would impose on the media. Justice White's majority opinion for the Court in *Cox Broadcasting* upheld the right of the media to publicize a rape victim's name without even a discussion of the harm to the victim. However, Justice White dissents in *Florida Star* stating,

> [I]t is not too much to ask the press, in instances such as this, to respect simple standards of decency and refrain from publishing a victim's name, address, and/or phone number. The Court's concern for a free press is appropriate, but such concerns should be balanced against rival interests in a civilized and humane society.
>
> . . . There is no public interest in publishing the names . . . of persons who are the victims of crime. . . .

Perhaps we should take heed from the Justice who started the Court down the path of curtailing rape victims' privacy rights with the *Cox Broadcasting* decision and now believes "we [have] hit the bottom of the slippery slope." Justice White maintains, and we agree, that a line can and should be drawn "higher on the hillside"—high enough to protect the rape victim's privacy rights but at the same time not to interfere with the reporting of matters of legitimate public concern.

"The harmful effects of publicity do not present a compelling argument in favor of withholding a victim's identity."

Rape Victims' Identities Are Not Protected by the Right to Privacy

Sarah Henderson Hutt

Some feminists and lawyers advocate revealing the names of rape victims, asserting that they should be identified just as victims of other crimes are. In the following viewpoint, Sarah Henderson Hutt agrees and argues that the public's right to know the identity of rape victims outweighs the victims' right to privacy. Hutt contends that this freedom of information helps maintain openness and public access, cornerstones of the criminal justice system. Hutt is a note editor for the *Duke Law Journal*, published by Duke University in Durham, North Carolina.

As you read, consider the following questions:

1. Under what circumstances would publication of a crime victim's name constitute invasion of privacy, according to Hutt?
2. In Hutt's opinion, how does protection of identity validate a rape victim's story?
3. Why are newspapers unlikely to print the names of rape victims, according to the author?

From Sarah Henderson Hutt, Note, *In Praise of Public Access: Why the Government Should Disclose the Identities of Alleged Crime Victims*, 41 Duke L.J. 368, 368-69, 371, 393, 396-401, 414 (1991). Reprinted with permission.

Recent events have made crime victims the subject of intense public attention and debate. The *New York Times*'s controversial decision on April 16, 1991, to publish the name of an alleged rape victim, caused a public outrage, prompting the state legislature to seek new ways to restrict public access to the identities of alleged crime victims. On July 19, the New York State Legislature passed a bill that requires police, prosecutors, and court officials to keep the identities of victims of sexual offenses confidential. The bill provides that "[n]o report, paper, picture, photograph, court file or other documents . . . which identifies such a victim shall be made available for public inspection"; disclosure of the identity can result in civil liabilities. Later that month, New York Governor Mario Cuomo signed the bill.

Two other states have restricted public disclosure of a rape victim's identity. In September of 1991, Alaska passed a bill that deems the name of a victim of a sexual offense not to be a matter of public record and that provides for the use of the victim's initials in all transcripts of otherwise open proceedings. Louisiana amended its public records law to exempt from public disclosure all law enforcement records that reveal the identity of a victim of a sexual offense.

Denying Public Access

As these state laws demonstrate, the most recent attempts to protect rape victims' identities have not been aimed at punishing the press who decide to publish a victim's name, but rather have been aimed at cutting off public access to identifying information that typically appears in complaints, incident reports, and transcripts of criminal proceedings. Traditionally, the government has not restricted access to the identities of persons appearing in these records unless disclosure of that information would place the victim in physical danger or would impede an ongoing criminal investigation. Now, the government is restricting access to victims' identities for the primary reason of protecting the victim's privacy. This viewpoint examines whether such restrictions are an impermissible infringement on the public's First Amendment right of access to information about the criminal justice system. . . .

The First Amendment right of access was announced by seven Supreme Court justices in *Richmond Newspapers, Inc. v. Virginia*, in which the Court invalidated a trial judge's decision to close a criminal trial to the public. In the plurality opinion, Chief Justice Warren Burger concluded that "a presumption of openness inheres in the very nature of a criminal trial under our system of justice," that "the right to attend criminal trials is implicit in the guarantees of the First Amendment," and that "[a]bsent an overriding interest articulated in findings, the trial of a criminal case must be open to the public." The *Richmond Newspapers* Court did not, however, announce a clear standard for assessing how the state could rebut the presumption of openness that attaches to a criminal trial.

Relying on *Richmond Newspapers*, a majority of the Supreme Court in *Globe Newspaper Co. v. Superior Court* invalidated a Massachusetts statute that mandatorily excluded the public from all sex-offense trials during the testimony of a minor victim. . . .

To determine whether a victim's privacy interest at the investigative stage of a criminal matter could be deemed a compelling reason to restrict access, it is important to consider the precise nature and scope of the victim's privacy interest in his identity after he reports an incident to the police. A victim's privacy interest at the investigative stage is too ambiguous to be compelling. It is not clear that the right has clear boundaries or a solid grounding in the law, that victims desire privacy at that stage, or that privacy is beneficial to victims or to society.

First of all, the precise source of the alleged victim's privacy right in his identity is murky, although there are three possible sources of derivation: the common law, constitutional doctrine, or the Supreme Court's interpretation of FOIA [Freedom of Information Act]. Under common law doctrine, all persons have a privacy interest in the private facts of their life. Rape victims who have sued over the publication of their names have a cause of action for the publication of a private fact. This tort relies upon the view that persons should not be subject to public disclosure of facts that would be "highly offensive and objectionable to a reasonable person of ordinary sensibilities," [according to W. Page Keeton and William Prosser]. In Texas, the Attorney General based a victim's privacy interest in certain public records on common law notions of privacy, stating that privacy adheres in the "highly intimate or embarrassing" details of a person's life. Therefore, according to common law, the disclosure of the victim's name is not, in itself, a violation of privacy; rather, the disclosure of a victim's name in conjunction with details of a crime that are highly offensive, intimate, or embarrassing violates the victim's privacy interest. . . .

Dubious Benefits of Protecting Identity

The policy debate about the public disclosure of victims' names has focused on the effect of publishing a rape victim's identity. This viewpoint argues that the harmful effects of publicity do not present a compelling argument in favor of withholding a victim's identity from the public.

First of all, not all crime victims, even rape victims, desire to remain anonymous. Some actively seek publicity to promote social awareness of criminal issues. Because restricting access to these names intrudes upon a significant public interest, the government does not have a compelling interest in protecting a victim's confidentiality unless the victim expressly requests it. Furthermore, the current victim's rights movement has not focused on obtaining privacy rights for victims. Instead, the typical "Victim's Bill of Rights" focuses on obtaining compensation and emergency aid for victims, information about the status of the case and the scheduling of proceedings, and increased participation in criminal proceedings.

Influencing the News

The paternalism of not naming names reinforces the idea that rape is anything more than a terrible act of violence, that women should be shamed. Moreover, it gives a figure in the news the power to decide what the news is; only if a rape victim grants permission will the press include her name. We rightly don't tolerate judicial or legislative attempts to make unilateral editorial decisions. We shouldn't permit it in the individual context either.

David A. Kaplan, *Newsweek*, December 16, 1991.

In the case of rape, commentators are split over which causes greater injury to a victim: public disclosure of identity, or the perpetuation of the stigma of being a victim caused by the secrecy surrounding a rape victim's identity. Paul Marcus and Tara L. McMahon, for example, argue that "routine disclosure" of rape victims' names to the media harms the victim by interfering with the healing process, focusing attention on the victim instead of on the source of prejudicial views (i.e., society), and burdening the victim with the task of educating society. Mental health experts have also argued that giving a rape victim control over the publication of her name helps the victim to regain a sense of control, thereby aiding recovery. Some victim advocates have compared media publication of a rape victim's name to the public "outing" of closet homosexuals because both are events in which a private fact about an individual is forcibly disclosed.

Many rape-victim advocates argue that victim confidentiality is essential to ensure that rape victims will not be afraid to come forward and report the crime. Susan Estrich wrote that "[t]o this day, women call my office for advice and are ashamed to leave their names, afraid to be identified as rape victims even to me [a famous rape victim advocate] or my secretary." In a stinging critique of the media's practice of interviewing and

50

scrutinizing a rape victim's credibility, Katha Pollitt wrote that the "chief characteristic" of the system's treatment of rape is that "it puts genuine rape victims (98 percent of complainants) through such an ordeal, with so little hope for justice, that most (90 percent, according to *Time*) don't even report the crime. . . . As a justice-achieving system, our approach to rape is a spectacular failure, but as a victim-deterrent system it works extremely well."

Reasons to Disclose Identity

The foregoing reasons, if valid, would offer compelling arguments for protecting a rape victim's confidentiality. On the other side of the issue, however, commentators have called the government and media's policy of withholding rape victims' names paternalistic. Nadine Strossen has argued that "if we are ever to get beyond the situation where rape is seen as stigmatizing, where the victim is seen as 'damaged goods,' then we have to stop mythologizing it and treating it as some kind of special crime." Furthermore, defense advocates have argued that it is unfair to publish the alleged assailant's name but not to publish the alleged victim's name. Such protection heightens the stigma attached to being an accused rapist, thereby chipping away at the accused's presumption of innocence. Such protection functions as a validation of the victim's story and also allows the victim to be an "anonymous accuser"—empowered to damage permanently the accused's public reputation without having to reveal his own identity. Alan Dershowitz wrote that the press's lopsided reporting policy is particularly unfair in rape cases because "false charges of rape are more frequent than false charges of any other serious crime."

It is important to emphasize at this point that the issue of the harm that results from *publishing* a rape victim's name is analytically distinct from the precise concern of this viewpoint, which is whether the names should be *disclosed* to the press. Routine disclosure of a victim's name does not automatically result in the publication of that victim's name. Even newspapers that have policies of interviewing crime victims and publishing their names in non-rape crimes do not publish the name of every victim in every crime. Metropolitan papers typically have space to report only the most serious crimes and will write stories about only the most egregious instances. Editors are not required to publish victims' names and can exercise discretion not to publish the name when the circumstances call for such discretion. Most commentators addressing the harmful effects of publication have ignored the distinction between disclosure and publication, assuming that "routine disclosure" of a victim's name will automatically lead to the routine publication of that name.

This is not a logical assumption, nor is it supported by the policy and practice of most media organizations in this country. In fact, the media in most states currently have access to the identities of rape victims but choose, in almost every case, not to publish the victims' identities. The media organizations that reported the name of the alleged victim in the William Kennedy Smith rape case drew tremendous criticism from the public and other media. The public reaction to this incident indicates that the media will probably not soon change their policy of respecting the privacy of rape victims who desire to remain anonymous.

Assuming that the media will continue to respond to overwhelming public sentiment to not publish rape victims' names, then the argument that publication of a victim's name will harm that victim is not a compelling reason to keep the victim's name confidential at the investigative stage of a criminal matter. Even if the media does change its policy, the government's interest in protecting a crime victim's privacy is, ultimately, outweighed by the threat of such protection to the integrity of the criminal justice system.

The Integrity of the Justice System

To determine whether the government has a compelling reason to withhold victims' identities, the victim's privacy interest should be balanced against the competing interests of the public, the suspect, and the criminal justice system. The public's primary interest in the criminal justice system at the investigative stage lies in encouraging the press to supervise the workings of that system to protect against state abuses of power. To this end, the victim's identity is significant information.

The suspect or arrestee's interest in disclosure of the victim's identity at the investigative stage is one of basic fairness. It is unfair to protect the victim's name when the suspect's is disclosed to the media. Furthermore, the accused criminal is in a far more vulnerable position than is the accusing victim. The accused must submit to the coercive powers of the state and stands to lose the privileges of freedom. At the very least, the accused will suffer from the lasting public stigma of having been an accused criminal. It is only fair that a victim who is willing to subject a person to the ordeal of a criminal trial be willing to stand publicly by his accusations.

Moreover, the integrity of the criminal justice system is at stake. The modern system is founded on the notion of public access. It cannot accommodate the interests of participants in the system who merely desire to protect their privacy without compromising the most fundamental check on the fairness of the system—the public's responsibility to act as overseer. Chipping away at public access to information about criminal investigations will only lead to greater government secrecy, greater abuse of power, and less public confidence in an already shaky system. In theory, the interests represented at the investigative stage of the criminal matter are fairly evenly balanced. The victim has an ascertainable—if nebulous—privacy interest that is offset by the suspect's interest in fair treatment. The balance is tipped, however, by the strength of the public's interest in access to information about criminal investigations. The integrity of the system depends on the public playing an active role in ensuring that the system is operating fairly.

A Drastic Infringement on Access

This viewpoint urges, therefore, that state and federal governments should not attempt to restrict access to victims' names merely to protect a victim's privacy interests. If a government does try to restrict access to victims' identities for privacy reasons and this restriction is challenged by the public, a court should not find that the government has asserted a "compelling interest.". . .

An Open Justice System

We must recognize that we live under a democratic system of criminal justice, open to public scrutiny by the press and the citizenry. Any compromise with that openness—even when done in the name of privacy or other important values—is a compromise with one of the most important safeguards of liberty: that no person shall be tried for a serious crime by an anonymous accuser who is unwilling to be confronted both in a court of law and in the court of public opinion.

Alan Dershowitz, *The Union Leader*, May 7, 1991.

In conclusion, a state government has never restricted access to a victim's identity for purely privacy reasons over a defendant's or the public's challenge to gain access to that identity at a criminal proceeding. Keeping information out of the public record is a drastic infringement on public access. It is only justified when the life of a participant in the trial is at stake, or when the fairness of the entire proceeding would be jeopardized by access. The privacy interests of an adult victim, although significant, are not worth the cost in public access. Finally, by protecting the privacy interests of a victim over the public's interest in overseeing criminal proceedings the state undermines the victim's own interest in seeing that the criminal justice system operates fairly. This viewpoint concludes that a victim's interest in privacy is not compelling because it is not equal in magnitude to these other interests.

Statutes recently passed in New York, Alaska, and Louisiana may reflect a trend toward increasing restrictions on public access to identifying information about victims. These new statutes, and similar statutes in existence in other states, should be challenged as posing unlawful restrictions on public access. . . . A victim's privacy interest is not sufficiently compelling to justify infringements on the public's right of access. The interest is nebulous, has an uncertain grounding in law, and undercuts the victim's and the public's interest in encouraging fairness and openness in the criminal justice system. As long as openness and public access are the cornerstones of the criminal justice system, vigorous public oversight, supported by liberal public access to information and proceedings in a criminal matter, operates to everyone's advantage—including the victim's.

"Workers, consumers, and citizens all suffer from the increasing encroachment of electronic surveillance."

Employees Need Privacy Rights Against Electronic Monitoring

Cindia Cameron

More than ever, worker productivity is monitored electronically with computers or telephone systems. In the following viewpoint, Cindia Cameron argues that electronic monitoring unfairly violates workers' right to privacy because it is used to spy on employees. Cameron contends that unethical employers can use monitoring systems to listen to workers' private conversations. Computer monitoring places too high a demand on workers' performance, diminishes their quality of work, and invades their privacy, she concludes. Cameron is a field organizer for 9 to 5, the National Association of Working Women in Atlanta.

As you read, consider the following questions:

1. Why does Cameron believe that employers should notify workers that they will be monitored?
2. How could electronic monitoring track an employee's activities inside a building, according to the author?
3. According to the author, how could a supervisor falsify a worker's computerized productivity records?

From Cindia Cameron, prepared statement to the U.S. Senate Subcommittee on Employment and Productivity, in support of the Privacy for Workers and Consumers Act, September 24, 1991.

In response to calls from our members about increasing problems with computer monitoring, 9to5 opened a hotline in January of 1989 to collect stories of workplace monitoring. The results were published in a report entitled *Stories of Mistrust and Manipulation: The Electronic Monitoring of the American Workforce.*

Carol Scott and Renee Maurel, who have testified today, are two individuals who called 9to5, looking for help to protect their dignity and privacy in electronically monitored jobs. I will share the experiences of others who could not be here in person, and describe how this bill will protect the estimated 25 million workers who are monitored at work, and the approximately 10 million whose job evaluations are based on computer-generated results.

Unethical Employers

The requirement that employers provide written notification of monitoring systems and visual or aural signals of telephone surveillance will provide urgently needed protections from some of the most serious invasions of privacy. Imagine how you would feel if the way you found out about your employer's monitoring practices was by having a co-worker tell you that your boss had been making a habit of listening in to your private conversations with a boyfriend. This is what happened to Sherry, a top-rated collections agent in Atlanta.

Loretta found out that her manager had the capability to listen in on telephone calls when she was fired after he overheard her making an appointment to interview for another job. Since he had overheard the name of her prospective employer, he went a step further, calling the company and giving false information about her work record.

It is not just isolated, unethical bosses who snoop at the electronic keyhole that we are concerned about. Computer journals advertise software which allows a boss to "look in on Sue's computer screen. You monitor her for awhile, in fact, Sue doesn't even know you are there." A software program called "Peek and Spy" allows you to look in on someone else's screen. When you let the person know you are looking, you are "peeking"; when you access their work secretly, of course, you are "spying."

The section of this bill providing an employee access to data collected about their work will allow them to challenge unfair disciplinary actions, and provide for some due process protection. Susan, an airlines reservationist who became involved in a union organizing drive, says that a computer was used to fire her. According to her account, her good results (called "runs") were deleted from her file, and other agents' poor statistics were added. After many years of outstanding performance, she was told her numbers were too low, and she was dismissed.

Becky, who worked for an insurance company, explained that at her office each employee uses a computer ID number to log into the system. After Becky filed a sex discrimination complaint against her employer, she found out that her ID number was routinely assigned to temporary replacement workers, who were always slower than experienced staff. When she complained about this procedure and asked to see her file and statistics, the company refused. Becky has since been fired, despite more than five years of above average evaluations.

Lack of privacy is at the heart of many complaints about the new electronic workplace. Maxine, a customer service representative who quit her job as a result of a serious stress-related illness, described her feelings, and those of dozens of hotline callers this way: "Monitoring makes you feel like less than a child, less than a thinking human being. It's a shame because they have a lot of intelligent people there. You have to stop and think that your ancestors did not cross the ocean in steerage and come through Ellis Island to be treated like this."

Relevancy to Work Performance

Electronic monitoring now goes beyond simply using computers to collect data on employee performance. In many cases, the technology allows an employer to cross a line from monitoring work, to monitoring the worker. The provision of this bill requiring that personal data collected be relevant to job performance is key to reestablishing a degree of dignity and privacy for large numbers of workers.

Sandra works for an express mail company. Her employer collects data not only about the number and length of calls she handles, but also on the length and frequency of trips to the restroom. She was told by her supervisor that four trips to the bathroom per day was excessive and that she obviously had a medical problem and needed to see a doctor.

Several large railroad companies in St. Louis use a system which records the location and length of time employees spend in any part of the building. Workers flash their ID cards through an electronic sensor in each doorway. A computer tracks how long the employee spent in the restroom, the payphone area, the smoking lounge or at a friend's work station. Employees have been disciplined based on these figures.

Kevin was a recruiter for an employment agency, which used a telephone call accounting system to track each outgoing phone call. Kevin's wife worked for the company, and they often consulted about work-related matters. Kevin's supervisor, using the daily telephone printout, regularly questioned Kevin about the number of calls made to his wife. Despite Kevin's protests that the calls were work-related, and actually improved his performance, the harassment continued. Kevin quit in frustration.

Having a computer count your every move, every keystroke, and phone call is difficult and stressful. But some employers go beyond the counting and tracking to public posting of employees' work results. In a survey of 700 employees at 49 companies carried out by the Massachusetts Coalition on New Office Technology, 23 percent of respondents said their individual statistics were posted publicly. Hotline callers report seeing their work records posted in the workplace with large red circles around certain statistics and written comments from the supervisors. The result is humiliation for the employee, and unnecessary, unproductive distrust and competition for high averages.

A Statute for Privacy Protection

A comprehensive workplace privacy statute is needed to limit computer surveillance, telephone monitoring, searches, physically invasive testing, audio/video surveillance and invasive questionnaires. Included in the privacy statute should be provisions stipulating that:

• All surveillance, testing and searches must be directed toward information that is demonstrably related to job performance.

• Any search for evidence of misconduct must be supported by a reasonable, articulable suspicion that such evidence will be found.

• Electronic monitoring of job performance must be accompanied by a simultaneous signal that such monitoring is taking place.

The American Civil Liberties Union, *A State of Emergency in the American Workplace*, 1990.

Most of us have had the experience of someone standing over our shoulder while we work. This is not usually when we give our best performance. With electronic monitoring, the supervisor is in the machine; watching and counting every minute. This supervisor does not take into account that anyone can have a bad day, a slow start, or a difficult afternoon. The provision of this bill that monitoring data may not be used as the sole basis for evaluation, will prevent ruthless human supervisors from hiding behind the myth of the "neutral, objective computer" as a way of harassing workers.

Limits on Data Are Required

Jean, a reservationist at TWA, told of handling a difficult caller and getting off the line; then cursing under her breath, as many stressed-out agents do. No one heard the comment, but Jean—and her supervisor—who picked it up through her headset monitoring device. Jean was called into the office, berated for unprofessional conduct, and required to sign a letter documenting the incident which went into her personal file.

Another reservationist told us, "One day I had a cold and had to make myself unavailable between calls to cough and blow my nose. I was monitored that day and got a very bad work report." Luckily that agent was not targeted for dismissal. Al, a reservationist in Miami, found out from a friend in management that the company monitored him constantly for six months, trying to find an incident with which to fire him. All they found was one 10-minute trip to the restroom.

A major theme of complaints by monitored workers is that trying to meet numerical figures, over which they have no control and no input, sets up a conflict between giving quality service and "keeping the time down." In the Massachusetts survey mentioned earlier, 65 percent of respondents said they could not do a quality job because they had to work too fast.

A "timer," or computer-generated work report, from an airline reservation agent illustrates the tyranny of computer monitoring. These agents receive scores on five different statistics per day; the number of calls handled, average time per call, average time between calls, "unmanned time" (usually meaning trips to the bathroom), and overall average. Agents are expected to take 150-200 calls per day, with a 96 percent success rating. They may be disciplined for any of the following: Calls longer than three and one half minutes, more than 12 minutes per day of "unmanned time," or too long between calls. One agent was put on warning for spending a total 23 seconds—over a full eight hour shift—between calls.

Sylvia, a data entry operator in Maryland, desperately needs protection from the use of computer-generated results as the sole basis for setting of work quotas. Her pay and evaluations are based on meeting the minimum requirement of 11,000 keystrokes per hour. Although she punches in and out of her worksite, she is paid only for the time logged on the computer. If, for example, she needs to go to the bathroom, she faces a quandary. If she turns her machine off, she is not paid for the time away from her desk. If she leaves her machine on, her keystrokes per hour will decline; she will get a lower rating and face a pay decrease.

Government Must Intervene

It is not just workers who suffer the effects of abusive computer monitoring. Each of us has likely had the experience of being cut off mid-sentence by a telephone operator whose goal seems to be simply to get us off the line as fast as possible.

Ask yourself whether, as a consumer, you are comfortable with the fact that when you call your insurance company to discuss your personal medical records, or ask an airlines agent for emergency rates to visit a relative dying of AIDS, there may be several people listening in on your conversation. You might also ask your wife, husband or best friend if their employer uses telephone monitoring, before you call them on their lunch hour at work to make a hot date, or discuss your legal or financial affairs.

The most enlightened employers will say that where monitoring becomes abusive, it should be left to labor-management relations to solve the problem, that government regulations are an unnecessary intrusion. I leave it to you to tell Sylvia, Jean, or Loretta, that government need not intrude on their behalf, that they should negotiate on their own behalf with management. The truth is that the vast majority of monitored workers do not have unions; and without that protection and collective voice in the workplace, the idea of labor-management negotiation is completely unrealistic.

Workers, consumers, and citizens all suffer from the increasing encroachment of electronic surveillance in the modern workplace. As Americans we believe strongly in the right to privacy. With this bill you have an opportunity to prevent serious erosions of this right in the workplace.

"Companies have been able to cut costs of production and boost quality through the use of [monitoring] equipment."

Electronic Monitoring of Employees Improves Productivity

Lawrence Fineran

Businesses such as manufacturers value electronic monitoring as a tool that can help them improve productivity. In the following viewpoint, Lawrence Fineran agrees and argues that electronic monitoring must be allowed to gauge workers' performance and to help protect company property. Fineran is the assistant vice president of government regulation, competition, and small manufacturing for the National Association of Manufacturers (NAM), a Washington, D.C., organization that works to protect manufacturers' interests.

As you read, consider the following questions:

1. How does electronic monitoring aid compliance with state and federal laws, in Fineran's opinion?
2. Why does Fineran believe that employees do not always have a right to privacy at work?
3. According to the author, how can monitoring help assess employee loyalty?

From Lawrence Fineran, prepared statement to the U.S. Senate Subcommittee on Employment and Productivity, in opposition to the Privacy for Workers and Consumers Act, September 24, 1991.

NAM opposes enactment of S. 516 [Privacy for Consumers and Workers Act] as both unnecessary and counterproductive. Effective electronic monitoring should pose little threat to employee privacy while ensuring employee compliance with Federal and state statutes as well as corporate policies. Employee privacy should be respected to the extent practicable. But employees should be expected to perform the work assigned and modem equipment should be allowed to assist employers in gauging performance. The proposed legislation goes well beyond telephone monitoring of customer service operators and will hamper security programs as well as efforts to regain domestic productivity and competitiveness. . . .

In addition to traditional manufacturing, many NAM members provide customer service through "800" telephone numbers, sell their products or services over the telephone, offer a variety of financial services, and operate retail outlets. And NAM itself markets directly to small manufacturers through our National Division office. Assurance of quality is critical for both products and services.

Harmful Impact on Businesses

The language of S. 516, however, makes clear that it is not limited to these activities. By its very definition, "electronic monitoring" includes all forms "of visual, auditory, or computer-based surveillance." This means, in effect, that any modern business—service or manufacturing—will be impacted negatively by S. 516.

NAM's primary objection is that the legislation fails to recognize a basic tenet of employment that has existed since the beginning of commerce: That one is expected to perform the work assigned according to the employer's standards in return for payment. A corollary of this is that employee interaction with customers reflects directly on the employer. Members of Congress constantly speak to the need for domestic businesses to be responsive to consumers if they expect to be competitive in the global economy. NAM's members agree with this, and many have implemented quality control, customer service, and internal security programs, which often rely on various forms of electronic monitoring to be successful.

NAM takes no exception to the parts of S. 516 that suggest that employees generally subject to monitoring should be so informed upon being offered the position. This is standard practice. Neither does NAM object to sharing information gleaned from monitoring with employees in a timely fashion. The legislation, however, goes well beyond this and will distort labor-management relations.

I have first-hand experience with this issue since my first job after college involved telephone solicitation. From there, I was moved into a supervisory position. While on the phones, I was subject to monitoring and generally found the comments of my supervisor helpful. It was one thing, though, to know that at any given time a supervisor could have been evaluating my performance versus knowing for certain that at a particular point I was being monitored. Had I known, I would easily have become nervous or flustered. From discussions with my colleagues at that time, I know that most if not all of them felt the same way.

An Effective Management Tool

Monitoring is the most effective management tool to ensure compliance with statutes such as the Fair Debt Collections Practices Act, which prohibits abusive, deceptive, and unfair tactics in the course of collecting debts. In addition, legislation now wending its way through Congress and various state legislatures dealing with telemarketing practices will make monitoring even more important if companies are to make certain that their employees are implementing the new laws correctly. Employees who perhaps do not follow new company policies mandated by such legislation will be aided by knowing when monitoring is occurring since they can "perform" for the supervisor.

For instance, some employees may decide not to change their practices in order to comply with new laws governing the use of marketing by telephone. But, they will certainly know to alter their behavior when a monitoring signal is activated. Without the ability to silently monitor, how does Congress expect employers to implement such statutory changes effectively? After all, the legislation holds the employer liable for compliance. While S. 516 makes a concession for signaling in cases where monitoring is continuous, there is no practical way for employers to handle these situations effectively except in periodic, random intervals.

In NAM's National Division, which again markets directly to small manufacturers by telephone, monitoring has been found to be a very effective management and training tool, with the support of the membership managers. They report that they find the feedback from supervisors helpful, especially during the initial training period. NAM also respects their privacy by providing them with a switch on their telephones that allows them to make calls that are not subject to the monitoring device while on breaks. Other companies provide either pay or employer-paid telephones for the same purposes.

The effect, if not the intent, of S. 516 on employees subject to periodic monitoring is likely to be misrepresented employee evaluations. Good employees who are unnerved when a signaling light or beep tone is activated will receive less stellar evaluations than they otherwise would have, while other employees may be able to mask their actions.

A Fine Line Divides Rights

Employees certainly have a right to privacy when it comes to dealing with problems of a personal nature, as long as they do so on time set aside by their employer and as long as their performance is not affected. While there may be anecdotal evidence provided of some abuses, the fact is that employees are paid for the time spent at work. Employers thus should be allowed to control the use of employer-provided equipment for non-work related purposes. There is a very fine line in this regard, but the legislation unfortunately will tie the employer's hands.

Suppose, for instance, that an employer decides to monitor the effectiveness of an electronic mail system, which was entirely paid for by the employer to increase efficiency, productivity, and customer service, and a gambling pool is discovered. Or consider an employee who uses employer-provided equipment to run a business on the side after hours and on weekends. To extend the hypothetical, let's assume that the employees involved have been performing their jobs generally well. Under the terms of this legislation, may the employer confront the employees with the information, or will this be considered personal data that "is not relevant to the employee's work performance?" In this case, apparently the bill would prohibit even the collection of such information even though the employees themselves entered it into the company's computer system.

There are many other hypotheticals such as these that may be raised. The point is, simply, that employers should and must be able to have free access to the computer equipment that they bought and paid for without fear of unintentionally having collected personal data arguably irrelevant to an employee's work performance. Still, such data may assist the employer in assessing an employee's character, productivity, or loyalty.

Corporate Security Concerns

Loyalty does, of course, become entirely relevant in the case of suspected corporate spying. This issue is a real concern of many companies, especially in high-technology industries. A business victimized by corporate spying will find itself at a strong competitive and strategic disadvantage. But S. 516 severely hampers the ability of employers to rout out such suspicions since the suspect employee must be notified that monitoring is taking place.

The bill also conflicts with security controls mandated by the

Department of Defense. Card keys or other authorizations measures, for instance, must be used to control access to areas containing classified data. Yet, card keys rely on personal identifying information and, by their very nature, track employee movements. In addition, the production and quota provision of the bill raises questions about the practice of having employees use electronic identifiers to differentiate time spent for the government and for the corporation on shared machinery.

Similarly, the use of personal identifiers for access to computers and computer files will be put in jeopardy since they have the potential of tracking employee productivity. But, these identifiers are obviously necessary features for controlling access to sensitive files.

Employers Do Not Abuse Monitoring

While employee privacy should be protected in certain situations, the privacy must be balanced against the need of businesses to maintain quality services in a competitive market.

On the whole, I believe most employers use monitoring to help ensure a quality product and quality workplace, and not for sinister eavesdropping purposes.

Strom Thurmond, statement to the Senate Subcommittee on Employment and Productivity, April 10, 1991.

And how is an employer expected to control the collection of "personal data obtained by electronic monitoring which describes how an employee exercises rights guaranteed by the First Amendment"? Sensitive or remote areas may be continuously monitored by video and audio surveillance for either corporate or employee security. Must the employer turn off the camera and sound if employees begin to discuss current events? Won't this leave the area exposed to possible non-First Amendment right abuses during the time when monitoring is not being conducted? Or consider video surveillance cameras in parking lots. Their purpose is employee protection, but the provision raises questions as to the permissibility of the practice since some employees will almost assuredly have bumper stickers on the cars expressing "rights guaranteed by the First Amendment."

New Technologies Streamline Industry

Of more concern to manufacturers trying to meet the challenge of global competition, the legislation also seems to

threaten the use of modern technologies and techniques by inhibiting the use of computers and high-technology machinery in
the manufacturing process. Many of NAM's member companies
have been able to cut costs of production and boost quality
through the use of equipment that automatically monitors the
productivity of employees and even entire factories. These advanced techniques may rely heavily on statistical process control, numerically controlled machines, and other closely monitored systems. This has helped streamline production processes
and make U.S. industry more competitive. Where a factory
once needed several layers of managers to keep manufacturing
lines running productively and efficiently, now it may need only
one. Corporate management should not be prohibited from using information obtained through computer-aided manufacturing (CAM) unless managers are physically on the shop floor
looking over the shoulders of employees.

An Orwellian World

We are moving toward an ever-increasing technological workplace. This has generated fears in some of an Orwellian world.
Some may promote the language of Section 6(b) that data "obtained by electronic monitoring [cannot be used] as the sole basis for setting production quotas or work performance expectations" as a way of saving employees from such a scenario. But
these fears are as unfounded as those of the Luddite movement
in early 19th century Britain, which wanted to keep England
out of the industrial revolution because machinery was performing work previously done by hand, and which refused to recognize that failure to modernize in and of itself would jeopardize
the availability of jobs for the very workers the movement pro-
fessed to protect.

Computer-aided manufacturing should be seen as helpful to
productive workers, since subjective perceptions—as personality
conflicts with a supervisor—will be overridden by the objective
analysis. CAM, for example, will be able to tell management
which workers or work teams are most productive and which
may need additional help. But if U.S. factories are somehow discouraged from moving forward with CAM, then American
workers will be the ultimate losers as domestic factories won't
be modernized even as overseas factories become increasingly
efficient.

Cash registers present a similar dilemma. Many of NAM's
members have divisions where they are commonplace. The
modern cash register requires employees to use an identification
number when signing on and is hooked-up to a central location
within the store or selling area. It used to be that managers
would count out each cashier's receipts and compare these with

66

the money taken in during the shift. Today, computers assist in this function and the time of managers has been freed for other duties. Yet, the legislation seems to require that we return to the days when cashier-register comparisons were done entirely by hand. Similarly, loss prevention and security efforts will be set back significantly should S. 516 become law. Video and audio surveillance has greatly improved the effectiveness of these programs—to the benefit of employees as well as employers.

Meeting the Global Challenge

Electronic monitoring, like any other management tool, can be used well and for lifting the overall quality of life in the workplace. Admittedly, however, it also can be abused. But, if used wrongly, employers will be confronted with morale problems and decreases in customer satisfaction, product standards, and even profits. It is certainly an area ripe for labor-management relations, but legislating in this area faces the prospect of creating more problems than it solves.

NAM opposes any legislation that will interfere with the ability of modern and future equipment that can aid in gauging either the effectiveness or the accuracy of employees or inhibit security programs. Otherwise, the United States may as well let the information age pass it by. In short, NAM views this legislation not only as unnecessary, but also as counter-productive. Effective monitoring not only ensures compliance with various federal and state laws and provides customers with the assurance that employees are following corporate guidelines, but also respects privacy to the extent practicable. It also helps domestic companies meet the global challenge through increased productivity.

Periodical Bibliography

The following articles have been selected to supplement the diverse views presented in this chapter.

André Bacard — "Privacy in the Computer Age," *The Humanist*, January 1993.

Randall C. Bertz — "Abortion 1990s: Contemporary Issues and the Activist Court," *Western State University Law Review*, Spring 1992. Available from 1111 N. State College Blvd., Fullerton, CA 92631.

Robert M. Byrn — "The Perversion of Privacy," *Human Life Review*, Winter 1993. Available from 150 E. 35th St., New York, NY 10016.

David Chaum — "Achieving Electronic Privacy," *Scientific American*, August 1992.

Terry Eastland — "Against Her Will," *The American Spectator*, July 1991.

Roy Furchgott — "Invasion of Privacy," *Self*, December 1992. Available from 350 Madison Ave., New York, NY 10017-3704.

Ken Gormley — "One Hundred Years of Privacy," *Wisconsin Law Review*, 1992. Available from 975 Bascom Mall, Madison, WI 53706.

Carey Haughwout — "Prohibiting Rape Victim Identification in the Media: Is It Constitutional?" *The University of Toledo Law Review*, Summer 1992. Available from University of Toledo College of Law, Toledo, OH 43606.

Richard Lacayo — "Nowhere to Hide," *Time*, November 11, 1991.

Erik Larson — "Attention Shoppers: Don't Look Now but You Are Being Tailed," *Smithsonian*, January 1993.

Gary T. Marx — "The New Surveillance," *National Forum*, Summer 1991.

Eileen Quann — "Safeguarding Employees' Privacy," *USA Today*, September 1992.

Roger Rosenblatt — "Who Killed Privacy?" *The New York Times Magazine*, January 31, 1993.

James B. Rule — "Where Does It End? The Public Invasion of Privacy," *Commonweal*, February 14, 1992.

Sallie Tisdale — "A Place of Her Own," *Harper's*, October 1992.

2 CHAPTER

Should Freedom of Expression Be Restricted?

Chapter Preface

One night in 1991, a group of teenagers in St. Paul, Minnesota, burned a cross in the yard of their neighborhood's only black family. After the incident, officials prosecuted one of the youths under the city's Bias-Motivated Crime Ordinance. The ordinance, later declared unconstitutional, prohibited the display of all symbols or objects that aroused, on the basis of race, creed, or gender, "anger, alarm, or resentment in others." City officials had argued that such anger could escalate into violence.

Many restrictions of free speech have the same, positive goal as the St. Paul law—eradicating hatred and violence, particularly against racial and ethnic minorities, homosexuals, and women. For example, cities and universities have attempted to outlaw racist or homophobic speech by the Ku Klux Klan and other "hate groups." Similarly, other laws seek to reduce violence against women by restricting the sale and distribution of pornography. Andrea Dworkin, a feminist writer who has helped draft such laws, states, "We see elements of pornography in the rape of women, including maiming and outright torture."

But these well-intentioned laws or codes are often challenged by those supporters of free expression who believe that all speech, no matter how offensive, must be protected. Many free-speech advocates, for example, condemned the St. Paul restriction as a violation of First Amendment rights. They share the belief of former U.S. Supreme Court justice William Brennan, who once stated, "Government may not prohibit the expression of an idea simply because society finds the idea itself offensive or disagreeable."

American law places many limits on freedom of speech and expression. Whether such limits are justified for society's well-being is one of the main questions examined in this chapter.

"There are circumstances in which material is justifiably censored."

Freedom of Expression Should Be Restricted

Richard W. Behling

In the following viewpoint, Richard W. Behling argues that a belief in censorship does not mean that censorship should be applied indiscriminately. Behling asserts that certain circumstances warrant censorship of speech or expression. Behling contends, for example, that material which could encourage illegal activity or which is repugnant should be censored. Behling is an associate professor of philosophy at the University of Wisconsin in Eau Claire.

As you read, consider the following questions:

1. How does the public view censorship advocates, according to Behling?
2. In Behling's opinion, why are nonfiction books more deserving of censorship than fiction?
3. Why does the author believe that newspapers should not publish unsubstantiated criminal charges?

Richard W. Behling, from a 1993 revision of the author's "In Defense of Censorship," which originally appeared in *Wisconsin Dialogue*, number 7, 1987. Reprinted with the author's permission.

He who defends either the practice or the institution of censorship is commonly thought to be un-American or (at the very least) uncool; but he who decries censorship is deemed both patriotic and hip. It is no wonder, then, that even those of us who secretly favor the institution of censorship are wont to deny publicly that we do. Members of the Student Feminist Alliance of the University of Wisconsin-Eau Claire, for example, circulated a petition which denounced "sexist" programming on the *Playboy* channel. But the five hundred signatories to the petition, themselves members of the *Pepsi* generation, sought to reassure the members of our community by stating as clearly as possible that ". . . the undersigned in no way want to facilitate needless censorship."

Censors and Their Opponents

Of course, it is a bit difficult to imagine anyone being in *favor* of needless censorship, and the bold claim that one steadfastly opposes *needless* censorship seems tantamount to favoring *needed* censorship! So let those of us who favor the institution of censorship come out with it, then. We who feel that Captain Queeg is not the one to lead the men of the *Caine* should *say* that he's unfit to command a paper-boat in a bathtub, not merely that we deem him *fit* to do so!

A common mistake is made by those who try to adjudicate the dispute between would-be censors and their opponents. Many view the disputation between the principals as, say, a boxing match where "points" are awarded for skillful defenses as well as for aggressive offenses: the perspicuous "jab" of one combatant is weighted against the erudite "feint" of the other. Each advocate is on equal footing, so to say, and we who judge eagerly await a "knock-out punch" (if there be one) when confutation becomes refutation, and when censorship is either once-for-all enthroned or forever banished from the American imagination.

But the goings-on in a debate on the propitiousness of censorship are, or *should* be, unlike those of a pugilistic contest. The censorship-proponent and the censorship-opponent are certainly *not* on equal footing from the get-go, for we all believe that there is nothing intrinsically good about the practice of censorship; on the contrary, we feel that, in the absence of compelling evidence in its favor, censorship is an evil, for the dissemination of information is a positive good. But just now the question arises: *Are* there "compelling evidences" to be presented? Let us consider carefully both what the opponent says and what he overlooks.

In his [*Playboy* article] "The Idea Killers," the astute and witty Kurt Vonnegut, Jr., invites his reader to view the dispute between censorship-proponent and censorship-opponent in a mistaken way. Vonnegut writes both in support of the uncensored word and against those who would "kill ideas." I quote at length from Vonnegut's essay. His "affirmative" case proceeds as follows:

> Teachers and librarians have been unbelievably brave and honorable and patriotic, and also intelligent, during all of the recent attacks on the First Amendment, which says, among other things, that all Americans are free to read or publish whatever they please. Slander and libel, of course, are excepted from the law's protection.

And later, Vonnegut (continuing to speak favorably of bravery, honesty, intelligence, and the American way) adds:

> [Teachers and librarians] defend my books, and anybody else's, because they are law-abiding and because they understand, as did our founding fathers, that it is vital in a democracy that voters have access to every sort of opinion and information.

> Thanks to our founding fathers, it is the law in this country that, once any idea is expressed here, no matter how repugnant it may be to some persons or, simply to everybody, it must never be erased by the Government. . . .

The philosopher Ludwig Wittgenstein was fond of speaking of those who operate on a "deficiency diet of examples." By the Wittgensteinian standard, Vonnegut's attack on censorship needs a large dose of *Geritol*. Vonnegut's entire case turns out to be an attack against those book-burners who would commit the "Dirty Thirty"—classic works of fiction that have fallen into disfavor in red-neck circles—to the flames. For my part, I wholeheartedly agree with Vonnegut that no title among the list of the Dirty Thirty should be removed from public bookshelves; indeed, I maintain that any work of fiction, properly so-called, is worthy of public scrutiny. And let me even go so far as to oppose the feminists who oppose pornography, for I do not! But are we to say that, if the work of fiction and the "X-rated" movie are to pass muster, then there is nothing left to discuss, and that we must go on record as opposing censorship? Hardly!

Again, let us learn from the master, Wittgenstein. In considering any case, Wittgenstein cautions: "Do not assume; . . . look and see." *Do not assume*: Look at *all* of the evidence. See it all!

A Case for Censorship

In what follows, I shall not present an argument, properly speaking, in favor of censorship, but I will present evidences which we should all consider. We should look at a few cases that are n'er dreamt of in Vonnegut's philosophy of censorship. Let us count the ways in which his position is deficient. Let us *look* and *see*.

Example No. 1: "The Press's Obstruction of Justice?" During the early-morning hours on Aug. 24, 1970, the campus of the University of Wisconsin-Madison was rocked by a bomb-blast which destroyed the Army Mathematics Research Center and killed a researcher who was at work in the building. Dwight Armstrong, his brother, and two others had planted the bomb in hopes of gaining support for the anti-war efforts which were gaining momentum and which called for the immediate withdrawal of American forces from South Viet Nam.

When state and federal law-enforcement officers learned of the involvement of Karlton Armstrong in this incident, his name appeared at the top of the FBI's Most Wanted list, and he fled Madison for Canada so as to avoid prosecution on state charges and on federal charges (which included sabotage, destruction of government property, and conspiracy). Slightly more than a year later (on Sept. 11, 1971), two Madison law-enforcement officers flew to Toronto, on a tip that Karlton was living there. And, indeed, the tip was correct, and plans were made to arrest Armstrong at the place of his now-known residence.

Unfortunately, newsmen at a Madison newspaper became privy to this "breaking story," and before Armstrong was to be arrested this newspaper printed the story of his imminent capture! More incredibly, journalists at a Toronto newspaper picked up this story and printed it in their newspaper! Karlton Armstrong, America's most-wanted felon, simply *read* of his imminent arrest, left his residence, and got on an airplane for Vancouver (on Canada's west coast). His capture was thus delayed by some 5¹/₂ years.

Comment: Should newspaper publishers be free to print *whatever* they please, on the theory that the citizenry of a democracy like ours should have access to *every* sort of information? Suppose that the American press had learned that Normandy was to be the site of the Allies' invasion of Europe a week hence. Should publishers have enjoyed the insouciant luxury of deciding for themselves as to whether or not to release this information days before the actual invasion?

Facilitating a Crime

Example No. 2: "A 'How-To' Book: *How to Kidnap Successfully.*" Imagine that a recent retiree from the government service has written a manuscript which he hopes to have published. This book, containing mostly anecdotal material, is a fascinating account of how he and his cronies, aided by sophisticated technological devices developed by the FBI, were able to "crack" some celebrated and not-to-so-celebrated cases of kidnapping. One chapter is devoted to the Lindbergh case, and another is devoted to the Leopold and Loeb crime. Detailed accounts are given as to how it was that evidence was gathered so that the kidnappers involved could be brought to justice. But, we go on to read, the devices used by the FBI in the olden days of Lindbergh are *nothing* compared to what the FBI has available now.

Imagine that each of the last five chapters of the manuscript is devoted to a detailed account of a currently-used device that was heretofore unknown to the public. The constitution and function of the instrument are carefully detailed, and a blueprint of it is presented. The text of the chapters make it clear, moreover, that each of these devices can be easily "foiled" in clearly defined ways.

Comment: Should a book publisher interested in making a buck be allowed to publish the book? And even if the sales of the book to would-be kidnappers don't make it a best-seller, at least we (as book publishers) could take solace in the fact that— true to Vonnegut—we have made available to American voters yet another source of information . . . without libeling anyone!

No Immunity from Legal Regulation

Not everything that can be labelled "speech," or "expression," or "utterance" is worth protecting. Much of it must be granted immunity for the sake of preserving the freedom of speech and press that serves the ends of the First Amendment. But not all of it need be or should be rendered immune from legal regulation for the general good. The ends of the First Amendment, broad though they are, are not compatible with everything that it enters into the mind of man to utter, in any way in which he chooses to utter it. The quest for rationality in interpreting the amendment's guarantees of freedom of speech and press forces us to ask, in the end, what the freedom is for.

Francis Canavan, *Freedom of Expression: Purpose as Limit,* 1984.

The reader will note that the examples presented thus far—non-fictional writings—seem never to occur to those who oppose censorship. But I suggest that (to paraphrase Percy Bysshe Shelley) when we talk seriously of the censorship of fiction, talk of the possible censorship of non-fiction should not be far behind. Books of fiction are *not* the recalcitrant cases; non-fiction books are the problem!

Examine now another kind of case, one in which Vonnegut's word "idea" (as in "Idea Killer") seems strangely out of place. Look at examples that involve the *image*, the *picture*.

Example No. 3: "Docudrama: An Execution." There was a public execution not long ago in a bullfighting arena in Mexico City, Mexico. The executed had been convicted of all manner of horrible acts, and the citizenry of Mexico had its revenge. (Those readers who are weak of stomach might well want to move along to *Example No. 4* at this point.)

The twenty-minute execution was of a man who was standing, with his arms and legs spread apart and tied. He was shot five times and at five-minute intervals. He was shot in each knee-cap, each shoulder, and, finally, between his eyes. His shrieks of pain, needless to say, inspired the large throng there assembled to great heights of ecstasy.

Repugnant Images

Now suppose that an American film producer seizes the opportunity to film the goings-on. And we all know how it would be done! Cameras would whir so that the slow-motion action of bullet-smashing-kneecap could be fully savored. And what is a bullet-smash without *Dolby* stereo?

Our film producers now wishes to distribute the film to American audiences as a commercial venture. The film, he asserts, is a bit of Americana, albeit Central-Americana, and, anyway, it's newsworthy!

Comment: Again, nobody is libeled. Should we hold that in the interests of *cinema verite, qua* art-form, that this "docudrama" be allowed to see the American light of day? Or, is it rather that the producer's venture is *so* repugnant that his film ought not be seen?

Example No. 4: "The Video-Tape of an Outrage." An actual criminal case, considered in a state court of Minnesota, involved a defendant who was charged with committing an unusually bizarre series of crimes. In brief, he was accused and later convicted of kidnapping a woman, torturing and sexually assaulting her. (The woman had committed the unpardonable sin years before of giving the defendant a grade of "B" in her geometry class.)

The defendant, lest he allow himself to forget his manly acts, made videotapes of the proceedings, and these tapes, later found by police, were introduced into evidence against the defendant at his trial. It was thus that the tapes became "matters of public record," "matters in the public domain."

Managers of the local television stations in the Twin Cities then stumbled over each other to petition the court for release of the tapes. Being in the public domain, the video records were of interest to the public, and (true to their civic duty) the station managers sought to show portions of the videotapes on the six- and ten-o'clock news broadcasts. The station managers *did* concede that the tapes were "sensitive," and they reassured His Honor that they would handle this material with discretion. (One only assumes that the woman assaulted was much comforted by this assurance!) The judge duly noted the station managers' request; he decided after brief deliberation to deny the managers their request for the tapes. Apparently, he felt the woman had suffered enough.

Comment: This case begs us to consider carefully a dangerous bit of verbal legerdemain that goes on in Vonnegut's brief against censorship. Recall his view that "Americans [should be] free to read or publish whatever they please." Regarding it, we might say simply that he has overstated his case and that if we restrict our discussion to works of fiction (properly so-called), we agree with him. . . .

Censorship and Unsubstantiated Charges

When we learn of a teacher being fired for, say, using *The Catcher in the Rye* in her English class, we are offended; we clamor, or *should* clamor, for her reinstatement. We feel that she has been unjustly treated, and that *The Catcher in the Rye* should see the light of the high-schooler's day. We are restored in our belief that censorship is dangerous, and we oppose it.

So far, so good! Indeed, censorship abuses *are* dangerous in a free society. But what many of us fail to realize is that the *absence* of any censorship can be equally dangerous, or more dangerous. Consider a final example:

Recently, a colleague was charged in a criminal complaint of sexually assaulting a young boy. The colleague's name and details of the allegations made against him were splashed on the front pages of the local and school newspapers. Before a trial was held, the accused was given an opportunity to "tell his side of the case," to explain himself! His rebuttal "testimony" was then carried in the school's newspaper.

Then the charges were dropped. There was insufficient evidence to bring the matter to trial, and we learned that the "case" against the accused was frivolous.

Vonnegut maintains that those who favor censorship are Iranians. I fancy myself an American who favors censorship. But if Vonnegut be correct—if the American way is, for example, to publish unsubstantiated charges against untried fellow-citizens—then I shall depart my beloved country for England, where such practice is not tolerated. Maybe in Iran, Mr. Vonnegut, are unsubstantiated charges to be printed, but (one hopes) not in America. . . .

Were one to say, "I oppose capital punishment, but Charles Manson should fry and Patricia Krenwinkle should be hanged," we would properly be confused; despite his disclaimer, the speaker is an advocate of capital punishment. Yet when one says, "I oppose censorship, but some published material may merit censorship" or ". . . but there must be some practical, *ad hoc* method of making [censorship] decisions," we somehow feel *unconfused,* as if these speakers are being consistent.

Does the proponent of capital punishment maintain that *everyone* ought to be executed? Or even that all criminals should be? Or even that all convicted felons should be? No! To defend capital punishment is precisely to believe that there is at least one case in which capital punishment is justifiably carried out. To believe in censorship is not to recommend that all printed matter be immersed in a huge vat of *Liquid Paper!* It is merely to maintain that there are circumstances in which material is justifiably censored.

My putative critics—"opponents" of censorship—write that ". . . there must be some practical, *ad hoc* method of making [censorship] decisions," and that ". . . examples must be considered on a case-by-case basis."

I would have thought that this is precisely what the censor *does!*

"Thought, followed by speech, followed by the written word, must be protected as a unit."

Freedom of Expression Should Not Be Restricted

Jean Otto

The First Amendment's freedom of speech guarantee is Americans' most cherished right and should be vigorously defended, Jean Otto argues in the following viewpoint. Otto maintains that restricting freedom of expression harms democracy by inhibiting people's inclination to express their views. Otto contends that all views, including those offensive to others, must be protected so that all Americans can hear or read them. Otto is the founder of the First Amendment Congress, a Denver, Colorado, organization that emphasizes the importance of First Amendment rights, and is a former associate editor of the *Rocky Mountain News*, a Denver daily newspaper.

As you read, consider the following questions:

1. In Otto's opinion, why should military information be free of government censorship?
2. Why does the author believe that censorship of school newspapers is harmful to students?
3. How could restrictions on expression lead people to become disinterested in politics and democracy, according to Otto?

From Jean Otto, "Freedom to Speak and Write," a speech delivered to the First Amendment Congress, October 27, 1991, Richmond, Virginia.

We Americans are ambivalent about many of our rights and privileges. We abhor censorship, yet many of us believe that certain information, or ideas, or art, or music, or plays ought to be censored. Information about birth control and abortion. Even our Supreme Court believes in this kind of censorship. Until recently, it said so in ruling that those who receive federal funds for family planning clinics may not even say the word abortion. Censorship.

State Secrets

Information about certain kinds of military weapons, as revealed in the prior restraint of the *Progressive Magazine* story on how to build an H-Bomb. A story kept out of that publication for months even though all the information had been gathered from public sources. Censorship. Information about the Stealth bomber. And how it works. Or doesn't work. The safety of military helicopters. Censorship.

Timely and accurate information about our military excursions. The military's assigning handlers to every reporter attempting to be an honest broker of information during the Gulf War constituted censorship. The public wanted to know what was happening. Their sons and husbands and brothers were there. Reporters tried to find out. But the military, as in Grenada and Panama, wrapped information in the opacity of intimidation and inaccessibility. Censorship.

Justice Hugo Black said that

> Paramount among the responsibilities of free speech is the duty to prevent any part of the government from deceiving the people and sending them off to distant lands to die of foreign fevers and foreign shot and shell.

To that, we might add also, looking at Vietnam and the Gulf War, "of our own shot and shell."

Some forms of censorship are more overt than others, of course. Some of it takes place in denying to the public and the press information sought under the Freedom of Information Act. And some of it takes place in the very setting where a new generation is learning what it means to be a citizen of this country.

I refer to the Hazelwood decision in which the Supreme Court ruled that it's OK for a school principal or superintendent to remove stories from a student newspaper. Justice Byron White, who wrote the majority decision, said:

> A school need not tolerate student speech that is inconsistent with its basic educational mission, even though the government could not censor similar speech outside the school.

Three justices dissented. William Brennan wrote for himself and Justice Thurgood Marshall and Harry Blackmun that the notion of letting public officials control newspaper content showed "unthinkable contempt for individual rights." And he added, "It is particularly insidious from (a high school principal) to whom the public entrusts the task of inculcating in its youth an appreciation for the cherished democratic liberties that our Constitution guarantees."

Ben Bagdikian, journalism professor at the University of California at Berkeley, warned:

> If freedom of expression becomes merely an empty slogan in the minds of enough children, it will be dead by the time they are adults.

The lesson of Hazelwood was that it is OK to limit what the press may report. In another year or two, when students were old enough to vote, they would have learned that government, perhaps in the form of the Defense Department, or the Department of Energy, or the President, was entitled to do likewise. They would not think it strange or unusual that someone could tell the press what to say and tell the public what they could read and hear. Is that how we grow citizens who insist on their right to information as the base for making decisions about the kind of city, state, or nation we are to be?

These are the same kind of young people surveyed by People for the American Way in a 1989 study called "Democracy's Next Generation." What it found was that young people between 15 and 24 are markedly less involved and less interested in public life than previous generations were. Like their parents, they believe that this is the best country in the world to live in. But they are singularly unaware of the responsibility to participate in the hard work of self-government.

The Value of Freedom of Speech

These young people were asked whether, if they had to trade off one of their rights or freedoms in order to keep all the others, which would they be most willing to give up. The first to go, for every age group, was freedom of the press. The one they most wanted to keep was freedom of speech, followed by the right to vote and then the right to pick their own careers.

Then they said that, if the U.S. were invaded by a foreign country that tried to take away some of our rights and freedoms, they would fight hardest to keep freedom of speech, followed by freedom of religion and the right to pick their own careers. At the absolute bottom of the list was freedom of the press.

Yet Walter Cronkite advises:

> Freedom of the press . . . is not just important to democracy, it is democracy.

Our next generation has not heard, or perhaps has heard but not understood.

In 1990, the Thomas Jefferson Center for the Protection of Free Expression commissioned a study on American attitudes toward free speech and free press. It found that 90 percent of those surveyed thought government should not be able to tell citizens what to say, but 28 percent said that freedom of expression should not cover newspapers. About 29 percent didn't think this freedom should apply to cable TV, and 33 percent would abolish this freedom for network TV.

© Nina Paley. Reprinted with permission.

Even as they recognized the importance of the press being permitted to print whatever information it could get, 58 percent said government should be allowed to censor. They saw no harm to personal liberty if government kept certain material off network or cable TV, in fact a solid majority thought government should be able to keep violence and sex off television.

As for advertising—commercial speech—94 percent thought it important that businesses be able to advertise their products, but 53 percent favored bans on advertising in order to protect the health of consumers. That explains of course the public outrage that Philip Morris, which makes, among other things, legal cigarettes, was allowed to sponsor the traveling Bill of Rights exhibit, or to mention its own name in the Bill of Rights ads it sponsored on television. People, it seems, feared that Philip Morris might be found innocent by association. Or the Bill of Rights somehow demeaned by association with a tobacco company. We may like a message but if we hate the speaker, we want no part of what he has to say. It seems to me that we Americans should get our act together. Either we mean the First Amendment, and the Bill of Rights, or we should toss them out and say that only a few of us should decide what is right for all of us.

The Principle of Free Thought

In 1991, the American Society of Newspaper Editors released a survey carried out by Robert Wyatt at Middle Tennessee State University. It observed that "Americans may be cultivating a belief in a new right, 'the right not to be offended'." This belief, the survey reported, was an attempt by people to protect themselves and their families from words, music, photographs and other forms of expression that they find offensive or distasteful.

Justice Oliver Wendell Holmes had a response to this:

> If there is any principle of the Constitution that more impera-
> tively calls for attachment than any other it is the principle of
> free thought—not free thought for those who agree with us
> but freedom for the thought we hate.

The study on Free Expression and the American Public reveals the narrowing of the American debate. Many of us, it says, have grown more and more reluctant to express our views. We learn by osmosis and enculturation what is acceptable, and refuse to stick our necks out with views that differ from those of current company. How many of us, for example, openly reject racial, or sexist, or ethnic slurs made in ordinary conversation? We may not like such speech, and we may recount it to others at some other time or place, but few of us challenge such speakers on the spot. We go along to get along. And now we have the phenomenon of "politically correct." Prospects of this are that fewer of us will say what we think to avoid the risk of offending, and so offend language and meanings and the currency of communication.

Reluctance to say what we think especially afflicts the young, the poor, and those who are not well educated. The study also found that women are less likely than men to speak out on political issues; they fear retribution and getting involved. They want things to go smoothly. Older people also frequently lack the self-confidence to refute ideas they dislike. Nonwhites also are more timid about expressing their views.

Certainly this undermines the First Amendment assumption that Americans would get their ideas out there for discussion, that the marketplace of views and ideas would hear and read them all, and from all the conflicts and contradictions be able to identify what is true and right. If a significant portion of Americans feel they cannot speak their minds, then that marketplace has gaps and empty places. Just as there are great empty places in voting booths on election day. Both bespeak citizens who, for whatever reason, prefer to remain uninvolved.

Protect the Right to Communicate

Uninvolved is what citizens cannot be in a democratic society if democracy is to thrive. If some of us decline to learn, to speak, to share our thoughts, then decisions are left to the vocal few, whose ideas may not reflect those of the majority at all.

Sen. William E. Borah, referring to the impact of inhibition and timidity in speaking out, noted

> If the press is not free, if speech is not independent and untrammeled, if the mind is shackled or made impotent through fear, it makes no difference under what form of government you live, you are a subject and not a citizen.

Justice Black said that

> Freedom to speak and write about public questions is as important to the life of our government as is the heart to the human body. . . . If that heart be weakened, the result is debilitation; if it be stilled, the result is death.

To speak and to write are opposite sides of the intellectual freedom that is the coin of democracy. A thought not communicated may have some value to the individual thinker, but it does nothing to enhance any community, whether that be one's city or state or nation. The right to communicate, honestly, openly, is the spine of the First Amendment. Thought, followed by speech, followed by the written word, must be protected as a unit, because to interrupt at any stage is to deny society its right to know and to understand.

"We can ban racist ideas without any damage to . . . the First Amendment and free speech."

Hate Speech Should Be Outlawed

Charles Brown

Some forms of speech, particularly that of racist groups, have been the target of restrictive laws. In the following viewpoint, Charles Brown argues that racist speech must be restricted because the ideas expressed by such speech have led to the murder and suffering of millions of people throughout history. Brown asserts that free speech is based on truth and that the lies of racist speech should not have constitutional protection. Brown is an attorney in Detroit and a member of the National Alliance Against Racist and Political Repression, an advocacy group in New York City.

As you read, consider the following questions:

1. How is fascism a threat in America, according to Brown?
2. In Brown's opinion, why should freedom of speech be balanced against the right to be free from racist insults and threats?
3. According to the author, how has fascist speech historically been condoned over leftist speech?

Charles Brown, "For Outlawing Fascistic Racist Speech," *Crossroads*, December 1992/January 1993. Reprinted with permission.

The U.S. Supreme Court decision in 1992 that overturned laws outlawing crossburning based on "freedom" of speech and assembly for the Ku Klux Klan makes it appropriate to place before the left some of the legal and philosophical arguments for outlawing fascistic racist speech, assembly and organizations.

Liberal and civil libertarian arguments for tolerating KKK, Nazi and similar groups' political speech rely on the part of the U.S. free speech and assembly tradition legally crystallized in the First Amendment to the U.S. Constitution, and on judge-made law originating in the early 20th century opinions of Supreme Court justices Oliver Wendell Holmes and Louis Brandeis. In that approach, an important, democratic legal doctrine is extended so far as to turn into its opposite, so far as to justify promotion of a political doctrine—fascistic racism—which advocates abolition of most of the historic achievements of democracy, including freedom of speech itself.

Racism: Crime Against Humanity

A left perspective must begin with material facts, with the actual history of the doctrine of free speech and the doctrine of racism. It is no exaggeration to say that racism and racist ideology have been critical factors in the deaths and horrible oppression of hundreds of millions of people. The genocidal usurpation of the Western Hemisphere, the genocidal enslavement of Africans, worldwide colonialism, the Nazi holocaust against the Jews and Eastern Europe, dropping the atom bomb on Japan, the Vietnam War, the War on Iraq—these are the bitter fruits of racism and racist propaganda. By this, although body counts give diminishing returns in measuring crimes, racism is arguably history's greatest crime against humanity. (See *The World and Africa*, by W.E.B. Du Bois.) As important as freedom of speech has been for modern political liberation, it cannot be said that repression of free speech has led so directly and critically to holocaustic crimes comparable to those briefly outlined above. Fascistic racist ideas have many times in history entered the Holmes-Brandeis "marketplace of ideas," and more often than we can risk again the result has been holocaustic crimes against humanity, with hundreds of millions murdered and suffering lifelong oppression.

The First Amendment or our cultural freedom of speech must not be understood abstracted from history. We do not have to keep debating whether the world is round or flat. Similarly, the solid evidence of history in the long and short term gives proof beyond a reasonable doubt, nay *any* doubt, that there is no greater social evil than racist acts and movements, and that racist ideas, ideology and speech create a clear and present danger of racist acts and movements. Racism is like smallpox virus.

The remote possibility that it might give some future benefit to the human species does not make it worth preserving now. Balancing the real threat of genocidal harm against the "good" of racist ideas' "free play" in the marketplace of ideas, we can ban racist ideas without any damage to even the bourgeois liberal, idealistic purpose and rationale of the First Amendment and free speech.

Fascism in America

The fascist threat has not been eradicated from the American political scene. (See *Old Nazis, the New Right and the Republican Party*, by Russ Bellant.) The large votes for openly fascistic racist David Duke are important evidence that the genocidal threat of materialized racist doctrine has not faded into the past—thus the continuing need for outlawing this doctrine and outlawing political organization for realization of racism. Given the gravity of the danger and destruction which is fascism, extremely "premature" anti-fascist alarm is sensible. We should not wait until fascism is close to reality to struggle vigorously against it. Self-admitted fascism is one political movement that justifiably can be nipped in the bud in exception to general freedom of speech and assembly. U.S. law provides many other content exceptions to First Amendment protection of speech—for example, crying "fire" falsely in a crowded theater, libel, slander, obscenity or announcing an airline hijacking.

Legal Attacks Against Hate Speech

We must think hard about how best to launch legal attacks against the most indefensible forms of hate speech. Good lawyers can create exceptions and narrow interpretations that limit the harm of hate speech without opening the floodgates of censorship.

Everyone concerned with these issues must find ways to engage actively in actions that resist and counter the racist ideas that we would have the First Amendment protect. If we fail in this, the victims of hate speech must rightly assume that we are on the bigots' side

Charles Lawrence, *San Francisco Chronicle*, September 9, 1990.

On the individual as well as the genocidal level the effects of racist speech justify its prohibition when balanced against some bizarre individual right to express racism. Why is individual freedom of speech never balanced against the individual right to be free of racist insult and threat? Professor Mari Matsuda has essayed this legal matrix with special attention to the individual psychic harm to the victim.

Racism Is a Lie

A progressive understanding of the First Amendment is that it should protect the working class and people's right to know the truth. The value of truth is the obvious basis for excepting the cry of "fire!" *falsely* in a crowded theater from First Amendment protection. Since racial supremacy is false as demonstrated by science (especially biology and anthropology—although there are new struggles in academe against "scientific" racist doctrines such as sociobiology; see *Not in Our Genes* by R.C. Lewontin et al.)—this is another basis for denying racist doctrine free speech protection. Ann Ginger wrote in *The New U.S. Criminal Statute, the First Amendment, and the New International Information Order*: "When the First amendment was adopted, everyone knew that libel was not free speech, that telling lies about someone was not protected speech. This was part of the common law of England because lies imperil the public peace. That common law was transmitted to the colonies and hence to the new United States. Now everyone will learn that genocide is not free speech, that inciting genocide is not protected because it imperils the public peace. It falsely cries "Fire!" in the crowded theater that is 20th century America, falsely blaming minority groups for problems the majority face."

An important pragmatic *left* argument for accepting free speech protection for fascistic racist speech sees protection of left political speech as dependent upon the rule of tolerating all minority political speech. The scope of this viewpoint does not allow full debate with this position, but I offer the following critical arguments against it.

First, in historical fact, if one looks beyond the rhetoric and word formulas of the judges' opinion, the communists and progressives are as often as not denied free speech and put in jail (Debs, the Palmer Raids, the McCarthy era) and the fascistic racists are freed by the courts or never arrested in the first place. Thus, protecting fascistic racist speech has not meant consistently protecting progressive speech. We must build protection for our speech not by this link in legal "logic," but through winning masses of people politically in the all around manner that is the left's general goal.

Second, the tradeoff for whatever role the courts have played or might play in protecting oppressed racial or political group members' freedom of speech is not worth the allowance of the existence and growth of fascistic racist groups which directly, physically threatens their ideological targets—oppressed racial, social and political group members. Every week this results in bigoted violence that extinguishes the freedom of speech of its direct victims and of others made fearful.

Enforcing Laws Against Racism

In 1988 the U.S. adopted as domestic criminal law the U.N. anti-genocide law. This international law was the legal basis for the famous *We Charge Genocide* petition of William L. Patterson, Louise Thompson Patterson, Paul Robeson and many others. However, since its adoption there have been no prosecutions under it. This is due in part to court protection of fascistic racist speech in line with the liberal doctrines described above. Despite these legal complications, the National Alliance Against Racist and Political Repression, in the tradition of the *We Charge Genocide* petition and other such efforts, has undertaken a campaign to guarantee enforcement of the new anti-genocide law and other old and new laws against racist organizing and violence. (See *Enforce the Proxmire Anti-Genocide Law: Stop Racist and Anti-Semitic Violence*.) This is not an easy task given the extreme racism of the U.S. Supreme Court. Shifting the law from its current liberal doctrine to the doctrine of prohibition of fascistic racist speech partially explained in this viewpoint must be won mainly as part of a mass political movement and overall radical change in this country. Perhaps this viewpoint will encourage political activists—through organizational programs, newspaper and university debates and discussions and the whole range of practice in protest, lobbying, voting, referenda, recall and constitutional amendment campaigns—to struggle more consciously against the intermingling of liberal and racist doctrine.

"It is not for government to decide which kinds of speech are more offensive than others."

Hate Speech Should Not Be Outlawed

Gara LaMarche

Free speech advocates contend that hate speech should not be restricted by law, no matter how offensive such speech may be. In the following viewpoint, Gara LaMarche agrees and argues that such laws are ineffective and selectively used. LaMarche states that other countries' hate speech laws have failed to achieve the goal of reducing racial conflict and that the United States should not enact similar laws. LaMarche maintains that lawmakers cannot single out offensive words based on race, religion, or gender for punishment, while ignoring other types of offensive speech. LaMarche is executive director of The Fund for Free Expression, an organization in New York City which promotes freedom of speech and human rights.

As you read, consider the following questions:

1. Why does LaMarche believe that distinctions should be made between hate groups' advocacy and action?
2. How could majority groups use hate speech laws to suppress the views of minority groups, in LaMarche's opinion?
3. According to the author, how can hate crime laws reduce interracial violence?

From Gara LaMarche, "The U.S. 'Hate Speech' Debate," *Peace and Democracy News,* Winter 1992-1993. Reprinted with permission.

The United States is in the midst of one of its periodic debates about the borders of free speech and equality. Most of the discussion has centered on the wave of "hate speech" provisions in disciplinary codes adopted by a number of colleges and universities. More recently it has been provoked by the Supreme Court's decision in a Minnesota cross-burning case—a decision that is controversial not so much for its outcome as for its reasoning, which may have altered the First Amendment landscape.

So many gallons of ink have been spilled about "hate speech" that it is daunting to consider adding more. Yet I believe that there are two important perspectives that have been missing from the debate—or, at least, that have not been articulated often or forcefully enough. The first is an international perspective: virtually every other country on earth punishes racist expression; what can the U.S. learn from that experience? The lesson drawn from that is closely related to the second missing perspective—how minorities and others who have lacked political power are disadvantaged by curbs on speech and expression, and how they have been targeted in many U.S. censorship battles.

Considering Speech Regulations

At the outset, I want to set forth four principles that govern my consideration of "hate speech" regulations and laws or any other curb on freedom of expression. First, there should be a careful distinction between advocacy and action. Second, expression should never be punished for its subject matter alone. Third, if speech is ever to be punished, there must be a direct and immediate connection to illegal action. Finally, any limitations on expression should be the least restrictive available.

These principles are shared by two organizations—Human Rights Watch and the American Civil Liberties Union—whose policies in this area I have had a hand in crafting. The other thing common to both groups, and to any institution that wants to deal credibly with "hate speech," is a strong commitment not just to freedom of expression, but to the eradication of inequality.

For example, the ACLU's 1990 policy statement on "Free Speech and Bias on College Campuses" asserts that "all students have the right to participate fully in the educational process on a nondiscriminatory basis." It also outlines eight steps to insure that all students "may participate fully in campus life," including adoption of affirmative action and dormitory desegregation plans and courses in "the history and meaning of prejudice." The ACLU is the foremost U.S. organization defending First Amendment rights; what is less well known is its extensive program (commanding many times the resources of the First Amendment work) on behalf of voting rights and non-discrimination in employment and education. The 1991 Human Rights Watch policy statement says that "freedom of speech and equal protection of the laws are not incompatible, but are, rather, mutually reinforcing rights." Like the ACLU, Human Rights Watch has an ongoing program of opposition to racism—for example, as the publisher of a series of reports on the persecution of ethnic minorities in Europe, Asia, and Africa.

Free Speech and International Law

The principles I have summarized above are closely related to U.S. First Amendment jurisprudence. This inevitably subjects me to charges of a narrow "Americanism" in my outlook. Yet international law contains apparently conflicting standards where "hate speech" is concerned. On the one hand, Article 19 of the International Covenant on Civil and Political Rights (ICCRP) holds that "everyone shall have the right to hold opinions without interference" and "everyone shall have the right to freedom of expression. This right shall include freedom to seek, receive and impart information and ideas of all kinds, regardless of frontiers, either orally, in writing or in print, in the form of art, or through any other media of his choice," subject only to those restrictions necessary "for respect of the rights or reputations of others" or "for the protection of national security or of public order, or of public health or morals."

On the other hand, Article 20 of the ICCRP requires the participating states to prohibit "any advocacy of national, racial or religious hatred that constitutes incitement to discrimination, hostility or violence." Article 4 of the International Convention on the Elimination of All Forms of Racial Discrimination (CERD) goes even further, calling on states to punish "all dissemination of ideas based on racial superiority or hatred" and to prohibit organizations "which promote and incite racial discrimination."

A number of countries have made reservations to Article 20 on freedom of expression grounds, including Luxembourg and Britain. When the United States ratified the Covenant, it did so with a reservation that "nothing in this Covenant shall be deemed to require or to authorize legislation or other action by the United States which would restrict the right of free speech protected by the Constitution, law and practices of the United States."

There is little connection in practice between draconian "hate speech" laws and the lessening of ethnic and racial violence or tension. Furthermore, most of the nations that invoke "hate speech" laws have a long way to go in implementing the provisions of CERD that call for the elimination of racial discrimination. Laws that penalize speech or membership are also subject to abuse by the dominant racial or ethnic group. Some of the most stringent "hate speech" laws, for example, have long been in force in South Africa, where they have been used almost exclusively against the black majority. . . .

U.S. Censorship Laws and Minorities

The invocation of hate speech laws against anti-apartheid demonstrators is a natural bridge to discussion of the second perspective largely absent from the current debate over hate speech: the way *all* censorship laws have been used to silence blacks and other minorities.

In 1976, for example, the board of the Island Trees school district on Long Island removed nine books from the school library as "un-American, anti-Christian, and just plain filthy." Little noted at the time or since was the fact that seven of the nine were by minority authors, including *Black Boy* by Richard Wright, *A Hero Ain't Nothing But a Sandwich* by Alice Childress, and works by Langston Hughes and Piri Thomas. The U.S. Supreme Court narrowly held that the First Amendment would be violated if it could be proven that those who removed the books were animated by a political motivation, but I have always felt that Island Trees was in effect a disguised exclusionary zoning case—a white suburban school district trying to fence out the ideas and the images of the urban ghetto.

Speech Bans Would Backfire

Any restriction on speech, no matter how narrowly drawn or well intended, is certain to lead to further restraints that will be broader and distinctly less benign. The precedent of today's ban on hateful speech is bound to be invoked tomorrow to justify constraints on other forms of expression. And when those constraints are imposed, their first victims are likely to be the very same groups who now call for rules and regulations—racial and ethnic minorities, women, lesbians and gays, political dissidents.

The Progressive, August 1992.

The theme of race re-emerges in the controversy over "offensive" song lyrics. Who are the only people to be criminally prosecuted over an allegedly obscene record? A black rap group, 2 Live Crew, and a black record store owner. What sparked the war over the National Endowment for the Arts? Robert Mapplethorpe's photographs of interracial lovers.

Given the persistence and pervasiveness of racism in American society, it is no wonder that many blacks find curbs on racist speech an appealing weapon. But we are all in the same boat where First Amendment rights are concerned. As Justices William O. Douglas and Hugo Black wrote in a dissenting opinion in the 1952 case of *Beauharnais v. Illinois*, upholding a "group libel" law: "The same kind of state law that makes Beauharnais a criminal for advocating segregation in Illinois can be utilized to send people to jail in other states for advocating equality and nonsegregation.". . .

The St. Paul Case

How has the Supreme Court's 1992 decision in *R.A.V. v. St. Paul* affected the constitutional framework that applies to racist and other bigoted expression? The St. Paul ordinance struck down by the Court prohibited displays that could arouse "anger, alarm or resentment" based on "race, color, creed, religion or gender." The law had been used to prosecute a young white man who burned a cross on the front lawn of a black family.

Before the Court ruled, the pro and con arguments for the constitutionality of the ordinance seemed to go as follows. On the pro side, the city of St. Paul's brief argued: "On balance, the minimal First Amendment rights of one who clandestinely burns a cross in an African-American's yard are far outweighed by the rights of the victims to live where they wish in peace." On the con side, the Association of American Publishers and the Freedom to Read Foundation filed a friend-of-the-court brief that did not dispute that cross-burning aimed at intimidating a particular family can be subject to prosecution under harassment or anti-terror laws, but argued: "If the St. Paul ordinance had been in effect in the South during the 1950s, it could have been used to prosecute a black family for putting a sign on their front lawn demanding : 'Integrate all-white schools now!'"

All nine of the justices agreed with the AAP/Freedom to Read Foundation view—also supported by the ACLU—that the ordinance was vague and overbroad, and therefore fatally flawed. But a majority of five, led by Justice Antonin Scalia, went even further. Even if the cross-burning constituted the kind of "fighting words" unprotected by the First Amendment, Scalia wrote, lawmakers cannot single out some kinds of fighting words for punishment (in the ordinance at issue, those which involved race, religion or gender) and not others.

Reinforcing the principle that it is not for government to decide which kinds of speech are more offensive than others, there is much in the majority opinion to cheer First Amendment advocates. It would certainly appear to sound the death knell for most campus "speech codes." But the sweeping analysis may also affect other kinds of anti-bias measures as well.

For instance, many states have adopted "hate crimes" statutes that enhance the criminal penalties for assaults where it can be shown that the victim was selected on the basis of race, religion or perceived sexual orientation. A number of free speech advocates, myself included, think that properly-drawn laws of this kind are an important tool against bias-related violence, and do not necessarily impede First Amendment rights. Others, like Nat Hentoff, disagree, claiming that the penalty enhancement is in effect a punishment for "bad thoughts." In any event, there is now reason to believe that the Supreme Court will be skeptical of such laws—not to mention regulation of sexual harassment in the workplace that is based on the creation of an "intimidating, hostile or offensive working environment."

Ugly Racist Acts

I don't believe that laws like St. Paul's or codes like the University of Michigan's are an acceptable remedy, but there is no denying the resurgence of racially-motivated violence all across the U.S. It recalls the nightmarish days when white lynch mobs roamed the South—only this time aimed at blacks who venture into predominantly white New York City neighborhoods like Bensonhurst and Howard Beach. The retreat from a national commitment to civil rights—after a dozen years of a government which sharply cut back the enforcement of anti-discrimination laws and seems more concerned about the rights of white "victims" of affirmative action programs than about the continuing paucity of minorities in professional positions and higher education courses—has legitimized uglier racist impulses. The fact that the Scalia majority in the St. Paul case is composed largely of justices better known for their opposition to affirmative action than their love of free speech will certainly leave many who care about the unfinished business of racial equality feeling even more angry and impotent.

I hope they will take their cue, as I will, from Eleanor Holmes Norton. As a young black lawyer working for the ACLU in the 1960s, Norton defended the segregationist governor of Alabama, George Wallace, when New York City tried to bar him from holding a rally in a public stadium. She went on to serve as President Jimmy Carter's chair of the federal Equal Employment Opportunity Commission, and now represents the District of Columbia as its delegate in Congress. She urges those concerned about hate speech to work on the root causes of racism and resist the temptation to make the First Amendment a scapegoat: "It is technically impossible to write an anti-speech code that cannot be twisted against speech nobody means to bar. It has been tried and tried and tried."

"Obscenity—commonly called hard-core pornography—and child pornography have never been considered protected speech."

Pornography Should Be Prohibited

H. Robert Showers

Many Americans think pornography is obscene and should be prohibited. In the following viewpoint, H. Robert Showers agrees and argues that pornography contributes to antisocial behavior and sex crimes, and that such offensive expression should not have legal protection. Showers maintains that since the drafters of the First Amendment never intended to protect obscenity, pornography is subject to regulation. Showers is president of the National Law Center for Children and Families, a group in Alexandria, Virginia, which aids communities and prosecutors seeking to outlaw pornography.

As you read, consider the following questions:

1. How has pornography become more widely available and increasingly degrading, according to Showers?
2. In the author's opinion, why would the purpose of the First Amendment be lost if all forms of expression were protected?
3. Why does Showers believe that antipornography laws should be modeled after child pornography laws?

From H. Robert Showers, "Pornography and the Law." This article appeared in the December 1992 issue and is reprinted with permission from *The World & I*, a publication of the Washington Times Corporation, © 1992.

Contrary to popular belief, obscenity—commonly called hard-core pornography—and child pornography have never been considered protected speech under either English common law or the U.S. Constitution. . . .

By examining the speeches of America's Founding Fathers, one can find no evidence that they considered obscenity to be a form of speech protected by the First Amendment. Rather, substantial evidence to the contrary exists. . . .

Thomas Jefferson declared the purposes of the speech and press clauses of the First Amendment to be: "1. To prohibit the Federal Government from passing laws making it a crime to criticize the Government; and 2. To keep the Federal Government from intruding into the right of the people of the several states to punish licentious speech according to local law."

In Jefferson's view, licentiousness meant slander, libel, fighting words, and obscene libel, which indicates that he never intended to protect what he considered unacceptable forms of expression. . . .

A Definition of Obscenity

In 1973, the Supreme Court handed down eight obscenity decisions that charted a new course of stricter regulation of obscenity, including the landmark *Miller* decision. In its ruling, the Court defined obscenity as:

> 1) a work, taken as a whole, that is directed toward a prurient (unhealthy, abnormal, morbid, or shameful) interest in sex;
>
> 2) a work that depicts or describes, in a patently offensive way, sexual conduct such as the ultimate sexual act, sex with animals, sexual violence, masturbation, and lewd exhibition of the genitals; and
>
> 3) a work that, taken as a whole, lacks serious literary, artistic, political, or scientific value.

This three-part obscenity test is to be applied by citizen juries according to local community standards of what is acceptable in their community where the criminal case is tried. Any review of history, political experience, and the law as it was developed in *Hickman, Roth,* and *Miller* will clearly demonstrate that, under Anglo-American system of jurisprudence, obscenity was never considered protected expression. Such a conclusion was provided by the Supreme Court in *Miller*:

> There are certain well-defined and narrowly limited classes of speech, the prevention and punishment of which has never been thought to raise any constitutional problem. These include the lewd and obscene. . . . It has been well observed that such utterances are of such slight social value . . . that any benefit that may be derived from them is clearly outweighed by the social interest in order and morality.

Other classes of "speech" that traditionally have never been constitutionally protected are libel, slander, false advertising, and perjury. Just as with obscenity, these forms of speech were clearly outside the contemplation of the drafters of the Bill of Rights and are subject to regulation. In *Paris Adult Theatre v. Slaton,* Chief Justice Warren Burger articulated the rationale on which all pornography legislation should be based:

> Mr. Justice Benjamin Cardozo said, "that all laws in western civilization are guided by a robust common sense.". . . The sum of experience, including that of the past two decades, affords an ample basis for legislators to conclude that a sensitive, key relationship of human existence central to family life, community welfare and the development of human personality can be debased and distorted by crass commercialization of sex. Nothing in the Constitution prohibits a State from reaching such a conclusion and acting on it legislatively simply because there is no conclusive evidence or empirical data. . . .

Miller and its seven companion cases cleared up some legal confusion concerning the regulation of obscenity. Nevertheless, circulation of obscene materials exploded. Illegal pornography, which was once a "black market" enterprise grossing in the mere millions of dollars a year and confined to the decaying areas of many large American cities, has now spread to suburban regions and small towns via the use of local video outlets, convenience stores, cable television, satellite television, telephone "dial-a-porn," and even home computers. The increase and availability of pornography has been accompanied by an ever-escalating severity of content, including increasingly degrading, violent, and exploitive depictions. . . .

The Supreme Court and Censorship

Many individuals, including law professors and members of the ACLU [American Civil Liberties Union], have strenuously argued that the Supreme Court's approach to obscenity is a mistaken interpretation of the First Amendment. They have argued that any criminal prosecution based on the distribution to consenting adults of sexually explicit materials, no matter how offensive and hard-core or devoid of literary, artistic, or scientific value, is impermissible under the First Amendment.

While some of these arguments concerning censorship and challenges to the Supreme Court's approach to obscenity have some merit, the least plausible is that the First Amendment is somehow an absolute protection of all speech. Even Justices Hugo Black and William Douglas, commonly known to be First Amendment "absolutists," have never protected all spoken or written acts. On closer inspection, those accused of or confessing to such "absolutism" would at the very least apply their absolutist view to a range of spoken, written, or pictorial acts smaller than the universe of all spoken, written, or pictorial acts. For example, it is doubtful that they would argue that taking pictures of a child who was violently and sexually abused, or falsely accusing someone of a heinous act and maliciously publishing the lie to destroy his reputation, should be protected by the First Amendment.

A more plausible argument might be that while not all spoken, written, or pictorial acts would be protected, there should be at least a higher standard of justification, often described as "a clear and present danger" or "compelling interest" to justify regulation of illegal pornography. People who espouse that view argue that the empirical evidence of harm and the reasons for regulation are not compelling enough to meet this especially high burden of justification.

A Wrong Interpretation

They would further extend the purposes of the First Amendment to include not just protection of political or social discourse against the government but any aspect of self-expression that takes the form of books, magazines, or films. They argue that, because the purpose of the First Amendment is to allow all points of view to be expressed, any attempt by the government to treat one point of view less favorably than another is unconstitutional for that reason alone, no matter how dangerous, offensive, or otherwise reprehensible the disfavored point of view may be.

Unfortunately, there are many problems with this interpretation of the First Amendment and with the argument to protect all pornography from regulation. First, the First Amendment was never intended to protect all forms of speech or expression, as is clearly shown by any brief historical review.

Second, the First Amendment itself would suffer if its essential appeal were dissipated on arguments that essentially favor crass commercialization of sex and violence. The strength of all laws cannot reside exclusively with the courts but must reside in the widespread acceptance of the importance of such laws. Thus, there is a risk that, in the process of protecting all expression and speech, the real purpose of the First Amendment may be lost and the likely losers will be those who speak out harshly and provocatively and often offensively against the prevailing order.

Third, the standard by which regulation should be justified is not "clear and present danger" but rather whether the state has a rational basis for regulating such offensive and harmful expression or conduct similar to the standard for libel, slander, perjury, and false advertising, which is to protect legitimate public health, safety, and morality concerns.

Finally, most arguments against regulation rest on the claims of the harmlessness of pornography, which, according to recent scientific evidence, law enforcement data, and the 1986 reports from the Attorney General's Commission on Pornography and the U.S. Surgeon General's Workshop, are simply not true. The pornography commission concluded:

> Both in clinical and experimental sex studies, exposure to sexually violent material indicated an increase in the likelihood of aggression. More specifically, the research . . . shows a causal relationship between exposure to material of this type and aggressive behavior toward women, parents, and children.

In the Surgeon General's Workshop, two dozen leading researchers gathered, including many critics of the pornography commission's report. Yet they also reached five consensus conclusions concerning the harm of pornography and its relation to sex crimes and antisocial behavior. . . .

Pornography Is Not Free Speech

With Catharine A. MacKinnon, I drafted the first civil law against pornography. It held pornographers accountable for what they do: they traffic in women (contravening the United Nations Universal Declaration of Human Rights and the Convention on the Elimination of All Forms of Discrimination Against Women); they eroticize inequality in a way that materially promotes rape, battery, maiming and bondage; they make a product that they know dehumanizes, degrades and exploits women; they hurt women to make the pornography, and then consumers use the pornography in assaults both verbal and physical. . . .

Pornographers do these things to women, and the public square is a big place—every newsstand and video store. A photograph shields rape and torture for profit. In defending pornography as if it were speech, liberals defend the new slavers. The only fiction in pornography is the smile on the woman's face.

Andrea Dworkin, *The New York Times Book Review*, May 3, 1992.

Recent public opinion polls reveal that many Americans want the government to crack down on pornography and restrict children's access to it. The discovery of evidence of pornography's harm and the change in public opinion has spurred many state and federal authorities to pass new antiporn laws and to enforce existing ones. . . .

Supreme Court decisions have also begun to provide more weapons in the regulation of pornography. For example, in *Renton v. Playtime Theatres* (1986), the Court gave cities a great deal more power to pass zoning, licensing, and other laws to help police regulate the secondary effects of pornographic outlets in communities. In *Arcara v. Cloud Books, Inc.*, the Supreme Court indicated that the secondary effects and evidence of harm were sufficient reasons to permit removal of peep show booth doors and to close pornography outlets because of public-health-threatening sexual activity in such outlets.

Finally, in two recent Supreme Court cases, *Fort Wayne Books v. Indiana* and *United States v. Pryba*, the Supreme Court found that it is fully constitutional to make obscenity (and child pornography) one of the base offenses in proving the existence of a criminal enterprise under the powerful racketeering laws that permit asset forfeiture and increased jail terms. . . .

On February 27, 1992, Canada's Supreme Court decided by a unanimous vote that it is legitimate to suppress materials that harm women (and children) even though freedom of expression may be involved. According to Yale University law professor Catharine MacKinnon, this means that what is obscene is what harms women and children and not necessarily what offends our values. Materials that subordinate, degrade, or dehumanize women and children could now be obscene in Canada. As Kathleen Mahoney, who argued the case, explained,

> The Court said that, while the obscenity laws limited the Charter's [Canada's constitution] freedom of expression guarantee, it is justifiable, because this type of expression harms women personally, harms their right to be equal, affects their security, and changes attitudes toward them so they become more subject to violence. . . . The Court also said the harm caused by proliferation of [such] materials would seriously offend the values fundamental to our society and is a substantial concern which justifies restricting the otherwise full exercise of the freedom of expression. . . .

While the *Miller* test is fairly simple to state and debate, the U.S. Supreme Court could end [legal] confusion by providing a set of crystal-clear definitions to augment this twenty-year-old test.

A Blanket Prohibition

The better solution, however, would be for Congress and the states to prohibit obscene material in a more objective per se manner, similar to what has occurred in the child pornography area. After *Ferber v. New York* (1982), for example, a jury could find a violation of child pornography laws if children under eighteen were visibly depicted as being involved in any sexually explicit conduct. Likewise, a simple, blanket prohibition of all hard-core pornography or even some of the more egregious categories of adult pornography would provide an easy-to-understand benchmark to slow commercial trafficking in the material.

Two options are available for the per se obscenity standard. One would be to prohibit commercial dissemination of any hard-core pornography, which means any explicit depictions of ultimate sex acts (vaginal, anal, or oral), masturbation or foreign object insertion, penetration or ejaculation, or sadomasochist abuse. Originally, *obscenity* and *hard-core pornography* were used interchangeably by the courts. But *Miller v. California* made it clear that even simulated depictions of sex acts and lewd exhibition of the genitals, neither of which were considered hard core, could be constitutionally prohibited. . . .

The other alternative is to further limit the per se approach to pornography that most researchers and the public agree are harmful and cause or contribute to antisocial criminal behavior. . . .

Since the largest age group of consumers of hard-core pornography are adolescents aged twelve to seventeen, and since the greatest effect of pornography is on more vulnerable and emotionally naive individuals such as children, such a law appears to be not only necessary but critical and constitutional.

While predictions are always uncertain, one thing is for sure: Indecision is a decision, and inaction is an action, where the lives of children and women are at risk, as has been proven to be the case with regard to obscene material. In the end, public opinion, not the legislatures or courts, will decide the degree to which pornography will be regulated.

"We need sexually explicit material produced by and for women, freed from the control of right wingers and misogynists."

Pornography Should Not Be Prohibited

Feminists Against Censorship

Feminists are divided on whether pornography should be censored. In the following viewpoint, Feminists Against Censorship argue that pornography should not be censored because a free, democratic society must accommodate such expression. Sexist and exploitive material such as pornography should be countered not through censorship, but through debate about sex and by creating more tolerant attitudes toward sexuality, the authors contend. Feminists Against Censorship maintain that women value some sexually explicit and erotic material and that it should be produced and openly available. Feminists Against Censorship is located in London, England.

As you read, consider the following questions:

1. Why do Feminists Against Censorship believe that women are at ease expressing disapproval of pornography?
2. According to the authors, why should people be trusted to decide for themselves whether to use pornography?
3. How can sexually explicit material be of value to women, according to Feminists Against Censorship?

From *Pornography and Feminism: The Case Against Censorship* by Feminists Against Censorship, edited by Gillian Rodgerson and Elizabeth Wilson. London: Lawrence and Wishart, 1991. Reprinted with permission.

Attempts are being made, in the name of feminism, to whip up public feeling against pornography and add to the laws that restrict its production and distribution. . . .

Ranged against the pro-censorship feminists is our group: Feminists Against Censorship. We founded the group in order to counter the increasing dominance of the censorship lobby and to ensure that an alternative feminist view is heard. . . .

Countering Offensive Images

As feminists we have a responsibility to be critical of those images we find sexist, racist or exploitative and to counter them in the most effective way there is, not by seeking to get them banned, but by initiating a much more wide-ranging debate about sex, by lobbying for better sex education in schools, by creating more informed, tolerant and responsible social attitudes to the expression of sexuality, and by supporting those who are creating an alternative body of sexual images for women. As we said in our first leaflet, issued in 1989:

> Women need open and safe communication about sexual matters, including the power relations of sex. We don't need new forms of guilt parading under the banner of political correctness. We need a safe, legal working environment for sex workers, not repressive laws or an atmosphere of social stigma that empowers police and punters to brutalize them. We need sexually explicit material produced by and for women, freed from the control of right wingers and misogynists, whether they sit on the board of directors or the board of censors. We need an analysis of violence that empowers women and protects them at the same time. We need a feminism willing to tackle issues of class and race and to deal with the variety of oppressions in the world, not to reduce all oppressions to pornography. . . .

Until feminism entered the debate, pornography and censoriousness were an inseparable couple. All our definitions of pornography depended upon this; an essential ingredient of pornography was the desire to shock, to cross the boundaries, to explore forbidden zones. Repressive sexual morality always tends to foster and feed its own 'worst enemies' in this way.

Into this traditional ritual of laws and law-breakers, feminism has tried to intrude with completely new considerations. Feminism has wanted to side-step the question of the boundaries of sexual decency and focus on the fact that most pornography is produced for heterosexual men, that it consists of masculine sexual fantasies, mainly about women. Some feminist writers have gone so far as to claim that pornography lies at the very heart of women's oppression, either because, as Robin Morgan put it 'pornography is the theory—rape is the practice' of male domination or because 'pornography *is* violence against women', as Andrea Dworkin says. Such writers have tended to paint a very lurid picture of pornography, as if it were all images of rape, sadism and degradation in which women are the victims.

Not Necessarily Oppressive

Anyone can see that much pornography represents a sexuality in which women are passive and men active, and women are desired and men desire. Pornography does contain stereotypes of women which feminism wishes to challenge. In this respect it is similar to many other genres, from Renaissance painting to *Vogue* magazine, which have been subjected to feminist critiques. This is not to say that pornography is good, simply that most of it is no worse than a great deal of the rest of the patriarchal and misogynist culture which it reflects.

If pornography is defined, as the Williams Committee [on Obscenity and Film Censorship] defined it, as representations that are both sexually explicit and have as their function the sexual arousal of their audience, then it is not *necessarily* oppressive to women. Indeed, many feminists have wanted to challenge the old taboos about sexual material, to talk more frankly about women's bodies—and men's—and to explore what we find arousing. It is certainly possible to imagine a pornography *for* women, though no one could guarantee that it would never be used by men in a misogynist way. . . .

Many women feel very ambivalent about pornography, welcoming images we find erotic but being quite disturbed by others. In a society where sex is so freighted with implications of non-conformity and disorder, it is difficult for women to express our pro-sex feelings in public. It is much easier to express the other side of the ambivalence: the disapproval. This has traditional respectability on its side and so is more likely to find a public voice and public support. Pornography is an area where there will be widespread support for further control but for reasons that are very foreign to feminism.

The pro-censorship, anti-pornography feminists are plugging into a pre-feminist debate although they claim to have gone beyond it. They are against *degrading* images of women, or images they consider to be degrading. But their allies are against *sexually explicit* images of any kind and against any material that aims to be sexually arousing. As Feminists Against Censorship we wish to challenge and to question this equation of the sexually arousing with the degrading. Otherwise the alliance of the anti-pornography feminists with the traditional moralists may succeed in reversing many of the gains that have been made during the twentieth century. . . .

Censorship in one area cannot be separated off from censorship in another area. A free and democratic society is one in which a diversity of views and behaviour is tolerated. That is not to say that there should or could be *no* restrictions on behaviour, or *no* regulation of what may be said, written or shown. We must recognize, however, that in a complex society, there is a wide range of views on matters to do with politics, sexuality and many other issues. Those who wield power can easily succumb to the view that they know best what is good for other people (people with less power normally) and seek to impose their views by preventing others from making up their own minds about allegedly 'seditious' or 'titillating' material, or material which will, in the minds of the legislators, 'undermine national character' or attack established religious beliefs. Scientists, secularists and many others have had to battle against the censors throughout the ages. Vested interests and established authorities always seem to want to keep the rest of us in ignorance. Whatever anyone's views about pornography in particular, the general approach should be that individuals may normally be trusted to make up their own minds. That, unfortunately, is not the view taken by current campaigns against pornography. . . .

Freedom to Offend

Pornography is often grotesquely offensive; it is insulting, not only to women but to men as well. But we cannot consider that a sufficient reason for banning it without destroying the principle that the speech we hate is as much entitled to protection as any other. The essence of negative liberty is freedom to offend, and that applies to the tawdry as well as the heroic.

Ronald Dworkin, *The New York Review of Books*, August 15, 1991.

If everyone had the right to ban all images and written material which happened to offend them, how much would actually be left? If we were all only allowed to see and read that which offended no-one, culture would be utterly insipid—or more likely non-existent!

The distinction between 'erotica' and 'pornography', which the anti-pornographers have taken over from a mainstream elitist debate about what is artistically justifiable, tries to draw a clear dividing line between 'good' sex and 'bad' sex. We are not saying that all sex is automatically 'good' or that pornography can never be horrible or violent; we do feel that responses to explicit material are very subjective and that 'erotica' is what 'we' like while pornography is what 'they' like. Yet sometimes it is the 'pornography' that is the most interesting, creative and exciting; which, after all, is the purpose of the sexually explicit.

Western society over-values stereotyped ideals of sexual attractiveness and emphasizes the importance of sex in what are often unhelpful and disempowering ways. One result of this is that our insecurities about sexuality can be confusing and threatening. In a society in which sex is both a dirty joke and the most important thing about us, the key to happiness and a dark secret, it is much easier to criticize sexual images produced by other people than it is to examine our own fantasies and desires and take the risk of producing and being turned on by the representation of those desires and fantasies in words and pictures. It is easier to claim that women's sexuality is so colonized and so threatened that we can't possibly afford to do anything except batten down the hatches and try to get rid of everything we find unpleasant and nasty. It's much easier to assume that women who work in the sex trade must be abused victims, than to accept that their work can in some circumstances be their choice, and support them in their calls for better working conditions and less oppressive legal interference in their lives.

Target Sexism and Male Power

The campaigns against pornography are losing the feminist impetus that they started out with as they reach a wider audience and gain support from the moral right. The campaign is no longer primarily a critique of sexism, masculine power or patriarchal society. First it becomes a critique of the pornography industry: a 'billion dollar industry', as we're often told. Well, the food and garment industries are 'billion dollar industries' too, so what's new? If some people feel that it's wrong to profit from the sale of sexual imagery, why don't they campaign against those who make vast profits out of feeding us, often with polluted and dangerous food? To point the finger at the industry is to ignore the more important critique of sexism and of male power, which is what feminists should target. Of course, when the campaign then gets taken up by the 'moral majority', the target of their attack becomes the 'permissive society', they want to *restore* patriarchal power, which they feel has been eroded by the greater freedom of choice, limited though it still is, that women have gained over the past thirty years.

We have seen the ways in which feminism has made a difference in the world. Women are taking control of their lives and at least some young women have more choices, including sexual choices, than they once did. We must defend those gains. We have a right to our own sexuality and many of us are taking the expression of our sexuality in public, in words and pictures, out of the hands of multinational corporations with their limited imaginations about what anyone does 'in bed'. Many women are taking risks to produce feminist sexual images, images which do not exploit either the viewer or the producer.

In the past decade, there has been an explosion of material produced by women, particularly by lesbians. In the United States, this began with the line drawings of the *Cunt Coloring Book* and there is now the explicit photography and stories of *On Our Backs* (the San Francisco magazine). The lesbian film *Desert Hearts* has received fairly wide distribution, sex scene and all. In Britain, the lesbian erotic short story book *Serious Pleasure* is in two volumes and the sex magazine *Quim* has published two issues. Both the production and the consumption of pornography can be erotic acts, and we have the right to participate in these acts.

The Real Battle

We must go on the offensive and stop being baited by those who call our defence of our sexual images oppressive, stop allowing them to set the agenda for what is and is not feminist. The battle against pornography, like the temperance movement at the turn of the century, is about much more than gin, videos, or 'vice'. To a disturbing extent, the present censorship campaigns could end up, as those former campaigns did, as one group of women attempting to control and regulate another, less privileged group. And all the while the real battle is elsewhere: it is the battle against public and private violence, against unequal pay structures, against a lack of opportunities for girls and women.

We support campaigns for greater freedom of expression in all forms of art and culture. We want better sex education. We want an end to the militaristic, imperialistic culture of our society, and an end to racist and sexist violence. These evils arise in part from poverty, exploitation and injustice, but also from the cult of the macho and the 'hard man'. Films and publications which glorify non-sexual violence probably do far more damage than 'Page Three' and *Hustler.*

It's time to name the real enemies.

"An indecency ban should apply to all art subsidized with taxpayer dollars."

Government Should Deny Subsidies for Offensive Art

Bruce Fein

People opposed to public funding of offensive art often state that the denial of funds does not preclude artists from creating controversial works and therefore cannot be considered a violation of freedom of expression. In the following viewpoint, Bruce Fein argues that the government should withhold grants for offensive art for the good of the nation. Fein asserts that government support of such art could arouse racial or religious bigotry, and send the public the message that the government supports such views. Fein contends that it is constitutional to deny grants for offensive art and that artists should adhere to funding restrictions. Fein, a former U.S. associate deputy attorney general, is a lawyer and newspaper columnist for the *Washington Times*.

As you read, consider the following questions:

1. How do artists influence public opinion, according to Fein?
2. Do you agree with the author that sponsoring religious art with tax dollars is unconstitutional? Why or why not?
3. In Fein's opinion, how is politics a fundamental part of art?

The issue involving legislation to reauthorize the National Endowment for the Arts raises a more important component of public policy and democratic philosophy than is frequently apprehended. For as the literary giant Shelley perspicaciously observed: "Poets are the unacknowledged legislators of the world." The reason is that the arts inform the evolution of public opinion; and in democratic governments like our own, public opinion or conventional wisdom, whether right or wrong, is an irresistible legislative juggernaut.

No Right to Subsidies

The Constitution does not compel governmental funding of artistic expression that is protected from censorship under the First Amendment. Writing for the Supreme Court in *Maher v. Roe*, 432 U.S. 464 (1977), Mr. Justice Lewis Powell underscored the fundamental difference "between direct state interference with a protected activity and state encouragement of an alternative activity consonant with legislative policy." Thus, while the Constitution, at present, recognizes a right to an abortion, it does not guarantee a right to have the government subsidize that choice; while the Constitution guarantees a right to private education, it does not insist on governmental funding of parental choice; and while the First Amendment protects the right to acquire and to display Vincent Van Gogh's *Irises*, it does not guarantee the owner a $55-million governmental bequest to foster exercise of the right.

The Supreme Court reiterated in *Regan v. Taxation with Representation of Washington*, 461 U.S. 540 (1983), that congressional decisions regarding allocation of public largess, tax exemptions, or deductions are generally shielded from judicial oversight in deference to the policy choices of legislators. A legislature's decision to decline subsidies for the exercise of a fundamental right, whether affecting abortion, free speech, or otherwise, is irreproachable unless animated by an illegitimate constitutional purpose, such as hostility toward a particular idea.

In sum, no artist is crowned with a constitutional right either to insist that NEA be reauthorized or to receive an NEA grant if the program is extended and funded. . . .

No Funding of Offensive Art

Congress should forbid NEA from funding indecent art. As defined by the Supreme Court in *FCC v. Pacifica Foundation* (1978), indecent compositions or performances are those that appeal to the prurient interest and describe or depict sexual acts or organs in a patently offensive manner. The Pacifica decision upheld a broadcast curb on indecency, at least if children were likely members of the audience. Writing for a plurality, Justice John

Paul Stevens emphasized that any idea worth hearing could be communicated without employing indecent elocutions. At the very least, an indecency ban should apply to all art subsidized with taxpayer dollars.

Nor is there justification for NEA subventions of art intended by the author or promoter to vilify or arouse hatred against a group based on race or religion. Certainly nothing in the First Amendment compels the expenditure of federal dollars on such artwork. And if Congress foreclosed NEA from doing so, there is strong justifying Supreme Court authority in *Beauharnais v. Illinois* (1952).

An Illinois state law made it a crime to defame any "class of citizens, of any race, color, creed or religion by exposing the class members to contempt, derision, or obloquy, or which [was] productive of breach of the peace or riots." The statute was invoked to punish the public distribution of an incendiary leaflet intended to arouse racial hatred. Speaking for the Court, Justice Felix Frankfurter noted that "[r]esort to epithets or personal abuse is not in any proper sense communication of information or opinion safeguarded by the Constitution." He upheld the group libel law and tacitly recognized that racially or religiously bigoted maledictions seek to close minds permanently, not to open them to ideas, and seek to exploit the human instinct to find vulnerable scapegoats to vent personal or professional unhappiness.

Grant Denials Do Not Breach the Constitution

Indeed, to the extent the Constitution comes into play at all with respect to prejudicial art inspired by race or religious hatreds, it is in the funding by the NEA, not in the denial of funding. In *Reitman v. Mulkey* (1967) and *Norwood v. Harrison* (1973), the Supreme Court denounced as unconstitutional any governmental action that might induce, encourage, or promote private persons to practice racial discrimination. Thus NEA funding of reproductions or exhibitions of the racist film *Birth of a Nation* would flout the Constitution if the intended consequence was an exacerbation of racial prejudice.

Similarly, the NEA could violate constitutional strictures by underwriting art that promoted or denigrated religion. The Supreme Court has repeatedly decreed that the First Amendment's establishment clause forbids use of taxpayer monies to sponsor either religion or nonreligion. Thus the NEA cannot subsidize the authorship or reproduction of a prayer book. Nor could it fund Madalyn Murray O'Hair diatribes against religion or, most probably, depictions of the crucifix upside down in a bowl of urine.

By placing off-limits to the NEA the funding of obscene art,

111

child pornography, indecent art work, and racially or religiously bigoted matter, Congress does not impose an overly prudish standard. Yet even if some might disagree on this point, a bar against grant awards for any such artwork is of no constitutional concern. To the extent President Bush and John Frohnmayer suggested otherwise as their ground for opposing legislative constraints on NEA funding, they hid behind an invisible shield. There is no First Amendment cover to be found.

Calvin and Hobbes, © 1992 Bill Watterson. Distributed by Universal Press Syndicate. Reprinted with permission. All rights reserved.

The idea that NEA must shun content-based evaluations of grant applications is fatuous. How can evaluations otherwise be sensibly made? NEA employees and consultants should be fired if they decline that task so indispensable to their useful employment.

NEA, of course, regularly does make content-based distinctions in the grant-making process. The General Counsel of NEA has publicly confessed, for instance, that one proposal was denied because it seemed to celebrate animal cruelty. How is that content-inspired decision any different from one refusing a proposal because it would depict children engaged in sexual acts?

A nation lives by symbols. When the government funds works of art, it necessarily gives tacit approval to the grantee and the goals he or she promotes with taxpayer dollars. As Justice Louis D. Brandeis lectured in *Olmstead v. U.S.* (1928), "Our government is the potent, the omnipresent teacher. For good or for ill, it teaches the whole people by its example."

The government, accordingly, must be scrupulously concerned with the messages it sends to the public by underwriting specific types of art. Bigotry, for instance, intended to arouse racial or religious prejudice should receive no governmental support. Suppose David Duke, a former member of the Ku Klux Klan, gubernatorial candidate, and current member of the

Louisiana legislature, requested a grant from NEA to paint a picture glorifying post-Reconstruction lynching of "niggers." To make the grant would signify governmental approval or indifference to racial bigotry and would inflame race relations throughout the country.

Suppose a neo-Nazi sought NEA funding of a mural applauding the Holocaust. To underwrite the applicant would foster anti-Semitism and suggest the government was phlegmatic about private persecution of Jews.

The government is vitally interested in suppressing, not promoting, bigotry because bigotry threatens democracy. Freedom and liberty cannot thrive in communities steeped in racial, ethnic, or religious prejudice, as the German Third Reich verifies. . . .

The individual fulfillment and enjoyment that stem from uncurbed expositions of ideas are not threatened by an absence of governmental funding. And that absence will not breed the hate and violence associated with censorship, because of the sweeping free-speech protection in the First Amendment of opposing or unconventional viewpoints, including flag-burning.

Politics and art inevitably intersect. Exemplary are Picasso's "Guernica" and "Peace Dove," Longfellow's "Paul Revere's Ride," Francis Scott Key's "Star Spangled Banner," Charles Dickens' *Oliver Twist* and *A Tale of Two Cities*, William Shakespeare's *Julius Caesar*, Thomas Nast's political cartoons, and Peter Seeger's folk songs.

NEA thus should consider how proposed works of art might enrich and strengthen democratic norms and aspirations in awarding grants. That task is comparable to that of the schoolteacher who selects readings from Alexander Pope over *Hustler* magazine in order to promote a mastery of the English language and a penetrating understanding of human nature.

NEA is ill-suited to administering statutory funding restrictions because its expertise is art, not law. Thus Congress should instruct NEA to obtain an affidavit from every grant applicant of an intent to adhere to the restrictions. A grantee who breaks the promise would be subject to claims of restitution or damages in cases initiated by a United States attorney and be permanently barred from NEA funding. In such proceedings, the federal judiciary would adjudicate the merits, including the question of whether any of the statutory curbs on art were unconstitutional. This enforcement procedure would obviate the potential of NEA bureaucratic censorship through misapplication of legal standards or through lead-footed decision-making. And it would leave final authoritative interpretation of the First Amendment where it belongs: the contemplative chambers of the United States Supreme Court.

"Without [offensive art] we do not have an index of whether the First Amendment is working."

Government Should Grant Subsidies for Offensive Art

John Frohnmayer

John Frohnmayer served as chairman of the National Endowment for the Arts from 1989 to 1992. In the following viewpoint, Frohnmayer argues that government should fund offensive art to raise public awareness of social problems and injustices depicted in such art. Frohnmayer contends that government's refusal to subsidize offensive art disrespects artists' freedom of expression. The author asserts that government should fund art without applying ideological standards and that doing so would strengthen the First Amendment.

As you read, consider the following questions:

1. In Frohnmayer's opinion, why should government promote the arts?
2. How can art benefit the public, according to Frohnmayer?
3. Why does the author disagree that offensive art has harmful effects on the viewer?

From John Frohnmayer, "Giving Offense," *The World & I*, December 1992. Reprinted with the author's permission.

Thomas Paine, the great pamphleteer and author of *Common Sense*, said regarding the Constitution:

> He that would make his own liberty must guard even his enemy from oppression; for if he violates this duty, he establishes a precedent that will reach himself.

This is an interesting quote because it calls not upon high-minded principle, but rather upon frank self-interest. I must protect another's liberty because someday I may need that person to protect mine. It recognizes the plastic nature of democracy; that it is constantly becoming, it is never fixed, secure, or comfortable. Each generation must reenfranchise both our democracy and the First Amendment, which I consider, incidentally, to be the absolute bedrock of our democratic system. It says:

> Congress shall make no law respecting an establishment of religion or prohibiting the free exercise thereof; or abridging the freedom of speech, or of the press, or of the right of the people peaceably to assemble and to petition the government for a redress of grievances.

The First Amendment tells us that religion, ideas, associations, and criticism of the government all belong to the people. The rub comes, then, when the government supports this individual free expression under the general welfare provision of the Constitution (Article 1, Section 8). All civilized governments through history have supported the arts, as should ours, but in doing so, the government must respect the speaker and provide a level playing field without blacklists or ideological preconceptions. When the artist as speaker, expresses what some deem as dangerous, radical, blasphemous, or crude ideas, we encounter the kind of free-for-all we in the arts have been experiencing for the last few years. Congress has gotten more mail, most generated by right-wing fundamentalist groups, on the arts issue than on the savings and loan scandal. To put that into perspective, the S&L scandal will cost each of you $2,000, at least. The arts cost $.68 per year for everything we do. The amount that you will have to pay for "controversial art" is a microcent.

The Tax Dollar Argument

The argument I have frequently heard is: "Artists can do whatever they please, but not with my tax dollars." (Actually, it's "hard-earned-tax-dollars" or, as that great sloganeer, Dana Rohrabacher, put it, they can do anything they want "on their time with their dime.") But they didn't read Thomas Paine. Much of what the government does is not to our liking—the agriculture policy, military policy, labor policy, environmental policy—name any one of them, and you will find that there is hardly unanimity. The point is that we as citizens do not have a

115

line item veto. It is fundamental civics that, in order to have order, to be governed, we give up some prerogatives.

What is not supposed to be subscribed in American democracy is the life of the mind. In another context (defamation law), Justice William Brennan of the Supreme Court said, "There is no such thing as a false idea."

Challenging Art Requires Public Funding

It is the public sector which is the most inclined to fund controversial projects and emerging artists. So once the public sector monies are taken away, and therefore the private sector support is impossible to obtain, you are left with no support of that challenging work. In totalitarian societies, censorship is conducted by throwing people in jail for ideas that do not conform with prevailing fashion. As a result, one finds bad state-sanctioned art: brawny men on tractors, and artists afraid to create, like Dmitri Shostakovitch, whose works were banned. In a capitalist democracy, censorship is easily effected by withdrawing financial support. It certainly is more subtle, but just as effective!

Kitty Carlisle Hart, from a speech to the Louisiana Cultural Caucus in Baton Rouge, November 2, 1989.

So what about the part that is offensive? Can citizens be compelled to pay for that? My answer is unequivocally, *yes,* with only one caveat. The government doesn't have to support the arts at all. Nothing in the Constitution says that there shall be a National Endowment for the Arts. If, however, the United States wants to be a leader in the realm of ideas and of the spirit, to help us as citizens to understand who we are, to humanize society, and to give to citizens, not just the right of physical protection from enemies, but the environment in which they can fulfill themselves in all of their intellectual, emotional, and spiritual selves, then the government absolutely should promote the arts. . . .

Art and Repression

Every great age of art has been followed by an age of repression. Girolamo Savonarola burned the works of Giovanni Boccaccio and Ovid in the first bonfire of the vanities. Michelangelo's *David* was stoned by the crowd and an arm broken off when it was unveiled in Florence. Georges Bizet was booed in Paris upon the debut of *Carmen.*

And in the United States, James Joyce's great novel, *Ulysses,* originally printed in France, was imported and immediately seized on the docks in New York. . . . More recently, the work of David Wojnarowicz in which a small portrait of Christ with a crown of thorns and a needle in his arm was excerpted from the main work and blown up and widely disseminated as blasphemous has, I fear, been widely accepted as such. Nowhere has there been discussion about the theological premise of Christ taking on the sins of the world. Likewise, Andres Serrano's *Piss Christ* has been the most frequent stalking horse of those seeking to find blasphemy. Mainline theological analysis, namely, that the cross is a symbol of man's inhumanity to the son of God, and that in our generation that might accurately be depicted by placing that symbol in human waste, has never been a part of the argument. That is too bad because we all lose by it.

I am not suggesting that either of these interpretations are what the artist intended. I am, however, strongly urging that art be a subject for discussion rather than invective since one of its primary purpose in our society is to help us better understand ourselves.

The First Amendment is in existence precisely to protect minority and unpopular ideas, and when we look only to offense, we are not protecting the speaker, but the hearer. Art, sometimes, ought to make us feel awful, to recognize social injustice, man's inhumanity, hate where there ought to be love, destruction of our world and its species. Art sometimes is meant to be confrontational; to blast us out of our lethargy. And the NEA, in its quest for safe art, cannot wish away our problems. The reflection will remain the same whether or not the mirror is allowed to exist. But in so doing, we lose the opportunity to heal ourselves because art not only can show us our problems, weaknesses, and inadequacies, but it can help us relocate our humanity, our charity, and our generosity of spirit.

Offensive Art Is Needed

Offensive art is as necessary as it is inevitable. Necessary, because without it we do not have an index of whether the First Amendment is working. To worry about the hearer is not only to doubt our ability to solve our problems by vigorous intellectual debate, but it gives rise to aberrations such as speech codes on campuses and other limitations born out of our fear that somehow, someone, might be offended.

One final point about offense. Those who are outraged, who are "preening in indignation"—and here I'm talking about the Pat Robertsons, the Donald Wildmons, and the Patrick Buchanans of this world—have not been assaulted by unexpected intrusions. They have gone looking for those offenses; they have rooted them out to fuel their outrage. Reverend Wildmon had the six lines from the poem about the "wilding incident" virtually before the obscure publication, *The Portable*

Lower East Side, hit the streets. That publication is one meant for a limited audience in the lower part of Manhattan and yet, Reverend Wildmon had it before we at NEA did and excerpted six lines about oral sex behind the altar, sending them to every member of Congress. It was, I am told, my defense of the literary merit of that long poem that was the final straw causing my firing. In case you care, it was about the incident in which a group of thirteen-year-old boys beat, raped, and nearly killed a female jogger in Central Park. The poet, attempting to understand how such an antisocial and horrible act could be committed by children so young, wrote this epic poem from the perspective of a fatherless, abused, socially discarded child. It was an attempt to understand the rage and disaffection and moral unchartedness of this youth. It is a serious poem that ought to have produced, on our part, a serious response (as should, incidentally, the charge of pedophilia by a priest; it is that act that is certainly obscene rather than the words that graphically describe it). . . .

No Harmful Effects

The suggestion that because an artist may deal with grizzly or gritty subject matter, we, or our children, will be influenced and polluted by it, fails to withstand scrutiny. Were this theory correct, those who have read Agatha Christie would have pantries full of dead butlers, and those seeing the interminable Terminator movies would be out causing mayhem. If we are going to ban something, let's try not selling handguns to children. That would promote a few family values I care about, like keeping our children alive.

Finally, I resent, as I suspect you do, the suggestion that only part of our society is wise enough to avoid the perils of being exposed to smut. Certainly if anyone should have become a raving lunatic and sex fiend, it would be Donald Wildmon, who wallows in what he sees as depravity twenty-four hours a day. Let's give ourselves some credit. The First Amendment does. It gives honor to our brains, our tongues, our hearts, our good sense. It allows us to order our lives instead of letting someone else do it. But as a famous track coach said, "You can't do the long jump without getting sand in your shorts." We all have to be involved, lest we be the generation to abrogate the rights so many Americans have died for.

Our common goal should be to reinvigorate the First Amendment—its protection of and from religion; the sanctity of ideas and the individual and the press, and our right to come together and decide what we value. In that context, the NEA about which I care so deeply can be easily and gratefully saved from its critics. We must simply reaffirm our desire, as a country, to be a leader in the realm of ideas and of the spirit. To kill the NEA because of a few disturbing lines or images poses a far greater threat to this nation than anything that has ever been funded. It would be a craven admission that we are not strong enough to let all voices be heard.

Truth as Artists See It

You and I don't have to like everything that the NEA supports because our government is not the sponsor of those ideas; it is merely an enabler. The ideas belong to our diverse and sometimes brilliant artists—patriots who are bold enough to tell the truth as they see it.

The motto of the old *Chicago Times* was, "It's a newspaper's duty to print the news and raise hell." Sometimes it is the artist's duty to tell the truth and raise hell, too. We need to face that truth, now, more than ever. Offense is necessary.

Periodical Bibliography

The following articles have been selected to supplement the diverse views presented in this chapter.

Robert Brustein	"Art Wars II: The Empire Strikes Back," *The New Republic*, October 12, 1992.
Barbara Dority	"Profile of a Censor," *The Humanist*, January/February 1991.
Ronald Dworkin	"The Coming Battles over Free Speech," *The New York Review of Books*, June 11, 1992.
Franklyn S. Haiman	"Stealing First: The Rehnquist Court Gags on Free Speech," *The American Prospect*, Winter 1993. Available from PO Box 383080, Cambridge, MA 02238.
Nat Hentoff	"Multiculturalism and Free Speech," *The Progressive*, November 1992.
Nat Hentoff	"When Students Teach Professors," *The Progressive*, February 1993.
John Irving	"Pornography and the New Puritans," *The New York Times Book Review*, March 29, 1992.
Wendy Kaminer	"Feminists Against the First Amendment," *The Atlantic*, November 1992.
Charles R. Lawrence III	"If He Hollers Let Him Go: Regulating Racist Speech on Campus," *Duke Law Journal*, June 1990. Available from Duke University School of Law, Durham, NC 27706.
Wendy McElroy	"The Unholy Alliance," *Liberty*, February 1993. Available from PO Box 1167, Port Townsend, WA 98368.
Catharine A. MacKinnon	"Pornography as Defamation and Discrimination," *Boston University Law Review*, November 1991. Available from 765 Commonwealth Ave., Boston, MA 02215.
The New Republic	"Speech Therapy," July 13 & 20, 1992.
The New York Times Book Review	"Pornography and the New Puritans: Letters from Andrea Dworkin and Others," May 3, 1992.
Cliff Stearns and Ted Weiss	"Should Congress Stop Funding the National Endowment for the Arts?" *The American Legion*, November 1992. Available from PO Box 1055, Indianapolis, IN 46206.
Phyllis Zagano	"Beyond the First Amendment: Censorship, Art, and Moral Responsibility," *Vital Speeches of the Day*, August 1, 1991.

Should Church and State Be Separate?

Chapter Preface

In the 1992 case *Lee v. Weisman*, the U.S. Supreme Court weighed the right of a public middle school to have a nondenominational prayer at a graduation ceremony against the right of students not to participate in such a prayer. The Court banned such prayers by one vote. This case is only one of many instances in which religion and government have clashed. Public schools, in particular, are battlegrounds in this controversy because many parents believe their children are highly impressionable and consequently susceptible to the benefits or harms of religious influences.

Many Americans favor including religion in public schools and other areas of public life because they believe all Americans have the right to express their religious beliefs in public. In addition, they blame the absence of religion in public schools for the moral decline of America's youth and call for schools to reflect more of the nation's Christian values. As Mississippi governor Kirk Fordice states, America "is a Christian nation. The less we emphasize the Christian religion, the further we fall into the abyss of poor character and chaos."

Yet chaos is what many people believe would occur if public schools were to advance Christianity over other religions. In this increasingly pluralistic society, many Buddhist, native American, Jewish, Muslim, atheist, and other parents of public school students fear their children could be coerced into expressing faith in religions not practiced by their families or be ostracized for not joining in such expression. This, they feel, would lead to more conflict in schools where tensions caused by ethnic and racial divisions are already high.

In America, where citizens revere both the right to practice and the right to be free of religion, issues of religion in public life bring into question the Constitution's separation of church and state. How this constitutional guarantee should be interpreted is debated in the following chapter.

"Jefferson and Madison held . . . that church-state separation would protect both religion and government. "

The Constitution's Framers Intended Strict Separation of Church and State

Rob Boston

The U.S. Constitution's First Amendment states that "Congress shall make no law respecting an establishment of religion." In the following viewpoint, Rob Boston argues that Thomas Jefferson, James Madison, and the other framers of the Constitution created this clause to keep church and state strictly separate. The author maintains that the framers favored strict separation to ensure total religious freedom and to prevent government from being dominated by religion. Boston is the assistant director of communications for Americans United for Separation of Church and State, an organization located in Silver Spring, Maryland, that promotes the principle of church-state separation.

As you read, consider the following questions:

1. Why was the Constitution written as a secular document, according to the author?
2. In Boston's opinion, why were the founders opposed to equal aid for all religions?
3. According to the author, why did Madison oppose an official church-state partnership?

From Rob Boston, *"In 1962 Madalyn Murray O'Hair Kicked God, the Bible, and Prayer Out of School": And Ten Other Myths About Church and State.* Copyright © 1992 Americans United for Separation of Church and State. Reprinted with permission.

"Separation of church and state isn't in the Constitution." "Separation of church and state is a communist idea." "Separation of church and state is anti-religion, and only atheists support it."

Misguided clerics and short-sighted politicians sometimes say things like this about the constitutional principle of church-state separation. But a quick review of history demonstrates that these charges just aren't true.

To help Americans be on guard against such distortions, Americans United for Separation of Church and State has compiled a list of the most common myths about separation of church and state along with the facts.

A Constitutional Concept

MYTH: Separation of church and state is not in the U.S. Constitution. It is true that the literal phrase "separation of church and state" does not appear in the Constitution, but that does not mean the concept isn't there. The First Amendment says "Congress shall make no law respecting an establishment of religion or prohibiting the free exercise thereof. . . ."

What does that mean? A little history is helpful: In an 1802 letter to the Danbury (Conn.) Baptist Association, Thomas Jefferson, then president, declared that the American people through the First Amendment had erected a "wall of separation between church and state." (Colonial religious liberty pioneer Roger Williams used a similar phrase 150 years earlier.)

Jefferson, however, was not the only leading figure of the post-revolutionary period to use the term separation. James Madison, considered to be the Father of the Constitution, said in an 1819 letter, "[T]he number, the industry and the morality of the priesthood, and the devotion of the people have been manifestly increased by the total separation of the church and state." In an earlier, undated essay (probably early 1800s), Madison wrote, "Strongly guarded . . . is the separation between religion and government in the Constitution of the United States."

As eminent church-state scholar Leo Pfeffer notes in his book, *Church, State and Freedom,* "It is true, of course, that the phrase 'separation of church and state' does not appear in the Constitution. But it was inevitable that some convenient term should come into existence to verbalize a principle so clearly and widely held by the American people. . . . [T]he right to a fair trial is generally accepted to be a constitutional principle; yet the term 'fair trial' is not found in the Constitution. To bring the point even closer home, who would deny that 'religious liberty' is a constitutional principle? Yet that phrase too is not in the Constitution. The universal acceptance which all these terms, including 'separation of church and state,' have received in

America would seem to confirm rather than disparage their reality as basic American democratic principles."

Thus, it is entirely appropriate to speak of the "constitutional principle of church-state separation" since that phrase summarizes what the First Amendment's religion clauses do—they separate church and state.

Jefferson's Letter

MYTH: Thomas Jefferson's 1802 letter to the Danbury Baptists was a mere courtesy and should not be regarded as important. Religious Right activists have tried for decades to make light of Jefferson's "wall of separation" response to the Danbury Baptists, attempting to dismiss it as a hastily written note designed to win the favor of a political constituency. But a glance at the history surrounding the letter shows they are simply wrong.

As church-state scholar Pfeffer points out, Jefferson clearly saw the letter as an opportunity to make a major pronouncement on church and state. Before sending the missive, he had it reviewed by Levi Lincoln, his attorney general. Jefferson told Lincoln he viewed the response as a way of "sowing useful truths and principles among the people, which might germinate and become rooted among their political tenets."

At the time he wrote the letter, Jefferson was under fire from conservative religious elements who hated his strong stand for full religious liberty. Jefferson saw his response to the Danbury Baptists as an opportunity to clear up his views on church and state. Far from being a mere courtesy, the letter represented a summary of Jefferson's thinking on the purpose and effect of the First Amendment's religion clauses.

Jefferson's Danbury letter has been cited favorably by the Supreme Court many times. In its 1879 *Reynolds v. U.S.* decision the high court said Jefferson's observations "may be accepted almost as an authoritative declaration of the scope and effect of the [First] Amendment." In the court's 1947 *Everson v. Board of Education* decision, Justice Hugo Black wrote, "In the words of Jefferson, the clause against establishment of religion by law was intended to erect 'a wall of separation between church and state.'" It is only in recent times that separation has come under attack by judges in the federal court system who oppose separation of church and state. . . .

MYTH: The United States was founded as a Christian nation. Those who make this assertion confuse the founding of the United States as a political unit with the settlement of North America. It is true that a number of the first Europeans to arrive on our shores were religious dissenters who sought freedom to worship. Many of these people believed they were establishing some type of Christian utopia, and many supported religious liberty only for themselves. Most of the early colonies were theocracies where only those who worshipped according to state orthodoxy were welcome.

Following the American Revolution, political leaders began to construct the new U.S. government. Although a minority clung to European notions of church-state union, a general consensus emerged that the new country should steer clear of officially established religion. States with government-favored religions gradually began moving toward separation also. Massachusetts, the last state to maintain an official religion, disestablished its state church in 1833.

An Absolute Barrier

The Founding Fathers knew precisely what they were doing in writing the First Amendment to the Constitution guaranteeing the separation of church and state. They did not want government meddling in religion in any fashion; they wanted the constitutional barrier between the two to remain absolute.

Lowell P. Weicker Jr., *Why We Still Need Public Schools*, 1992.

During the Constitutional Convention, a minority faction favored some recognition of Christianity in the Constitution. In a report to Maryland lawmakers, delegate Luther Martin asserted that "in a Christian country, it would be at least decent to hold out some distinction between the professors of Christianity and downright infidelity or paganism." His views were rejected, and the Constitution was adopted as a secular document.

Incidentally, Ben Franklin did indeed urge the delegates of the Constitutional Convention of 1787 to open their sessions with morning prayers, as many Religious Right activists point out. However, the Convention, which had been meeting for a month without invocational prayers, did not concur. The Convention's records show that the delegates voted to adjourn rather than debate the issue. The matter was not brought up again when the Convention reconvened.

Further proof that the founders did not intend for the government to be Christian is found in the Treaty of Tripoli, a trade agreement signed between the United States and the Muslim region of North Africa in 1797 after negotiations under George Washington. The document, which was approved by the Senate under John Adams, states flatly, "[T]he Government of the United States is not, in any sense, founded on the Christian religion. . . ." (The assertion remained a part of the trade agreement for eight years, until the treaty was renegotiated.)

The framers wrote the Constitution as a secular document not because they were hostile to Christianity but because they did not want to imply that the new federal government would have any authority to meddle in religion.

Barring All Establishment

MYTH: The First Amendment's religion clauses were intended only to prevent the establishment of a national church. If all the framers wanted to do was ban a national church, they had plenty of opportunities to state exactly that in the First Amendment. In fact, an early draft of the First Amendment read in part, "The civil rights of none shall be abridged on account of religious belief, nor shall any national religion be established. . . ." This draft was rejected. Following extensive debate, the language found in the First Amendment today was settled on.

The historical record indicates that the framers wanted the First Amendment to ban not only establishment of a single church but also "multiple establishments," that is, a system by which the government funds many religions on an equal basis.

A good overview of the development of the language of the First Amendment is found in scholar John M. Swomley's 1987 book *Religious Liberty and the Secular State.* Swomley shows that during the House of Representatives' debate on the language of the religion clauses, members specifically rejected a version reading, "Congress shall make no law establishing any particular denomination in preference to another. . . ." The Senate likewise rejected three versions of the First Amendment that would have permitted non-preferential support for religion. The founders wanted to bar *all* religious establishments; they left no room for "non-preferentialism," the view touted by today's accommodationists that government can aid religion as long as it assists all religions equally. . . .

MYTH: The First Amendment was intended to keep the state from interfering with the church, not to bar religious groups from co-opting the government. Jefferson and Madison held an expansive view of the First Amendment, arguing that church-state separation would protect both religion and government.

Madison specifically feared that a small group of powerful churches would join together and seek establishment or special favors from the government. To prevent this from happening, Madison spoke of the desirability of a "multiplicity of sects" that would guard against government favoritism.

Jefferson and Madison did not see church-state separation as an "either or" proposition or argue that one institution needed greater protection than the other. As historian Garry Wills points out in his 1990 book *Under God,* Jefferson believed that no worthy religion would seek the power of the state to coerce belief. In his notes Jefferson argued that disestablishment would strengthen religion, holding that it would "oblige its ministers to be industrious [and] exemplary." The state likewise was degraded by an established faith, Jefferson asserted, because establishment made it a partner in a system based on bribery of religion.

Madison also argued that establishment was no friend to religion or the state. He insisted that civil society would be hindered by establishment, charging that attempts to enforce religious belief by law would weaken government. In his 1785 Memorial and Remonstrance, Madison stated flatly that "Religion is not helped by establishment, but is hurt by it.". . .

The constitutional principle of church-state separation has given Americans greater religious freedom than any people in history. Thanks in large part to this concept, citizens from many different religious backgrounds live together in peace. The right of each individual to join and support a religious group—or not do so—is protected.

2 VIEWPOINT

"Evidence . . . offers no support . . . that the First Amendment erected a 'high and impregnable' wall between church and state."

The Constitution's Framers Did Not Intend Strict Separation of Church and State

Robert L. Cord

Some scholars assert that the words and actions of the Constitution's creators imply that strict separation of church and state was not their intent. One such scholar is Robert L. Cord who, in the following viewpoint, argues that America's first legislators and presidents actively used religion to achieve certain secular goals, such as national unity. Cord contends that this fact proves that the framers wanted a limited, rather than absolute, separation of church and state. Cord is a political science professor at Northeastern University in Boston and the author of *Separation of Church and State: Historical Fact and Current Fiction*.

As you read, consider the following questions:

1. Why did the First Congress employ congressional chaplains, according to Cord?
2. According to the author, why did Jefferson exempt churches from paying taxes?
3. How are states prohibited from establishing an official religion, according to Cord?

From Robert L. Cord, "Church, State, and the Rehnquist Court," *National Review*, August 17, 1992. Copyright © 1992 by National Review, Inc., 150 East 35th Street, New York, NY 10016. Reprinted by permission.

When Clarence Thomas took his place on the Supreme Court, making the 1991-92 session the first one dominated by Reagan-Bush appointees, many expected the newly constituted Rehnquist Court to perform a historical re-examination of the doctrine of an "impregnable wall" between church and state. A suitable case was pending—*Lee* v. *Weisman*, in which the Court was asked to determine whether a non-sectarian invocation of God at the graduation ceremony of a public middle school in Providence, Rhode Island, violated the Constitution.

In a surprise 5 to 4 split decision handed down in June 1992, the Court decided that it did. The key vote was most likely that of Justice Anthony Kennedy, who wrote the opinion of the Court. Kennedy's opinion several times asserted that the only issue before the Court was the constitutionality of prayer *in public schools*. The Court's decision was compelled, wrote Justice Kennedy, "[by] the controlling precedents as they relate to prayer and religious exercise in primary and secondary public schools."

The fountainhead of these precedents is a 1947 case called *Everson* v. *Board of Education*, in which the Court first maintained that the Constitution was intended to, and still does, require a virtually absolute separation of church and state. "In the words of Jefferson," wrote Justice Hugo Black for the *Everson* majority, "the clause against establishment of religion by law was intended to erect a wall of separation between church and state. . . . [t]hat wall must be kept high and impregnable. We could not approve the slightest breach." Although the justices in *Everson* disagreed (5 to 4) on the disposition of the case, all agreed that the Constitution required virtually absolute separation.

A Challenge to Separation Doctrine

This doctrine was not challenged by any sitting Justice for 38 years—until Justice William Rehnquist (now the Chief Justice), in a dissenting opinion in *Wallace* v. *Jaffree* (1985), called for a reexamination of all Establishment Clause case law beginning with *Everson*. Specifically, Rehnquist challenged the version of history promulgated in *Everson*, which all Court majorities since have used to legitimize their church-state decisions. For Rehnquist, the historical evidence was clear, that the Founding Fathers and the Framers of the First Amendment did not construe the Establishment Clause as absolutely prohibiting government from using sectarian means to reach constitutional secular goals. Rehnquist, in *Wallace* v. *Jaffree*, called upon the Court to consider carefully all the historical evidence, and finally to probate it, even if the outcome ran counter to the "impregnable wall" metaphor.

Nor was Justice Rehnquist a lone voice in the wilderness. In a subsequent case that term, *Grand Rapids School District* v. *Ball* (1985), Justice Byron White, who also dissented in *Wallace* v. *Jaffree*, took the position that he too would be willing to review the Establishment Clause's history to see if it supported the sweeping prohibitions of *Everson* and its progeny.

In *Lee* v. *Weisman*, the Court had the opportunity to inquire anew into the meaning and intent of the religion clauses of the First Amendment, examining the events that occasioned James Madison's introduction of the Amendment in the first House of Representatives in 1789. Several of the State Ratifying Conventions had urged greater protection of individual liberty, especially religious liberty. Specifically, the Maryland Ratifying Convention had proposed an amendment stating: "That there be no national religion established by law; but that all persons be equally entitled to protection in their religious liberty."

The Virginia Ratifying Convention proposed a "Declaration or Bill of Rights" as amendments to the Constitution, of which Article Twenty stated, among other things, "that no particular religious sect or society ought to be favored or established, by law, in preference to others." The New York Convention similarly declared: "That the people have an equal, natural, and unalienable right freely and peaceably to exercise their religion, according to the dictates of conscience; and that no religious sect or society ought to be favored or established, by law, in preference to others." Resolutions passed by the North Carolina and Rhode Island Conventions echoed Virginia's "Bill of Rights."

Madison's Interpretation

Madison's first draft of what ultimately became the Establishment Clause clearly reflects these specific concerns: ". . . the civil rights of none shall be abridged on account of religious belief or worship, nor shall any national religion be established. . . ." Even after Madison's draft was changed by congressional-committee deliberations, when he was asked in debate on the House floor what the reworded Clause meant, the House record indicates that Madison said that he "apprehended the meaning of the words to be, that Congress should not establish a religion, and enforce the legal observation of it by law, nor compel men to worship God in any manner contrary to their conscience. . . . [T]o prevent these effects he presumed the amendment was intended, and he thought it as well expressed as the nature of the language would admit." Further, Madison thought "that the people feared one sect might obtain pre-eminence, or two combine together, and establish a religion to which they would compel others to conform."

This evidence all supports the interpretation that the First

Amendment was intended to forbid the establishment of a national church or religion, or the placing of any one religious sect, denomination, or tradition into a preferred legal status. It offers no support to those, like Justice Black, who claim that the First Amendment erected a "high and impregnable" wall between church and state.

America's Founders Would Be Shocked

If the Founding Fathers were alive today they would roll over in their graves (to use a Yogi Berraism) at the thought that tolerance of all religions, or of no religion, would be interpreted in modern America to mean that we must abandon religious observance in public activities!

Jim Finnegan, *The Union Leader*, June 29, 1992.

What truly makes the Supreme Court's "original intent" arguments in *Everson* absurd is some of the words and deeds of the very people who wrote the religion clauses in the First Congress, and the actions of our early Presidents and Congresses.

If the basic purpose of the Establishment Clause was "to create a complete and permanent separation of the spheres of religious activity and civil authority by comprehensively forbidding every form of public aid or support for religion," as Justice Wiley Rutledge wrote in his dissenting opinion in *Everson*, then why did the first House of Representatives, after voting up the amendment, ask President Washington to issue a proclamation recommending to the people of the United States "a day of public thanksgiving and prayer, to be observed by acknowledging, with grateful hearts, the many signal favors of Almighty God"?

Views of the First Presidents

It was certainly not a commitment to absolute separation of church and state which led President Washington to issue the new nation's first Thanksgiving Day Proclamation. And it was not adherence to an absolute Establishment Clause when Presidents John Adams and James Madison also issued Thanksgiving Day Proclamations. (Jefferson did think they violated the Establishment Clause *and* federalism. Unlike his two immediate predecessors and Madison, his successor, he refused to issue them.) No commitment to absolute separation of church and state is evident in the First Congress when it set up a congressional chaplain system and voted a $500 annual salary for the Senate and House chaplains. Their principal duties were to offer audible public prayers in Congress. Did the authors of the religion amendment not know what it meant, or if they did, did they immediately proceed to violate it?

Further, no absolute interpretation of the principle of separation of church and state led President Thomas Jefferson to sign a tax-exemption bill for the churches in Alexandria County in 1802. And it was not an absolutist action when in 1803 Jefferson—one year *after* he wrote his famous "wall of separation" letter to the Danbury, Connecticut, Baptists—concluded a treaty with the Kaskaskia Indians which, in part, called for the United States to build them a Roman Catholic Church and pay their priest.

It seems axiomatic that the original principle of separation of church and state in the First Amendment must be one which reconciles the prohibitions of the Establishment Clause and the sectarian practices of the Republic's earliest Administrations and Congresses. A "non-absolute" interpretation of separation of church and state seems to do just that.

The crucial difference between an absolute separationist such as Justice Rutledge, and a non-absolute separationist such as Thomas Jefferson, has little to do with the goals of government. *Under our amended Constitution the goals of government must be secular.* On this point, I doubt that many constitutional scholars would disagree. Additionally, while the First Amendment initially prohibited a *national* religious establishment, the Supreme Court's incorporation of the First Amendment into the Fourteenth now similarly binds the states.

Using Religion for Secular Goals

Starting with the First Congress, the concept of separation of church and state was, I believe, mainly addressed to the constitutionality of using *sectarian* institutions or activities associated with religion as *means* to achieve appropriate *secular* governmental goals. When the authors of the First Amendment requested President Washington to issue his first "Thanksgiving Day" Proclamation, they were pursuing a secular goal, hoping that Washington's action would help unite the nation behind the new government and the new Constitution. I submit that their intent is reasonably clear from the debate in the first House of Representatives and the content of Washington's 1789 Proclamation.

Similarly, I think that members of the First Congress voted for paid prayer in Congress because they were a religious people who thought prayer an appropriate means to reach the secular goal of enlightened legislation and policies yielding a prosperous nation and stable government.

When Thomas Jefferson thought it desirable to provide tax exemption to benevolent institutions, including churches, he did so because they were viewed as legitimate means of serving the community. And when Jefferson used the Catholic Church in the Kaskaskia Treaty to provide for friendship with those Indians and to get them to cede their lands to the United States, he did not see his act as impermissibly aiding religion.

One post-*Everson* decision that did recognize this point was *Marsh* v. *Chambers* (1983). In that decision, sustaining the constitutionality of the Nebraska legislature's right to a chaplain and public prayer, Chief Justice Warren Burger, joined by Justices White, Harry Blackmun, Lewis Powell, Rehnquist, and Sandra Day O'Connor, cogently argued:

> historical evidence sheds light not only on what the draftsmen intended the Establishment Clause to mean, but also on how they thought that Clause applied to the practice authorized by the First Congress—their actions reveal their intent. . . . It can hardly be thought that in the same week Members of the First Congress voted to appoint and to pay a Chaplain for each House and also voted to approve the draft of the First Amendment for submission to the States, they intended the Establishment Clause of the Amendment to forbid what they had just declared acceptable. . . .

The lineup of the Court has changed since the *Wallace* v. *Jaffree* case in 1985. The dissent in *Lee* v. *Weisman*—written by Justice Antonin Scalia and joined by Chief Justice Rehnquist and Justices White and Thomas—indicates the willingness of four members of the current Court to embrace the historical evidence which would lead to a *narrower* definition of acts prohibited as "respecting an establishment of religion." Should this in fact be the case, any one additional vote will render an interpretation of the Establishment Clause that is much more in harmony with the words and actions of those who wrote it and added it to the supreme law of our land.

"The ultimate ground for the separation of church and state is that liberal democracy and conventional religiosity . . . [are] incompatible."

Church and State Should Remain Separate

Aram Vartanian

The separation of church and state was critical for the birth of democracy and the right to individual opinions, Aram Vartanian argues in the following viewpoint. Vartanian contends that church and state should be kept as separate as possible because their values are incompatible and because both function better apart. Vartanian maintains that religion's rigid dogmas and process of indoctrination would constrict an individualistic, free-thinking political system. Vartanian is a French literature professor at the University of Virginia in Charlottesville and the author of *Diderot and Descartes: A Study of Scientific Naturalism in the Enlightenment.*

As you read, consider the following questions:

1. Why do some religious factions assert that religion is essential to democracy, according to Vartanian?
2. In the author's opinion, how is democracy harmed by those who rely on the Bible to support their convictions?
3. Why does Vartanian believe that the Bill of Rights is incompatible with Christianity?

From "Democracy, Religion, and the Enlightenment" by Aram Vartanian, which first appeared in the November/December 1991 issue of *The Humanist* and is reprinted with permission.

In recent years, a religious militancy—the American avatar of Voltaire's *Infame*—has been bent on tearing down the constitutional barrier between church and state. From the birth of our republic, the principle of separation relegated clerics to the sidelines of public power. The Cold War changed that by giving to the religious right an opportunity to exploit a popular but false syllogism: if communism, the arch-enemy of the United States, is an atheistic ideology opposed to democratic government and individual freedom, then it follows that religion is a bulwark of American democracy and its Bill of Rights. This paralogism was accompanied by a deliberate distortion of history, allowing the promoters of religious politics to claim that the United States had been founded on religion and to paint their secular or agnostic critics as politically unreliable, even unpatriotic.

The Religious Agenda

The motive behind these assertions is obvious. If the public accepts that religion is essential to the survival of our form of government and our rights as citizens, the separation of church and state would no longer make sense and the First Amendment could be reinterpreted accordingly. Religious leaders would become political leaders, expanding their authority from the moral and spiritual to the material and temporal sphere. The idea of the United States as a religiously conceived nation has therefore spurred various assaults on the principle of separation. These have not attacked the First Amendment head-on but have tried, more prudently, to subvert the establishment clause by noisily raising tangential issues that insert religious considerations into politics. One example is the controversy over school prayer. It has nothing to do with prayer itself, since American youth is free to pray to whatever deity it chooses in a church, synagogue, or mosque, where God's hearing is as good as in a school auditorium. The official sponsoring of prayer sessions on public property is a Trojan horse by means of which its backers, once they have their way, could inject other components of their religious agenda into the law. More generally, the equating of God and religion with loyalty to the political values and traditions of the United States had much success during the Reagan administration and continued under his successor.

Against these trends, I shall defend a "strict construction" of the separation rule for reasons that, despite their importance, are seldom discussed openly. Not being a jurist, I will leave aside the history of the Supreme Court precedents concerning the establishment clause. As a historian of ideas, I will instead refer the origin and intent of the principle of separation to the philosophy of the Enlightenment, which was influential not only in France and England but in the American colonies on the eve of their independence. Contrary to the myths fabricated by zealots, the republic of the United States and its Constitution were inspired not by religious faith but by a critical attitude toward religion and the related aim of secularizing national life. The ultimate ground for the separation of church and state is that liberal democracy and conventional religiosity—in the eighteenth century and since—have been not merely different but *incompatible* systems of thought and behavior.

Eighteenth-century thinkers knew the reality of an establishment of religion, along with the intolerance, inequities, and persecutions it fomented—a situation to which, incidentally, the American colonies owed much of their settlement. Because the Catholic church in France was monolithic, the criticism of religion there took its most radical form, but enlightened individuals in France, England, and America all looked forward to ending the consecrated abuses of religion by *disestablishing* it; in this regard, the founders of the United States were closer to the French than to the British example. Disestablishment was first legislated, thanks to Thomas Jefferson, in the Virginia Constitution, and soon thereafter in a Bill of Rights ratified almost simultaneously with the declaration of the *Droits de l'homme et du citoyen* [*Rights of Men and of Citizens*] by the French revolutionaries. Today, history is being reversed: a successful tradition of disestablished religion is being challenged by revisionists who want to remove the wall between church and state, bring articles of faith out of the private and into the public sector, and once again confer the status of law on sectarian beliefs and practices—preferably, of course, those of their own sect.

The Principle of Religious Liberty

It was the divorce of church and state that first brought into being the principle of liberty of conscience, which granted to all members of society an equal and absolute right to their own opinions, theological or otherwise. This reform should not be confused with the older policy of "toleration." Tolerance is no doubt better than intolerance, but it is never as good as freedom. There is always a negative or restrictive overtone in toleration which presupposes the existence of an official orthodoxy that indulgently (and sometimes not so indulgently) "puts up with" unofficial beliefs. It was in this sense that Christians were "tolerated" in the Ottoman Empire, Jews in Christendom, Protestants in Catholic countries, and Catholics in Protestant lands. Religious liberty, by contrast, assumes that, because no scheme of worship enjoys a demonstrable monopoly of truth, no civil sanction should privilege one belief-system at the expense of others deemed to be "in error." Religious liberty requires that all creeds be viewed, in the neutral eyes of government, as imperfect human creations rather than as infallible divine revelations. This attitude—the result of the Enlightenment critique of religion—was, and remains still, deeply alien—indeed, anathema—to the devout consciousness. . . .

Some definitions are needed at this point. I will use the expression *liberal democracy* in contradistinction to *totalitarian democracy*—not to contrast a *liberal* with a *conservative* type of democratic government. Anyone committed to the freedoms and rights inscribed in the United States Constitution, and to the imperative of popular sovereignty, is for the present purpose a *liberal*, or a supporter of political rights and civil liberties designed to protect the citizen against abuses of power by the state.

I will also narrow the meaning of *religion*, henceforth, to "Christianity.". . .

Let us turn now to a logical examination of several key features of Christian thinking. That religion was founded, and its theology elaborated, under political circumstances altogether different from those of the United States. Shaped by the dual influence of Jewish theocracy and Roman imperialism, the origins of Christianity left on it an indelible stamp which a mere two centuries of forced cohabitation with a democratic and liberal ethos have not erased. Its very conception of truth reflects the political environment in which it evolved. The sort of "truth" proclaimed by Christians—like the fiats of theocratic and imperial authority—brooks no disagreement. It has thus crystallized as an orthodoxy, or a core of inalterable dogmas, that its followers are expected to steadfastly profess.

Democracy and Education

Now, it is precisely such a notion of truth that is inappropriate, even dangerous, to a liberal democracy, where it is essential that all citizens hold to personal *opinions* but not to collective *dogmas* on public issues. Dogmas, by their nature, are nondiscussable and nonnegotiable; whereas an open exchange of ideas, a readiness to give and take, and the possibility of reaching agreement through persuasion and compromise are vital to the operation of popular government. Yet, that is not how a pious Christian regards his or her credo, for religious education tends to be a process of indoctrination in unshakable beliefs. But it is evident that, if democratic education inculcated in everyone a set of beliefs qualified as eternal truths immune to doubt or change, it would defeat its own purpose, which is to prepare people to think for themselves. Education as indoctrination is suited to a totalitarian regime intent on *not* having people think independently. By contrast, a liberal education suited to a democracy must have as its aim the liberating—not the closing

—of minds. To be sure, Americans accept in principle the freedom to choose one's religion. But this does not mean that a religion, once freely chosen, is eager to cultivate habits of intellectual freedom among its rank and file. As regards the goals of education, religion and democracy in the United States have had little of positive value to offer each other, despite the existence of innumerable sectarian schools.

© Signe Wilkinson/Cartoonists & Writers Syndicate. Reprinted with permission.

When a religious group takes a position on a political issue, it typically does so by claiming divine inspiration. Not only does this inhibit debate, but it replaces rational discourse and the rules of evidence by obscurantism and willfulness. Citing "God's will" in a discussion is meant to silence, not convince, an opponent. The basic premise of the anti-choice movement is that God himself has prohibited abortion, the "proof" of which is to be found in the scriptures. However, the entire history of biblical exegesis shows that almost any personal or collective conviction can find support in divine revelation; not only are the contents of the Bible heterogeneous and inconsistent but they are often couched in vague, ambiguous, or figurative language. Thus, the Bible always obliges a true believer by miraculously saying whatever he or she *wants* it to say—even if nothing resembling one's belief can be discovered *verbatim* in the Old or New Testaments (as is the case for the alleged divine ban on abortion). When the true believer quotes "God's word" to confirm an opinion, what he or she expresses is the wish to raise personal opinion to the level of absolute and incontrovertible truth. Put more bluntly, the true believer pretends to speak with Godlike authority, as if he or she *were* God. Public discussion, so intrinsic to a democratic society, requires that everyone speak in his or her own human voice and with the duty to support by fact, reason, and eloquence—not by self-serving divine fiat—the views that he or she would like others to accept. A democracy is degraded when its members, seduced by the desire to play God, get in the habit of pontificating infallible truths on subjects of public policy. Such a practice must culminate, if unchecked, either in a theocracy or in chaos. . . .

The Shackles of Religion

Few have had the candor to point out the awkward fact that neither personal liberty nor civil rights have biblical sanction. On the contrary, scripture is at pains to tell us just the reverse: that we must submit in all things to the will of a supreme ruler against whom we have no assertable rights. Both the Old and New Testaments, if read from a political perspective, are undemocratic and anti-libertarian texts. The Ten Commandments, like the parables of Jesus, say nothing about individual freedoms and rights but a great deal about obedience and pleasing God so as to avoid the direst penalties. The *raison d'etre* of all religion is to lay down a "law" that all must obey, whether or not they like or even understand it. The essence of religion is thus constraint, not freedom; duties, not rights.

Some have attempted to sugarcoat this pill with the doctrine of free will; however, while it affirms that we enjoy the priceless gift of freedom, it warns us, in the same breath, that we must never use it independently of God's wishes. Adam found out, to his sorrow, the exorbitant cost of his "free will" to eat a certain apple! That kind of freedom is found also in the most despotic states, where people are free to do what they are told; no one would confuse it with what Americans call liberty, which is meaningless without rights. We are also informed that, in the divine courts on the day of judgment, justice will be summary, not litigable, because the Christian is not protected by anything like a "Bill of Rights" with which to defend any of the freedoms he or she has exercised in life. The very idea of such a self-defense seems ludicrous; yet, what is more American than the right to a fair trial? . . .

Surrender to an Absolute Power

What one does *not* find in the Judeo-Christian outlook is a conception of human beings as having both the right and the ability—through the free exercise of their reason and will—to

140

control their own destinies. What biblical religion gives us, in contrast, is a picture of human nature caught powerlessly between two cosmic forces—God and Satan—along with the caveat that no "salvation" in the short or long run is possible without total dependence on, and obedience to, God's wishes. Concepts such as individual freedom, civil rights, human initiative, and secular progress are basically foreign to holy writ and suspect to the mentality patterned on it. This is understandable. Liberal democracy is still a recent creation, barely 200 years old, and confined to a small area of the earth's surface. There is no compelling reason why all Americans should feel at ease with it; nor is there cause for surprise if many of them feel nostalgic for "old-time religion." The surrender of personal prerogatives to an absolute power—whether God or the state—which will act as an almighty protector and provider is a human reflex that goes back to the earliest times and still determines the behavior of the majority of our species. Conventional religiosity thus coexists among us with the new faith in freedom, rights and self-rule. There is a natural fear of freedoms and rights because they entail risks, struggles, responsibilities, and uncertainties. Religion allays anxiety by offering, in its place, conformism, obedience, and certainty. For most believers, the offer is irresistible. But torn between the kingdom of God and the republic of the United States, they never quite know whether they are docile vassals of the "Lord" or self-governing citizens of a democracy. It is essential, no doubt, in any society to lay down "commandments" about what everyone must do or not do; and no society, whatever its form of government, fails to do so, on pain of becoming extinct. But a list of rights and freedoms—of what no one can be made to do or may always do if one wants—is something altogether different, and relatively few societies promulgate such a list for the benefit of their members. Religion furnishes only the first but not the second set of rules. The Ten Commandments of the Bible should not be confused with the ten amendments of the original Bill of Rights, for the two decalogues are distinct and incommensurable.

Church and State Are Incompatible

What conclusions follow from the foregoing remarks? A partisan of religious politics would probably object to them on the grounds that it is wrong to draw ideological parallels between politics and religion by translating the mental structures and discourse of the one into those of the other. This devout adversary would add that religious thinking, the beliefs it holds on faith, its ideas of justice, its criteria of truth, and the ultimate goals it pursues are all so profoundly different from their seeming counterparts in the world of politics that it is pointless to construct, as I have done, political equivalents of such dogmas as original sin, eternal damnation, the absolutism of the kingdom of God, and the rest. I agree with such objections, and that is precisely the reason why religion and politics should remain separate. The truths of religion belong to a universe of discourse that is essentially symbolic, metaphorical, mythic, allegorical, and homiletic; when they are transposed to the province of politics, their meanings are transformed into an ideology that is at odds with the basic compact of American society.

The moral of my story is that liberal democracy and Christianity (or, indeed, any religion) represent incompatible modes of thought and irreconcilable value systems; that secularism (or secular humanism) is the appropriate context for a political system dedicated to individual freedoms and rights; and that church and state should be kept separate in the United States—not simply because the Bill of Rights so prescribes but because they do not in fact mix. A forced marriage of the two would be doubly regrettable. If politics were sacralized and religion politicized, we would get the worst of both dispensations: an emasculated Christianity and a debased democracy. Strict enforcement of the separation clause of the First Amendment is in the interest of all Americans, even the most ardent fundamentalists, because, to quote the wisdom of a common-sense poet: "Good fences make good neighbors."

"The time has come to restore the vital relationship between Church and State, between religion and law. "

Church and State Should Not Remain Separate

Anthony Bevilacqua

Anthony Bevilacqua is the archbishop of Philadelphia and a lawyer. In the following viewpoint, delivered as the homily at Washington, D.C.'s Red Mass, Bevilacqua argues that religion has much to offer government by affirming the fundamental values and rights of democracy. Bevilacqua contends that America's moral crisis demands an infusion of religious ethics. A close relationship between church and state, he concludes, can achieve this goal.

As you read, consider the following questions:

1. Why does Bevilacqua believe that the founding of the nation called for a strong church-state relationship?
2. Do you agree with the author that religion can protect democracy? Why or why not?
3. How could religious values address crises such as teenage promiscuity and drug abuse, according to Bevilacqua?

Anthony Bevilacqua, "Church and State: Partners in Freedom," *The Catholic Answer*, July/August 1990. Reprinted with permission.

It is fitting that in the capital of our nation, officials of government and members of the legal profession assemble today in prayer with leaders of religion.

The Red Mass, called such because of the color of the vestments worn, has been a tradition of many centuries. It is a spiritual reflection and celebration of the symbiosis of religion and law, of Church and State.

It is a religious expression of gratitude for the many blessings God gives us through government leaders and the law.

It is a time of reconciliation with God, asking forgiveness for our failure to acknowledge our dependence on Him, our Supreme Lawgiver.

It is a time of petition asking God to bless, strengthen and enlighten our civic and religious leaders, all servants of the law and all people of faith, so that in cooperation and mutual trust, we may more effectively achieve justice and freedom for all peoples.

Rediscovering Religious Principles

It is a time of challenge to religion and law, to Church and State, to government officials and religious leaders, to all citizens and to all faithful, to rediscover those basic moral premises, those essential religious principles that our Founding Fathers brought to the birth of this nation in the Declaration of Independence and in the Constitution.

It is a time of recommitment to those values of life, liberty and justice that are the protection of the sacred dignity and freedom of every individual human life.

It is a time when religious leaders call upon you in public office and in the legal profession to be in your role, as we are in our calling, prophets of the law "of nature and nature's God," teachers of moral values, evangelizers for justice and true freedom. . . .

Two hundred years ago in 1789, the American nation began a journey along a new path under the Constitution. In that same year, the Catholic Church in the United States also began a journey along a new road. For the first time, it began to walk under the leadership of its own hierarchical shepherd when John Carroll was appointed its first bishop.

(At this point, I wish to alert you that, though I speak as a Roman Catholic archbishop and, at times, as a civil lawyer, I will use the reality of the Catholic Church in the United States primarily as a metaphor for religion in general, as an image of all religious faiths.)

The new road that the Church and this nation began to walk together in 1789 was primitive and perilous, with mystery always ahead. But the journey was filled with hope, illumined by law and God's word, protected by His angels.

For the most part, it has been an odyssey in which both travelers, Church and State, survived and flourished, largely because of mutual trust and friendship. In spite of attempts to separate one from the other, to put an impenetrable barrier between them, the two knew from the beginning that they needed each other, and along the way they became even more convinced of this truth.

In Mutual Support

From the very first step, it was the intent of both the State and the Church that they would walk the path not as strangers, and certainly not as enemies, but as friends in mutual support of each other. Thus it was that George Washington unabashedly stated that "of all the dispositions and habits which lead to political prosperity, religion and morality are indispensable supports." James Madison, often called the Father of the Constitution, said that we cannot govern without God and the Ten Commandments. Thomas Jefferson, never labeled as a full-fledged Christian, nevertheless recognized the pragmatic necessity of religion when he asked: "Can the liberties of a nation be thought secure when we have removed their only firm basis, a conviction in the minds of the people that those liberties are the gift of God?" President John Adams echoed the sentiments of the writers of our fundamental law when he said: "Our Constitution was made only for a religious and moral people. It is wholly inadequate for the government of any other."

Alexis De Tocqueville, the French political sociologist, recognized during his voyage to Jacksonian America in 1831 the intimate fellowship of Church and State. He called religion "the first of America's political institutions" mainly because he saw religion as the leading defender of freedom.

The affirmation of the Church, on its part, for the fundamental values, rights and freedoms secured in the Constitution is echoed by the voice of the psalmist: "Legem tuam dilexi"—"I have loved your Law."

While the relationship between the companions traveling together, Church and State, has for the most part been one of mutual support and a true blessing for both, the conversation and attitude between them have not always been the most amicable. More recently, there have been times of misunderstanding and dispute. These in turn have led to exchanges of accusations and periods of chilled silence. Especially in the last three decades, it is the perception of many that Church and State, religion and law, are adversaries instead of companions, enemies instead of friends, antagonists instead of partners. In their quest for their respective kingdoms, Church and State are seen as walking with an inviolable, impenetrable and towering wall between them. The two pilgrims are further portrayed as shouting at each other over the wall in a cacophony of irate disagreements. Some have even suggested that the clash has become a babel of conflicting postures so that neither can understand the other.

The Wall Must Vanish

This opposition, this impregnable wall between two friends traveling the road of our American experiment cannot endure much longer. If it does, both will suffer and crisis will be upon us. If there is discord between Church and State, the consequence will be a wall between religion and society that can only lead to moral decay.

© Jerry Barnett/The Indianapolis News. Reprinted with permission.

A noted weekly news magazine judged the '80s, "a time of moral disarray." I am no prophet of doom, but even a casual observer of the American scene must admit that there is an undue obsession with self-interests and self-pleasures, that the trend is to eliminate from society and law those religiously-based moral values which were formerly co-natural to them. The clear direction today is toward a secular, antireligious, humanistic consensus in society and law.

Symptoms of this moral crisis are evident in the high rates of child abuse; the 1.5 million abortions a year; the increase in the divorce rate; teenage promiscuity and pregnancy; racism; drug and alcohol abuse; scandals in the world of finance, business,

146

politics and even religion. And this is far from an exhaustive list.

Still relevant today are the words that Will Durant uttered 50 years ago: "We move into an age of spiritual exhaustion like that which hungered for the birth of Christ. The great question of our time . . . is whether men can bear to live without God."

Neither you nor I, not society, not the state, not this democracy, can bear to live without God. Not if we want to remain a people of "life, liberty and the pursuit of happiness."

De Tocqueville again observed, "Despotism may be able to do without faith but freedom cannot. . . . How could society escape destruction . . . if it is not subject to God?"

The psalmist also warns us: "If the Lord does not watch over the city, in vain does the watchman keep vigil."

My dear friends, how long will it take us to learn this truth. The time has come to restore the vital relationship between Church and State, between religion and law. We must all read the signs of the times and recognize that more and more people are questioning the secularistic, relativist response to the issues that touch our very life. In education, science, politics, the press, medicine, law, business, family relations and the world of entertainment there is an increasing recognition of the need for ethical and moral values based on religion. Our nation is still predominantly a religious people. A poll taken in 1987 reported that 61 percent of adults over 18 have high confidence in religion. Religion ranked significantly higher than banks, public schools, newspapers, television, unions, and even, with all due respect, the Supreme Court of the United States—though it did come in second. We must realize—as Peter Berger, a sociologist of religion, put it—that we live "under a sacred canopy."

Time for Unity

Has the time not come for Church and State, the two travelers along the path of our republic, to stop shouting at each other and start conversing again in a language both can understand?

Should we not engage anew in a dialogue to rediscover those basic values found especially in the Judeo-Christian tradition and in the natural law? I am speaking of those religious values that defend the sacred dignity and inviolable value of every human being. I am speaking of those values which inspired our Founding Fathers to begin the American odyssey, "Sub Deo et Lege," "under God and the law." I am speaking of those religious values embodied in the fundamental law of our nation.

If Church and State journeying together are to engage in friendly conversation, there cannot be a towering, impregnable wall between them. Always needed is a clear line of demarcation, between Church and State, but it should be one which will still allow their supporting hands to reach out to the other in time of need, which will still allow them to look at the face of the other and see friendship and love in each other's eyes. The total effect of such a synergetic friendship could very well be greater than the sum of what each could do separately.

The words of the Jesuit philosopher and scientist, Teilhard de Chardin, resonate the benefit that will flow from this fellowship of Church and State, religion and law: "Someday after mastering the winds, the waves, the tides and gravity, we shall harness for God the energies of love. And then, for the second time in the history of the world, man will have discovered fire."

"Cases involving . . . serious claims of interference with religious liberty are often denied and forgotten."

Government Must Support the Public Expression of Religious Beliefs

Michael McConnell

U.S. Supreme Court decisions during the last few decades have strictly limited religion's influence in the public sphere. In the following viewpoint, Michael McConnell argues that government and the courts are wrongly upholding secular ideals and favoring a right to freedom from religion, while deciding against clear violations of people's constitutional right to public religious expression. McConnell states that the U.S. Supreme Court must no longer refuse to consider complaints of freedom of religion violations. McConnell is a law professor at the University of Chicago and a legal consultant on appellate and constitutional matters.

As you read, consider the following questions:

1. Why are freedom of religion claims a low priority for the U.S. Supreme Court and the media, according to McConnell?
2. Why does the author believe that freedom of religion must be given the same protection as freedom of speech?
3. According to McConnell, how have intellectuals tended to view religion in the last two hundred years?

From Michael McConnell, "Freedom from Religion," *The American Enterprise*, January/February 1993. Copyright © 1993, *The American Enterprise*. Distributed by The New York Times/Special Features.

The Supreme Court decided an important freedom of religion case in 1992 concerning a graduation ceremony in Providence, Rhode Island. The principal of the Nathan Bishop Middle School, following the school's practice of choosing clergy from various denominations to participate in its graduations, invited Rabbi Leslie Gutterman to deliver the invocation and the benediction. Rabbi Gutterman said the following prayer:

"God of the free, hope of the brave, for the legacy of America where diversity is celebrated and the rights of minorities are protected, we thank you. May these young men and women grow up to enrich it. For the liberty of America, we thank you. May these new graduates grow up to guard it. For the political process of America in which all its citizens may participate, for its court system where all may seek justice, we thank you. May those we honor this morning always turn to it in trust.

"For the destiny of America, we thank you. May the graduates of Nathan Bishop Middle School so live that they might help to share it. May our aspirations for our country and for these young people who are our hope for the future be richly fulfilled. Amen."

Objection to a Prayer

Two in the audience, Deborah Weisman and her father, Daniel, had tried to obtain a restraining order from the local court to prevent inclusion of a prayer in the program. Later, they filed a lawsuit in federal district court to make sure it wouldn't happen again. They objected to being subjected to this (or any) prayer as part of the public graduation ceremony. The case worked its way up to the Supreme Court, where the justices, in a very close decision with numerous separate opinions, held that the Weismans' constitutional rights under the First Amendment had been violated by the delivery of this prayer and that the school officials should be enjoined from sponsoring a prayer during future graduation ceremonies.

In an opinion by Justice Anthony Kennedy, the Court explained that the injury caused by the government's action—in this case the rabbi's prayer—is that the state, through the school setting, in effect required participation in a religious exercise. The Court explained that the school district's supervision and control of a high school graduation ceremony placed public and peer pressure on attending students to stand as a group or at least maintain respectful silence during the invocation and benediction. The Court went on to state that the Constitution forbids the state to exact religious conformity from a student as the price of attending her own high school graduation.

This is what I would call "freedom from religion" taken to its logical extreme. It is an example of the exquisite care with which our legal system now treats the right to be free from any possible imposition of religion upon our lives. Deborah Weisman was not required to be present at the graduation at all. Nor was she required to stand, or if she stood, she was not required to bow her head. If she bowed her head, she was not required to fold her hands. Even if she folded her hands, she was not required to enter into the prayer other than to remain silent during it. But the Court said that putting her through the experience at all was enough to violate the Constitution.

The decision was greeted in the press with extensive front page coverage and widespread acclaim. The extraordinary attention given to this case demonstrates what the press and the dominant culture think is at the heart of the religion clauses of the First Amendment.

The Constitution Requires Neutrality

The First Amendment bars the government from either "establishing" religion or prohibiting the "free exercise" of religion—in essence, requiring the government to remain neutral and leave decisions about religious matters to the people. Substituting the so-called "wall of separation" and other misleading metaphors for the language of the Constitution, many government officials and courts have transmuted the principle of freedom of religion into a rigid doctrine that everything in the public sphere must be secular—in effect, replacing the ideals of pluralism and neutrality with the quite different ideals of secularism and separation. In an opinion in one recent case, Justice Harry A. Blackmun went so far as to use the term "secular liberty" as his description of what the religion clauses are all about. This is what I call freedom from religion.

Lee v. Weisman is not an unusual case. The courts have lavished extensive time and attention on the detection of undue religious influence on expression in the public sphere. For example, in three separate cases in the past decade the Supreme Court has issued multiple lengthy opinions telling us when it is permissible for a state to display a nativity scene or a menorah. And there have been over a dozen lower federal court decisions on this question. Official city seals have come under similar scrutiny, with at least five courts of appeals holding that depictions on seals contained some element that could be construed as religious symbolism and therefore were unconstitutional.

These cases have two things in common. First, they have been widely reported and treated as issues of great constitutional significance. Second, they have nothing to do with freedom of religion. There is not a single person in these cases who has been hindered or discouraged by government action from following a religious practice or way of life. These cases are about freedom from religion, or the secularization of the public sphere.

My point is not that *Lee v. Weisman* or any of these other cases was wrongly decided. But the Supreme Court and the news media are so preoccupied with the finer points of freedom from religion that far more important cases of genuine freedom of religion have been almost completely neglected.

Freedom of Religion Cases

The Supreme Court has discretion to choose which lower court decisions it reviews, and the major criterion for that selection is the importance of the case. Here is a sampling of cases the Court has indicated are less important than the right of Deborah Weisman not to be subjected to Rabbi Gutterman's prayer.

In Colorado a public school principal told a teacher that he could not read silently from the Bible for his own interest during silent reading periods in the classroom. There was no evidence that the students were aware of what book the teacher was reading. The principal was concerned that the students might be influenced by the teacher's choice of reading materials. The principal also ordered two books of Bible stories removed from a classroom library of nearly 400 books.

Imagine the outcry if this teacher had been reading a biography of Robert Mapplethorpe or if the books had been removed from the library because they contained what someone decided was vulgarity. In either case, the American Civil Liberties Union (ACLU) would have taken up the case immediately, and it would have been a major news story.

Yet a federal court held that not only was the principal justified in prohibiting the teacher from reading the Bible silently and in removing these two volumes from the library, but that the establishment clause required these actions. One week after devoting 37 pages (four opinions) to *Lee v. Weisman*, the Supreme Court refused to hear the case.

Another recent case involved a tenure-track professor of physiology at the University of Alabama, Phillip Bishop, who offered an optional after-class lecture entitled "Evidences of God in Human Physiology." About six people attended this lecture, including a few of his colleagues and several graduate students. The professor also occasionally commented in class to his graduate students about how his Christian faith helped him deal with academic stress and set priorities for his life.

Several students complained, saying that they thought his integration of religious opinion was inappropriate, and the university ordered him to end his after-class lectures on the subject and not to present any comments "from a Christian perspective" during class.

What if Professor Bishop had been a Marxist and he had offered an optional lecture on the scientific basis for the movement toward socialism? Can you imagine how the American Association of University Professors would react if a professor was told that he could not make comments in class on the basis of his particular ideology? A federal court of appeals upheld the university, however, and the Supreme Court refused to hear the case.

"OUR INVOCATION WILL BE GIVEN BY REV. BEEKER AND ROY, OUR SOUND MAN, WHO WILL BLEEP OUT 'FATHER', 'GOD' AND ALL THE THEES AND THOUS!"

Reprinted by permission: Tribune Media Services.

In another case, the New Orleans Baptist Theological Seminary dismissed a student after police reports that he had abused his spouse. The student was studying for a degree in marriage and family counseling. The Louisiana courts held that he had a contract right to continue his studies and to be awarded a degree if he met all academic qualifications for the degree, and it ordered the seminary to give him a degree in marriage and family counseling because the student's conduct did not "touch upon theological or ecclesiastical matters."

This was particularly troubling because in the Baptist tradition there is no further screening process for the ministry. Once you have your degree, you can submit your résumé to any congregation, and the congregation may or may not choose to call you to serve in its church. This makes the seminaries the central institutions for screening candidates for the clergy. In effect, this important function was usurped by the state of Louisiana. Again, the Supreme Court refused to hear the case.

Tenets of Faith

These cases involve freedom of religion, not freedom from religion. In each, an individual is trying to live his life, or an institution is trying to conduct its spiritual mission, according to the tenets of their faith. In each, government power has been brought to bear to prevent them from doing that. In each case, the courts have provided no help, and the Supreme Court has chosen to allow those decisions to stand.

Another thing these cases have in common is their obscurity. You probably have not heard about them on the news or read about them in the newspaper. They don't receive coverage because the press does not consider them close to the heart of the First Amendment.

Inconsequential cases chasing the last vestiges of religious reference from public life are heard by the Supreme Court and placed on the front pages of the newspapers, while cases involving vastly more serious claims of interference with religious liberty are often denied and forgotten. But even when the Supreme Court hears cases involving genuine claims of freedom of religion, it doesn't necessarily reach a proper conclusion. The leading free-exercise case, *Employment Division of Oregon v. Smith,* was decided in 1990. It is frequently called the "peyote case" because the issue was whether a member of the Native American Church has a right to ingest peyote, a hallucinogenic derivative of cactus, notwithstanding the drug laws of Oregon.

The Supreme Court held that the free exercise clause does not preclude the government from enforcing what it calls "neutral laws of general applicability." And since Oregon's drug law was not passed specifically against the Native American Church or religion in general, it is a law of general applicability and thus can be enforced even though it makes the central ceremony of this small but ancient religion illegal.

What will the Court rule in dry states or dry counties when churches attempt to administer wine as part of the holy sacrament? What will the Court say when a fully qualified individual applies to become the first female priest in the Roman Catholic Church and claims that the free exercise clause does not protect the right of the church to decide whom it is going to hire? What will it say when a state fails to make a provision in its laws exempting kosher slaughterhouses from its ordinary regulations regarding meat packing?

Governments are probably not going to require major religious denominations to comply with laws that will destroy essential elements of their religious practice. Twenty-three states have even exempted peyote used in religious ceremonies from the drug laws. Most states exempt kosher slaughterhouses explicitly in their laws. The employment discrimination case has not yet come up. The effect of the *Smith* decision, though, is to leave these questions in the hands of legislators, so that freedom of religion now depends upon the legislatures and city councils. In a large proportion of cases, this will pose no problems, because respect for the religious practices of others is firmly ingrained in our political life. But there will be instances when this will not be the case.

Less Judicial Intervention

Will the San Francisco City Council decide, as did a court prior to *Smith*, that a Presbyterian Church can decline to hire a gay organist to conduct its worship services? We know that the school authorities of New York City will not allow Roman Catholic and other religious objectors to remove their children from those portions of the sex education curriculum that distribute and advocate the use of condoms. And we know that court intervention has been necessary to protect private religious schools in some states from overreaching state education bureaucracies.

The "peyote case" is consistent with the general movement of a more conservative Supreme Court toward greater deference to the decisions of elected officials and less judicial intervention in public affairs. And it has been accompanied by a similar restrained approach to the Establishment Clause, where the Court has retreated from some of the more extreme separationist doctrines of the past. No longer are religious institutions and religious citizens automatically excluded from participation in public programs or relegated to the margins of public life. To this extent, the conservative approach to the religion clauses might be thought to be a move in the right direction.

But it is a mistake to confuse "judicial activism" in defense of express constitutional freedoms for the wide-ranging power activist judges have asserted to impose their own values in place of democratic decisions. It is just as important for the courts to give full force and effect to principles expressly articulated in the Constitution as it is to allow democratic decision making where the Constitution is silent.

The religion clauses were enacted not because the people in 1789 had faith that the new federal government would not infringe on their liberties. They were enacted not to give a wide degree of discretion to the government in religious matters. They were enacted largely at the behest of small denominations that had not gotten a fair shake from the government: by Baptists who were taxed to support other people's churches, by Presbyterians who were denied licenses to preach or perform marriages, by Quakers who resisted military conscription. The people of the United States did not want this new, potentially threatening federal government to be able to oppress them in the same way that the colonial and state governments had in many instances. The principles of free exercise and nonestablishment are important constraints on government power and deserve the same sort of vigilant protection given to freedom of speech or press. . . .

Driving Religion Underground

Since the Enlightenment, intellectuals have tended to view religion as an irrational impulse—a form of tyranny over the mind. This has typically been coupled with a high degree of toleration for religion in its place, but its place has turned out to be confined to the home and church. Religion must be excluded from the public sphere or in any area the government touches. A wall of separation has been built, but it was not built in the middle of the playing field. It was built on the five-yard line.

This was not the impulse of those who demanded the addition of religion clauses to our Constitution. The Quakers, the Presbyterians, and, above all, the Baptists agitated for the addition of both free exercise and establishment clauses. They believe true piety to be the product of a free and unfettered conscience, which meant that there must be a freedom from religion because there cannot be a free and unfettered conscience to accept religion without there also being a free and unfettered conscience to reject religion. They understood this, and they were as enthusiastic as any ACLU member could be about this proposition today.

But they did not intend to create a society in which religion was driven underground, where secular ideologies are given a privileged position. They did not intend a society in which the full brunt of government power could be used to disadvantage those who did come to the free and unfettered choice to believe and worship God, as they put it, "in the manner and season most agreeable to their consciences." They would find the current state of First Amendment law bizarre and unrecognizable.

"Government sponsorship of religious activity cannot avoid preferring some religions over others."

Government Must Protect Citizens from the Public Expression of Religious Beliefs

Edd Doerr

Many early Americans of various religious denominations settled in the colonies to escape governments dominated by religion. In the following viewpoint, Edd Doerr argues that the colonists' freedom *of* religion depended on freedom *from* other religions. Doerr asserts that while everyone has the right to practice his or her own religion privately, the government must never sponsor a religion or support the public expression of religious beliefs. Doerr is the executive director of Americans for Religious Liberty, an organization in Silver Spring, Maryland, that advocates separation of church and state.

As you read, consider the following questions:

1. According to Doerr, how has the federal government strengthened separation of church and state in recent decades?
2. Why does the author believe that government assistance toward religion is unnecessary?
3. How could participation in public school prayer violate the rights of some students, according to Doerr?

"Freedom of Religion, Freedom from Religion" by Edd Doerr first appeared in the May/June 1993 issue of *The Humanist* and is reprinted with permission.

On March 8, 1993 a committee of the Maryland Senate held a hearing on a bill that would compel public school teachers and principals to "require all students to be present and participate in opening exercises on each morning of a school day and, voluntarily, . . . to meditate and pray silently." I presented testimony against this bill, for reasons to which I will return later, on behalf of organizations dedicated to defending freedom of religion.

Some people would undoubtedly say that I testified on behalf of freedom *from* religion and not freedom *of* religion. They would probably argue that freedom of religion is not the same thing as freedom from religion, that the former but not the latter is a fundamental right. On the other hand, some secularists who object to certain public manifestations of traditional religion might express a mirror image viewpoint, that freedom *of* religion is not enough and that freedom *from* religion is a right that should be specifically protected.

Freedom from Other Religions

It seems to me that freedom *of* and freedom *from* religion cannot and should not be distinguished. Let me explain.

Puritans and Pilgrims were Protestants who immigrated to New England largely because they desired freedom from the Anglican establishment in England. They disliked Anglicanism because it was, to them, too much like Roman Catholicism. They wanted freedom from Anglicanism. So too, Roger Williams and his followers set up shop in Rhode Island because they sought freedom from the Puritan establishment in Massachusetts. Sephardic Jews settled in Rhode Island to escape various European religious establishments. Anglicans and Baptists in Connecticut opposed that colony's Puritan establishment.

English Catholics settled Maryland to get away from Protestant establishments in their home country, while French Protestants came here to escape the Catholic establishment in France. Many British Anglicans came to Virginia and the Carolinas because they did not like Oliver Cromwell's Puritan establishment, while Quakers settled in Pennsylvania to avoid impositions on their freedom in England. In 1825 a boatload of Norwegians, many of them Quakers, arrived here for freedom from the Lutheran establishment in their land.

In short, many of our early immigrants came here for freedom of religion, which was, to them, the same thing as freedom from some other religion and from the imposition on them of someone else's religion. Unfortunately, many of those who came here for freedom of religion for themselves were reluctant to extend that freedom to others. As one wag put it, the Puritans so loved religious freedom that they wanted to keep it all to themselves.

Monuments to transplanted European establishmentarianism

and intolerance are the statues on the lawn of the Massachusetts state capital of Anne Hutchinson, expelled from the colony in 1638 for the crime of holding unauthorized religious gatherings in her home (and, though the legend on her statue's pedestal does not mention it, being of the wrong gender to lead religious discussions), and Mary Dyer, executed on Boston Common in 1660 for the crime of being a Quaker.

To a great many Americans of the colonial and immediate post-colonial periods, freedom of religion was equivalent to freedom from someone else's religion. And by the time of our armed struggle for independence from Great Britain (1775-1783) substantial numbers of Americans were ready to break with colonial and European establishmentarianism. They traded in the outworn "divine right of monarchs" for the Jeffersonian republican view that "governments are instituted among men" in order to secure inalienable equal fundamental rights, that governments "derive their just powers from the consent of the governed," who have the right to "alter or abolish" a government that does not protect their rights and/or enjoy their consent.

The Constitution's Separation Principle

When the state delegations met in Philadelphia in 1787 to—as it turned out—design a national government based on the principles articulated in the Declaration of Independence, they carefully crafted a constitution for a secular government of limited and delegated powers, one which gave to government no authority whatsoever to meddle in religious matters and which specifically prohibited mandatory oaths of office and religious tests for public office. Thus, the Constitution itself implied the separation of church and state, the theoretical basis for which had been spelled out in the 1785 Memorial and Remonstrance Against Religious Assessments (in Virginia) by James Madison, who emerged as the principal architect of the Constitution and the 1789 Bill of Rights.

The adding of the Bill of Rights to the Constitution, begun in 1789 and finished in 1791, made the separation principle an explicit part of the Constitution, as Jefferson noted in his famous letter to the Danbury Baptists in 1802 when he wrote, "I contemplate with sovereign reverence that act of the whole American people [the First Amendment] which declared that their legislature should make no law respecting an establishment of religion or prohibiting the free exercise thereof, thus building a wall of separation between church and state." While the First Amendment was initially applicable only to the federal government, the Fourteenth Amendment, proposed and ratified shortly after the Civil War, applied it to state and local government as well.

159

There are, generally speaking, two schools of thought about precisely what the First Amendment means. "Accommodationists" argue that the First Amendment was intended only to bar government preference for one religion or some religions over others, while permitting "nonpreferential aid" to all. "Separationists" would argue, in contrast, that "nonpreferentialist" or "accommodationist" language for the First Amendment was considered and rejected by the First Congress, and that the Amendment was aimed not merely at barring European-style establishments of religion, which had disappeared from the United States by 1789, but, rather, the types of multiple or nonpreferential establishments which lingered in some states until the early nineteenth century.

Freedom from Proselytizing

Parents who enroll their children in public schools, for the secular education mandated by the state, have every right to expect that their children will not be proselytized away from their own faith and into a sect which may be abhorrent to them. This could happen without their knowledge, let alone their permission.

Samuel Rabinove, *Why We Still Need Public Schools*, 1992.

Since the 1940s the federal and state courts have generally taken the separationist position, though some decisions in recent years have moved toward the accommodationist stance.

There is ample evidence that there has been a consistency of support in our country for separationism from Madison's day until our own. Not only have the courts generally supported separation, but legislatures and the people have also.

Congress: Adamant Toward Separation

With only rather minor deviations Congress and the state legislatures have remained separationist. Congress has never approved an amendment to the First Amendment to authorize government sponsored or mandated devotions in public schools and has never approved direct or substantial tax aid to pervasively sectarian private schools. State laws (in Arkansas and Louisiana) requiring schools to include the fundamentalist doctrine of creationism in science classes were readily struck down by federal courts during the 1980s. State laws or proposed amendments to provide tax support for sectarian schools have been defeated in referenda in Massachusetts, New York, Maryland, the District of Columbia, Michigan, Missouri, Nebraska, Colorado, Idaho, California, Oregon, Washington State, and Alaska since 1957. It is worth noting that at the time that the Supreme Court struck down school sponsored prayer as unconstitutional in 1962 and 1963, the practice was only found in about one-half of the nation's school districts.

In 1952 Congress considered and approved a constitution for the Commonwealth of Puerto Rico which not only reiterates the religious freedom clauses of the First Amendment but explicitly stipulates that "There shall be complete separation of church and state." In 1959 Congress approved the constitutions of the last two states admitted to the Union, Alaska and Hawaii, both of which bar tax aid to religious institutions and require public education to be religiously neutral, which is the pattern set by the other forty-eight states.

Let's return to the Maryland Senate committee hearing on March 8, 1993, to the bill to compel teachers and principals to "require all students to be present and participate in opening exercises" at which they would "meditate or pray silently." In my testimony to the committee I pointed to the inconsistency between the bill's word "voluntarily" and its stating that teachers shall "require" students to do something. I added that the bill, if passed, would put the state and its employees in the position of deciding when students should pray or meditate, that the state would be deciding that it is best that students pray or meditate at the same time, that the state prefers certain religious acts, such as praying or meditating, to other sorts of religious acts, such as doing good deeds, assisting the less fortunate, comforting the afflicted, etc., and that the bill would intrude the state into the province of the family and the church or synagogue.

Freedom from Government Coercion

My argument, in short, was that students and teachers should be free from government coercion, however mild or heavy-handed, in the area of religion, free even from the sort of government sponsored, watered-down, lowest-common-denominator religious activity envisioned by the sponsor of the bill. I concluded by citing Benjamin Franklin's statement to the effect that there is something wrong with any religion that must call for the help of "the civil power."

Views similar to mine were expressed by a wide spectrum of religious leaders in 1984 when President Reagan tried to get Congress to approve a "voluntary" prayer amendment to the First Amendment. One prominent church leader even denounced government sponsored prayer as "blasphemous."

In pleading that a "naked public square" results when government remains respectfully neutral toward religion, advocates of government support for religious activities or symbols overlook the fact that government neutrality has proven to be the best guarantor of individual religious freedom and interfaith harmony. When government shows preference toward some religions, it cannot help but discriminate against others and to create resentment or even fear among adherents to non-preferred groups. Have we learned nothing from the experiences of other countries and of our own colonial period? Can anyone really believe that "free exercise of religion" requires government assistance? Is religion so weak and fragile that believers cannot celebrate sacred days or seasons without special recognition from government? Reasonable adjustment of work or school schedules to accommodate free exercise should be possible without involving actual sponsorship.

How much controversy and ill will has been stirred up by what is supposed to be the annual celebration of the birth of Jesus? Colonial New England strongly disapproved of celebration of a "Romish" holiday. Non-Christian children are often upset and feel left out when their public schools have a religious Christmas celebration. Even many Christians are upset by Christmas celebrations because they do not believe there is a Biblical warrant for celebrating Jesus' birth on December 25.

It is argued by some that government neutrality toward religion is really hostility. But neutrality is not hostility. And anything other than neutrality is, ipso facto, government preference toward some and discrimination against others.

Public schools have been criticized for inadequate attention to religion. Yes, it is quite legitimate for public schools to present instruction *about* religion, as long as it is objective, academic, and balanced. But agreeing on the necessity of objectivity and balance in the abstract is far from achieving it, as anyone familiar with public education should well know.

Back to our subject of freedom of and freedom from religion, I could maintain that each person's freedom of religion, freedom of conscience, and free exercise of religion necessarily involves freedom from government preference for any other religion and freedom from any discrimination against that person's religion.

Graduation Prayers

Considerable discussion of freedom of/from religion has been stimulated by the Supreme Court's June 24, 1992, ruling in *Lee v. Weisman*, in which the Court held that public school graduation prayers coerced students into participating in religious exercises in violation of the First Amendment's prohibition of government acts "respecting an establishment of religion." As Justice Anthony Kennedy wrote, "The Constitution forbids the state to exact religious conformity from a student as the price of attending his or her own high school graduation. This is the calculus the Constitution demands." Government, Kennedy held, may never coerce the religious opinions of individuals, even indirectly. "The undeniable fact is that the school district's supervision and control of a high school graduation ceremony places public pressure, as well as peer pressure, on attending students to stand as a group or, at least, maintain respectful silence during the invocation and benediction. This pressure, though subtle and indirect, can be as real as any overt compulsion. . . . [T]he state may not, consistent with the Establishment Clause, place primary and secondary students in this position."

Not only did the graduation prayers in *Lee v. Weisman* put pressure on students, but the school district, in an effort to try to minimize possible student or parent discomfort over the prayers, issued guidelines to participating clergy to get them to be as nondenominational as possible. Presumably a clergyperson not amenable to offering as bland a prayer as possible would be disqualified from participating. Not only would subjecting the person invited to offer the prayer to a content-based test offend the constitutional clause barring religious tests for public office, but it certainly ought to be interpreted as insulting to the clergyperson.

Public Prayer Alternatives

But what about the freedoms or rights of the majority of students who presumably might want to have a prayer at their graduation? There is no bar to any student's praying silently at his or her graduation ("Thank God it's over. Now on to Harvard.") or his or her attending a special graduation service at a church or synagogue where no one questions the right of those present to participate in a lengthy and totally religious exercise.

What is needed, finally, is a little clarity of thought. Short of activity which would violate the equal rights of others, such as hurling maidens into a volcano to appease a thunder god, individuals are free to exercise their religions privately, as Jesus recommended in the Sermon on the Mount, or publicly, as in an outdoor pageant, but government sponsorship of religious activity cannot avoid preferring some religions over others, thereby rendering some or many people second class citizens.

Your freedom *of* religion necessarily implies your freedom *from* my religion.

Periodical Bibliography

The following articles have been selected to supplement the diverse views presented in this chapter.

Khoren Arisian	"The Supreme Court Violates Our Democracy," *The Human Quest*, November/December 1992. Available from Churchman Co., 1074 23d Ave., St. Petersburg, FL 33704.
William Bentley Ball et al.	"How to Restore Religious Freedom: A Debate," *First Things*, April 1992. Available from PO Box 3000, Dept. FT, Denville, NJ 07834.
James J. Conn	"Graduation Prayers and the Establishment Clause," *America*, November 14, 1992.
Edd Doerr	"Backward or Forward?" *The Humanist*, March/April 1992.
Marvin E. Frankel	"Religion in Public Life—Reasons for Minimal Access," *The George Washington Law Review*, March 1992. Available from 716 20th St. NW, Suite 302, Washington, DC 20052.
J.D. Gruenberg	"The Free Exercise Clause: An Illusion of Freedom for Those Who Need It Most," *Criminal Justice Journal*, Spring 1992. Available from 2121 San Diego Ave., San Diego, CA 92110.
Richard John Neuhaus	"A New Order of Religious Freedom," *First Things*, February 1992.
Michael Novak	"Prayer in School: An Intolerant Supreme Court," *The American Legion*, December 1992. Available from PO Box 1055, Indianapolis, IN 46206.
Daniel Pilarczyk	"Church and State: Attic or Living Room?" *Vital Speeches of the Day*, May 1, 1991.
L. Anita Richardson	"Tomorrow's Jericho?" *Human Rights*, Fall 1992.
Antonin Scalia	"Prayer Decision Violates Constitutional Traditions," *Human Events*, July 11, 1992. Available from 422 First St. SE, Washington, DC 20003.
John M. Swomley	"Movement for Theocracy," *Christian Social Action*, April 1992. Available from 100 Maryland Ave. NE, Washington, DC 20002.
James M. Wall	"Religious Freedom: Tensions and Contentions," *The Christian Century*, January 15, 1992.

4 CHAPTER

How Can Civil Liberties Be Protected?

CIVIL
LIBERTIES

Chapter Preface

The Ninth Amendment to the U.S. Constitution states that "the enumeration in the Constitution, of certain rights, shall not be construed to deny or disparage others retained by the people." The Fourteenth Amendment, ratified in 1868, declares that "no state shall make or enforce any law which shall abridge the privileges or immunities of citizens." History, however, reveals that such constitutional rights were far from guaranteed. Despite the Ninth Amendment, for example, blacks were enslaved for decades, and neither amendment acknowledged women's right to vote.

Eradicating such injustices became the ambition of civil rights pioneers such as Frederick Douglass and Susan B. Anthony, whose years of diligence helped sway public opinion and finally convinced the government to abolish slavery nationwide, in the Thirteenth Amendment in 1865 and to grant voting rights to women, in the Nineteenth Amendment in 1920.

The leadership of Douglass, Anthony, and others spurred the creation of organizations dedicated to protecting civil liberties. In 1920, for example, two of America's most influential civil rights groups, the American Civil Liberties Union (ACLU) and the National Association for the Advancement of Colored People (NAACP), were created and have since won many civil rights victories, including due process for suspected criminals and the end of segregation laws.

Despite such marked progress, the protection of individual rights and liberties remains an ongoing endeavor. In the words of former House Judiciary Committee chairman Peter Rodino Jr., "The task of protecting the people's rights, both specific and general, is neither an easy nor a one-time job." Recognizing this, the authors in the following chapter debate how best to protect civil liberties.

"*It is unlikely that problems will vanish until children's rights appear.*"

Children Should Be Given More Legal Rights

Charles D. Gill

Many child advocates believe children should be accorded many of the legal rights adults have. In the following viewpoint, Charles D. Gill agrees and argues that children today are essentially property and unprotected by the U.S. Constitution. Gill proposes a constitutional amendment that would guarantee that children receive education and health care, among other rights. Gill states that America should follow the lead of the United Nations, which in 1989 adopted the Convention on the Rights of Children, by granting more rights to children. Gill is a superior court judge in Hartford, Connecticut.

As you read, consider the following questions:

1. How could including the term "love" in a children's rights amendment be problematic, according to Gill?
2. Why would Gill exclude older teenagers from constitutional protection?
3. In the author's opinion, why should government meet children's needs when parents cannot?

From Charles D. Gill, "Essay on the Status of the American Child, 2000 A.D.: Chattel or Constitutionally Protected Child-Citizen?" *Ohio Northern University Law Review* 17 (3): 543-79. Reprinted with permission.

We hold these truths to be self-evident, that all men are created equal, that they are endowed by their Creator with certain unalienable Rights. . . .

These magnificent words, largely the inspiration of Thomas Jefferson, a slave owner, and signed by fifty-six white males, are the philosophical cornerstone of our democracy. This compelling phrase is permanently enshrined in each of us as school children and is frequently recited in emotional tones to hushed audiences at anniversaries and events of national significance. This belief in certain "rights" is also the foundation for the Constitution of the United States and is reflected in its preamble.

During Constitution Week of 1990, a day was set aside for each town to ring its steeple bells to celebrate the existence of our Constitution. And the bells rang. But while they were pealing for adults; the children of this country had few rights to celebrate.

The truths, the rights, justice and the blessings of liberty were not extended to all people by our fundamental documents. Slaves, children, and, to a large degree, women were excluded. They were property, mere chattel, in varying degrees. Slaves had no rights, since they were property, and the child-citizens, similarly, had no rights except to someday succeed to the rights of their fathers.

The thirteenth, fourteenth, and fifteenth amendments elevated the status of black citizens in the United States. One constitutional amendment, the nineteenth, improved the status of women by granting them voting rights. However, the American child remains essentially property, and its constitutionally unprotected status is more and more likely to produce disastrous consequences that threaten the viability of our democracy. . . .

A Children's Amendment

It is hardly a novel idea in the world to include protections for children in national constitutions. Unlike America, the constitutions of seventy-nine nations at least mention children. Every new idea has to start with words reduced to writing. The National Task Force for Children's Constitutional Rights has done this. This idea is not presented as a final, unchangeable, document of perfect content and draftsmanship. It is presented as a starting point only. An agenda to initiate discussion, constructive criticism and even unconstructive criticism. The language of section one is no more than a description of the basic needs of children as generally agreed upon by reasonable people. Sections two through four are an attempt to equalize the child in the courtroom and to put a child's developmental needs in a position of understanding and respect in the adult arena.

Read this not with cynical eyes of the lawyer, but with the eyes of a child. Your eyes as a child in need, or those of your child. This is the amendment that is proposed for discussion and dialogue on the American agenda as we approach the year 2000 A.D.:

Section 1
All citizens of the United States who are fifteen years of age or younger shall enjoy the right to live in a home that is safe and healthy; the right to adequate health care; the right to an adequate education and the right to the care of a loving family or a substitute thereof, which approximates as closely as possible such family.

Section 2
All citizens of the United States who are fifteen years of age or younger shall be allowed to testify in any legal proceeding without having to view any person accused of abusing said citizen, notwithstanding any other provision of this Constitution.

Section 3
All citizens of the United States who are fifteen years of age or younger shall enjoy the right in any legal proceeding to have the trier receive evidence as to such citizen's developmental level as it pertains to that citizen's credibility.

Section 4
All citizens of the United States who are fifteen years of age or younger shall enjoy the right to counsel in any legal proceeding that affects that citizen's interests. . . .

It may well be that a final amendment would exclude the word "love." It is fascinating to watch law colleagues squirm at the concept of that term which other professions have no difficulty evaluating. This mysterious and indefinable term is promised by adults at the time of their marriage contract, used to describe their acts of sexual intimacy, sworn to exist for their children in custody proceedings and recited as being absent in their divorce hearings. Scientifically, we know babies die without it and adults die for it. My legal colleagues will also be disturbed by section four of the suggested amendment, which provides for legal counsel for children. Imagine! A quasi-chattel having the right to counsel in any legal proceeding that affects that "helpless" child-citizen's interests! Outlandish!

Adults Versus Children

Or is it? Do we not provide counsel or representation for a "helpless" adult in any legal proceeding affecting the adult's interest? Does not modern society provide protection rights for adults who are retarded, mentally ill or so disabled as to be helpless?

169

Sections two and three give rise to "adult" concerns over "adult" trials of "adults." Adults can see no farther than their Bill of Rights of 1791. Even the drafters of the Constitution knew it was imperfect and expected change. They provided for two amending processes within the Constitution itself.

Take Heed of Children's Life Choices

How many of the structures, institutions and practices established to 'protect' children actually do so? Think of the juvenile court, the care system, observation and assessment centres, reporting systems where abuse has been identified, 'child protection' registers for children 'at risk', and ask whether the 'official' version of the truth withstands critical examination. But ask also whether, and to what extent, we are prepared to encourage children to participate in decisions regarding their life choices. It is much easier to assume abilities and capacities are absent than to take cognizance of children's choices.

Michael Freeman, *Children, Rights, and the Law*, 1992.

In 1991, some adults may feel that justice for an adult accused in a criminal case includes the right to force a five-year-old child witness to look the adult defendant straight in the eye. All capable adults can easily avoid such a process. Some adults feel this is just. Others feel that, based upon our depth of modern knowledge of child development, it is court-sanctioned child abuse.

Some may feel that section three works an injustice to adults while providing justice to children. Would a judge or jury more likely reach an unjust result by having access to information that facilitates the fact-finding process?

Would evidence as to a child's development level help or harm a jury trying to determine credibility? Is it fair to say that the jurors' present ignorance of the child witnesses' developmental level has produced unjust verdicts? Has juror ignorance in this area helped in the search for truth that we claim is the goal of the American trial?

Ignorance of developmental and cultural norms has led many a good jurist astray. One colleague of this writer was always able to "size up" youthful offenders of a certain ethnic group who appeared before him. He noted how they were afraid to look him in the eye. One wonders how many children suffered incarceration or were not believed by this judge. He did not realize that young men of that culture were trained not to look an older man in the eyes, because it would be disrespectful.

According to Professor Phillip Alston, other countries of the world have given children the following rights in constitutional form:
1. The right to health care.
2. The right to protection.
3. The right to education.
4. The right not to be exploited.
5. The right of "special consideration in judicial and administrative procedures. . . ."
The proposed amendment intentionally creates exclusions. It does not protect fetuses. The amendment's proponents certainly do not intend to confer these rights on children, only to have them delayed or defeated by the national "fetus rights" battles. Supporters of the proposed amendment have diverse positions on the fetus issue. They have chosen to shelve these positions in this effort so as not to deny protections to those who have been born and who are now suffering.

Excluding Older Children

The proposed amendment defines a citizen, as does the Constitution, as a person *born* in the United States. The proposed amendment likewise excludes children ages sixteen and seventeen. It is fully realized that children of those ages have special needs also, and are often found in dire circumstances "slipping through the cracks." (Sixteen and seventeen year olds can be the Achilles heel of this movement.) The example of a seventeen year old drug dealer, in a BMW surrounded by money and possessions, who cries for protection under this proposed amendment in a courtroom would surely insure the defeat of the amendment for those children who clearly need it—the proposal's "Willie Horton" if you will.

Discussions of this proposed amendment invariably lead to a comparison to the Equal Rights Amendment (E.R.A.). Some immediately rush to the conclusion that "equal rights" for children are sought here. Obviously, such is not the case. The rights here, like the needs, are special. They fulfill those basic needs of children and protect them from adults and adults courtroom procedures.

The proposal does not ask, for example, that four-year-old children have the right not to incriminate themselves. It does ask that these children have the right to avoid people or circumstances that constitute dangers to them at home or in a courtroom. . . .

It is unlikely that problems will vanish until children's rights appear. Any group that proposes a substantial change in the status quo must be ready to present concrete advantages to the change. A "No One Knows" position will not do. The proposed amendment initially entitles American children to receive that which all reasonable people believe to be their basic needs; health care, education, safety, and a nurturing environment seem beyond dispute.

Once entitled, the satisfaction of these needs is not obtained from the bended knee of the child advocate at a legislative hearing. The legislature would be no longer able to choose which bone is thrown to the child, along with the highway department, the state police, and the university basketball team. The child advocates can leave their well worn knees and demand that government provide for these needs where parents cannot, or will not, provide.

Dialogue on Children's Rights

The proposed amendment is merely to initiate dialogue. It is offered for concept rather than legislative detail. Does the reader agree that American children should be protected? Are these protections and entitlements generally palatable? If so, let the dialogue begin. Let the drafters, the word mechanics, the debaters, and the philosophers loose their weapons and skills. In doing so, let them remember that the adult protective rights are already in the repository of the United States Constitution. Let them remember that speculation and flyspecking did not prevent the passage of the adult Bill of Rights. For example, speculation as to whether yelling "fire" in a crowded theater or burning the flag constitutes free speech was not an impediment to the adoption of the first amendment. . . .

Protections have recently been extended to children internationally. On November 20, 1989, the United Nations (U.N.) unanimously adopted the U.N. Convention on the Rights of the Child:

> Whatever the reason for the final form of the convention on the rights of the child, it is, indeed, a Magna Charta for children. It does not matter that it was drafted without reference to a comprehensive theory of children's rights. Now that it exists, it creates a theory of its own, a theory which upholds the right of the individual child to dignity and respect.

This Magna Charta provides for a number of rights, some which mirror the proposed amendment. Some relevant provisions are present here:

Article 2
1. *State Parties shall respect and ensure the rights set forth in the present Convention to each child within their jurisdiction* without discrimination of any kind, irrespective of the child's or his or her parent's or legal guardian's race, colour, sex, language, religion, political or other opinion, national, ethnic or social origin, property, disability, birth or other status.

Article 3
1. *In all actions concerning children,* whether undertaken by public or private social welfare institutions, courts of law, administrative authorities or legislative bodies, *the best interest of the child shall be a primary consideration.*

2. *States Parties undertake to ensure the child such protection and care as is necessary for his or her well-being,* taking into account the rights and duties of his or her parents, legal guardians, or other individuals legally responsible for him or her, and, to this end, shall take all appropriate legislative and administrative measures. . . .

This Convention went into force as international law on September 2, 1990 when it was ratified by the twentieth nation. Approximately seventy nations have now ratified the Convention thus becoming legally bound by its standards. Another seventy nations have indicated their intent to ratify it.

The notable hold-outs are Iran, Iraq, Libya, South Africa and the United States of America. Since we are "known by the company we keep," our administration has raised several strawmen as impediments. All of these impediments can be resolved by merely taking reservations and thus allowing American children to be brought into the twenty-first century in the safety of the majority of the Convention provisions.

It is supremely ironic that American children now, theoretically, have more protective rights under international law than they have here in the land of the free, home of the brave.

Ending Children's Second-Class Status

The notion that young people even have rights comes as a shock to many parents. "Portable property" was Emerson's term for children, and most people believe kids do belong to their parents, body and soul. As a practical matter, the courts have tended to uphold that view. But in recent years, lawyers have won cases affirming the constitutional rights of children. It has become distressingly clear that all too many kids need such protection—they may be the nation's last second-class citizens.

Pat Wingert and Eloise Salholz, *Newsweek*, September 21, 1992.

The Convention is a remarkable document. It tells us that a "worldwide consensus has emerged that children are indeed persons, that they are entitled a fortiori to respect and protection, and that nation-states should ensure the fulfillment of such rights with the force of law.

There are those who believe that the United States Supreme Court has fully declared children to be persons. These beliefs were shaken when that Court allowed unadjudicated juveniles to be detained in a locked facility because "[j]uveniles, unlike adults, are always in some form of custody."

The Convention makes a total break from previous approaches to children's rights. Previous "rights" were paternalistic, whereas the Convention makes the state directly responsible to the child. The pervading themes of the Convention are the dignity of the child and the individual child's best interests. [As Cynthia P. Cohen and Edith Naimark write:]

> This is true even when the child's interest may come into conflict with the rights of parents. The child has a right to be brought up by his or her parents, but he or she also has the right to be placed in an alternative family setting should this be necessary. The child has a right to be protected from all types of abuse, including that which occurs within the family unit. Under the Convention, the rights of the individual child are paramount.

The Convention also requires that nations ratifying it shall have two years and thirty days from ratification to submit the extent of their acts of compliance. Presuming eventual ratification, ways must be sought in which to implement its proposals.

Constitutional Protection

Do we need state by state legislation? Do we need federal legislation? Or shall children's rights be placed alongside the adult's rights in the Constitution? Professor Alston suggests that in lieu of a specific, constitutional amendment as is suggested here, a simple constitutional amendment such as the following may be sufficient: "Children shall enjoy the protection provided in international agreements which safeguard their rights." [According to Stuart N. Hart:]

> Children's rights are now the central issue in the human rights movement. Child rearing at home, in school, and in the community will determine both the course of society, nationally and internationally, and the dignity accorded all persons. During the last few hundred years, children have progressed through property and potential person status, with protection and nurturance rights, to partial personal status, with some self-determination rights. Public opinion, policies, and laws are converging in support of assuring self-determination rights for children to validate their person status.

"*Equal rights would . . . undermine [families'
teaching] role without offering anything but the
school of hard knocks to replace it.*"

Children Should Not Be Given More Legal Rights

Laura M. Purdy

Families and society would face serious consequences if children were given more legal rights, Laura M. Purdy argues in the
following viewpoint. Purdy asserts that if children had such
rights, they would endanger their future by discounting their
parents' wise advice and making bad decisions, such as quitting
school or engaging in drug abuse or irresponsible sexual activity. Purdy maintains that because parents play an important role
in shaping their children's lives and teaching them self-control,
they are best suited to decide a child's best interests. Purdy is
an associate professor of philosophy at Wells College in Aurora,
New York.

As you read, consider the following questions:

1. How are parent-child interactions based more on persuasion
   than power as children grow older, according to Purdy?
2. In the author's opinion, how should conflicts of interest
   between parents and children be resolved?
3. What problems do teenage mothers face, according to Purdy?

Julie, fourteen, wants to quit school; her parents think she should stay. Their disagreement illustrates two complex and difficult questions: How much control should children have over their lives? Are they capable of making decisions about their own best interest?

Julie thinks she is. . . .

She does not now have a right to leave school. Should she have it? A surprising array of people, not just budding fourteen-year-olds, agree that she should have, along with all other adult rights, the right to decide for herself whether to go to school or not. . . .

At present, children are for the most part dependent on their parents, although certain factors in contemporary life provide some children with sources of power with which to counteract the resulting dependence. A good deal of power, however, still generally rests with parents.

Equal Rights and Control of Children

If children had equal rights, some of this power would remain in parents' hands; their attitudes would determine to a considerable extent how it would be wielded. "New breed" parents would be assisted in their approach by the liberation program. They would get social approval for their relaxed handling of children, and they would not be held responsible when their children got in trouble. If, on the contrary, parents believed in shaping their children, and if they had a good relationship with them, then their home life might not be too different from that enjoyed by similar families today. These parents' power would in many cases be noticeably attenuated by social changes, however, even when legal rights were not at issue. The more children expected to run their own lives, the more difficult it would be for parents to persuade them to practice appropriate self-control; and since, as children grow older, more and more interactions must be based on persuasion rather than power, the base-line of expectation about compliance with parental preferences would drop. . . .

Lacking Vital Traits and Virtues

If children had equal rights, they would be sent a strong message that adults' greater experience is not a crucial difference between children and adults. Young children would presumably be relatively unaffected by that message, although their parents might be still less willing than at present to provide the [right] kind of structure. Under these circumstances, we might reasonably expect teenagers to experience more difficulties growing up, and awareness of their new rights would most likely still more increase resistance to parental attempts to instill self-control, enabling virtues, and moral behavior. Less fundamental but still valuable traits such as neatness and organization, or love of learning, would quite likely go by the boards as parents struggled just to pass on the basics without being pasted with unpleasant labels. Only those children with especially determined and energetic parents would get the training and support necessary to take the harder path. So even if the legal changes inherent in equal rights for children might not directly affect family relationships, they could, at the very least, be expected to accelerate the kind of troubling trends already examined.

In jeopardy, in fact, is the teaching role of families. Now, as I have suggested, what is important is that the teaching get done, not who does it. Equal rights would, I believe, undermine that role without offering anything but the school of hard knocks to replace it. Substantially gone would be social support for parental transmission of self-control, enabling virtues, and moral values, for as John Sommerville points out, "under pure egalitarian theory, few propositions are more reprehensible than those authorizing some to control or even to influence significantly the value choices of others." What follows from this theory is that we ought not to be influencing children, let alone using authority to tell them what to do, even for their own good. It would therefore seem to be just as wrong to pressure them to develop good study habits as to push them into drug dealing, just as wrong to raise them to help cripples as to turn them into racists.

Parents: Deciding in a Child's Interest

Now the power to shape children carries with it awesome responsibility, and we know that it is sometimes used in unreasonable ways. Howard Cohen, attempting to rebut the idea that equal rights would much alter parental power, admits that equal rights wouldn't even protect children from religious indoctrination. I suspect he is right. Parents who are determined to inculcate specific religious or political beliefs usually realize that success depends on an early and emotionally laden start. Young children are likely to take such teaching for granted and hence won't rebel. Older children may do so, but their only recourse may be to leave home. In this case, there would be no benefit to liberation, since for many children independent life would not be a realistic option. Moreover, children do not need equal rights to be rescued from bad homes.

The central issue here is *who* decides that a given family is bad for a child. Liberation puts the decision in children's hands. And although we might agree that some children need an escape hatch, it does not follow that they are usually the best judges as to when this is the case. As we have just seen, they could well be satisfied with circumstances that are not in their best interest; conversely, they may rebel against those that are.

Cohen begs us to consider the case of Jenny, a twelve-year-old who wants to exchange her rather strict home for a friend's more easygoing one: "The parents have done nothing which could legally be described as child abuse or neglect, . . . they have genuine concern for the child's development, . . . and they are rather strict disciplinarians." Cohen judges that it would be paternalistic for them to prohibit Jenny's moving in with a friend because of the implication that they know better than she what is good for her. Who are we, asks Cohen, to say what she needs? But what if she hasn't yet learned the importance of honesty or responsibility, and just wants to get away from her parents' attempts to help her to do so? What if, in fact, there is ample reason to believe that without her parents' warm but appropriately firm discipline she will fail to learn self-control and moral behavior? Letting children leave home under these circumstances amounts to saying that they should be free to escape the hard labor required for maturation. . . .

"AND AS FOR THE *PROPERTY SETTLEMENT,* LITTLE BILLY GETS THE HOUSE AND STOCKS, BUT YOU RETAIN THE *BATMAN ACTION FIGURES.* . . . "

© Bob Gorrell/*Richmond Times-Dispatch.* Reprinted with permission.

It hardly needs saying that once children become teenagers, tinder piles multiply: skipping school, homework, curfew, sex, drugs, dress, loud music, and simple courtesy often become battlegrounds. Conflict seems almost a foregone conclusion. The difficulty with the liberation point of view is that conflict has a tendency to become conflated with conflict of interest. A conflict of interest occurs when two individuals have legitimate interests that cannot both be satisfied. I have suggested that morality calls upon us to satisfy the stronger interest. I think it is probably also generally recognized that special relationships, such as parent-child relationships, can involve commitments on the part of parents to subordinate more of their own interests than would otherwise be required. As any thoughtful parent knows, translating this theory into practice is no easy task; we find ourselves asking time and time again: Is *this* something I owe my child?

Liberationists rightly point out that protectionism has a way of covering up possible conflicts of interest between children and adults. The underlying suggestion is that there is an analogy with the case of women, whose interests, until recently, were thought to be adequately protected by laws that left their affairs in the hands of men. The answer, for women, was to give them the power to protect their own interests. But women are adults who can handle their own affairs; given children's immaturity, there is little reason to think that the same approach would benefit them.

Neglected Children

We know that some of children's interests ought to have priority for parents; getting parents to behave accordingly is essential for children's well-being. Any decent society must have a backup system for children whose parents are not meeting their basic needs. Contemporary Western societies have mostly relied on the state for this protection, although, as liberationists rightly emphasize, the record of that alternative is to some degree a sorry one. However, it is far from clear that liberating children is the answer to this problem.

Equal rights promise children the power to ensure that their basic needs are met without direct reliance on the good graces of other adults. What they deliver, instead, is a weapon that in the short run helps children get their own way, whether the conflict in question is one of interests or not. It might be reasonable to accept this result if the bad consequences of children's running their own lives were outweighed by the guarantees for their important interests. I think that by the end of this viewpoint it will be absolutely clear that this is not the case and is not likely to become so in the foreseeable future.

Some disagreements between parents and children involve true conflicts of interest. For example, a parent with a demanding work schedule needs some free time, which might have to come at the expense of a child's desire for the parent's attendance at a school function. In general, as I have suggested, the stronger interest ought to prevail here, although it isn't always easy to see which it is. . . .

Consequences of Dropping Out

What about schooling, for example? What if a teen refuses to take school seriously or wants to drop out? The consequences will depend in part on outside circumstances; some would be able to do these things with impunity, for their situation permits them to make up work or return to school without any major penalty. But many children would not be in such fortunate circumstances and they would quite likely find themselves trapped for life in low-paying, dead-end jobs; they would also be deprived of whatever cultural enrichment further schooling might provide. These probable consequences of a poor school record are well known, but they are unlikely to be taken seriously by adolescents who want to drop out. Parents and other adults can help by painting graphic pictures of the consequences; they can also require a child to work if she drops out, giving her a taste of reality before getting too far behind in school. To be sure, by the teenage years, parents must exercise most of their authority by stating acceptable alternatives and sticking to them, even if that means throwing a child out of the house. In a sense, then, we are no longer talking about the kind of parental control liberationists object to, but more subtle pressures generally compatible with their stand except insofar as they think teens have a right to financial support no matter what their behavior.

Teens might also insist that drinking or doing drugs should be their own choice, just as it is for adults. But the reverberations both for themselves and for those about them suggest the desirability of pressing them to limit such activities in a way that might not be appropriate for adults.

Sex Carries Risks

The same is true for sex. Taboos on early sexual activity are breaking down: according to *Newsweek* "a recent [1987] Harris poll of U.S. teenagers indicated that more than half have had intercourse by the time they are seventeen." But only a third used contraception regularly; a third admitted to never using it, despite its availability. Consider the story of Vantra and her boyfriend, both sixteen. She used contraception only sporadically until recently, but after two months on the pill, her boyfriend asked her to quit using it: "He wants a child. And I don't know, in a way I want one, and in a way it's just too early for one." But she did quit, despite the fact that they have sex at least twice a week. Sadly, many people attribute the increase in sexual intercourse to peer pressure and our sexualized culture, not to affection or even desire.

180

The consequences are no less serious or real, whatever their causes. Sexually transmitted diseases are epidemic, and one might reasonably expect to see an increasing number of AIDS victims in this age group, especially among poor minorities. One could hardly call this consequence either trivial or self-regarding.

Children Need Guidance, Not Legal Rights

The most compelling argument against excluding any group from full citizenship is that people learn responsibility only by exercising it. But this argument breaks down in the case of children, who need a long period of tutelage before they are able to take care of themselves. Even John Stuart Mill, who based his political philosophy on the principle that individuals know their own interests and did not hesitate to draw the logical consequence in the case of women, never thought to extend legal rights to children. His common sense told him that it would be quite inappropriate to treat children as if they were adults before the law.

Christopher Lasch, *Harper's*, October 1992.

Another result of irresponsible sexual activity is substantial teenage motherhood. Yet the consequences of early childbearing are extremely damaging. Pregnancy doubles the risk that a girl will drop out of school; most such girls never return, regardless of their financial situation or ethnic background. Once the child is born, the girl is unlikely to be in a position to earn more than welfare would offer her and she has the responsibility of a child to boot. But if she chooses to go on welfare, her sense of agency and independence is seriously damaged. If she marries instead, she is not only unlikely to finish her schooling but also faces a significantly higher probability of divorce than a woman who waits until her twenties to marry. Thus girls who engage in unprotected sex and who elect to keep their babies are at serious risk of a worse life than they could otherwise have expected.

But the damage does not stop there. The plight of their children is painful. Neither parent may take responsibility: they may be ignored by their fathers and handed to some female relative by their mothers. For the child, this may be a blessing in disguise, as the most irresponsible teens are those least likely to possess the qualities required for good childrearing. As these babies get older, however, they show the effects of their unfavorable environment. Children of teen mothers score worse on ability tests, get worse grades, and expect less in the way of education than children of older women. They also get less education, marry earlier, and divorce more often. . . .

Some such kinds of irresponsibility may well boomerang on parents themselves. Who spends a lifetime helping instead of being helped by a son or daughter whose lack of employment skills was caused by failure to take school seriously? What about parents who must pick up the pieces of their children's drug-shattered lives? What about those mothers who wind up taking care of their daughters *and* their offspring? Do we want to reduce parents' power to protect themselves from these kinds of foreseeable consequences of irresponsible behavior on their children's part? There has been some discussion of what children owe their parents but it has tended to focus on the source of children's duty (based on enlightened self-interest) to obey their parents while they live at home or on what they owe them once they are gone.

In general, it seems to me that although parents' interests must often take a back seat to the duties created by children's needs during the years of active parenting, there is a limit to what should be expected of them afterward. The answer that parents can simply ignore their offspring's needs does not satisfy: it overlooks the bonds of love and caring we hope are inherent in such relationships. There is something radically wrong with this picture of family, and indeed of the society of which it is a part.

"The Bill of Rights has done little to protect gays against . . . laws . . . which serve to promote discrimination."

Homosexuals Should Have Increased Legal Protection

Marshall Kirk and Hunter Madsen

Many homosexuals assert that they should have the same legal rights and protections against discrimination as other oppressed minorities. In the following viewpoint, Marshall Kirk and Hunter Madsen agree and argue that homosexuals need protection against an assortment of discrimination, such as that from employers and landlords. The authors contend that legal protection would reduce the suffering that discrimination causes gays and help eliminate homophobia in society. Kirk is a Cambridge, Massachusetts, writer and researcher in neuropsychiatry. Madsen is a public communications consultant in New York City.

As you read, consider the following questions:

1. Why do Kirk and Madsen believe that job discrimination against gays is difficult to confirm?
2. In the authors' opinion, why is there a large proportion of homosexuals among schoolteachers?
3. How is hiding one's homosexuality to escape discrimination as wrong as discrimination itself, according to Kirk and Madsen?

On his best days, the recognizable gay person is treated as a harmless freak, enjoying all the respect accorded to the Bearded Fat Lady at the circus. On not-so-good days—which, since AIDS, have been most every day—he is treated more as a leper, menace, moral cretin, and third-class citizen.

Beliefs and actions go hand-in-glove. A small, sinful, and dangerously diseased band of sex addicts is easily subdued: just impose laws that criminalize their practices; keep them out of your neighborhood, workplace, school system, church, government, and—if they're foreigners—your nation; and do not forbear to taunt and beat them from time to time. This is the way to control an undesirable minority.

Promoting Suffering and Homophobia

We must concern ourselves with these actions for two reasons. First, they bring profoundly unjust suffering upon gays. Second, these actions, perfectly visible to the friends and enemies of gays, are thus powerful symbols for manipulation by both sides. So long as antigay discrimination is encouraged to persist in its most overt forms, the public is reassured that homohatred itself must be appropriate and virtuous; whereas the opposite message is conveyed when antigay aggression is deplored and outlawed.

For this reason, our battle for the hearts and minds of Americans must take place both above and below the surface. Antigay actions are the brutal tip of an enormous iceberg otherwise submerged. An effective plan to smash homohatred must steer directly at the great mass underneath: hostile feelings and beliefs among the general public. But our success will be judged by how well we topple the exposed peaks of blatant discrimination and violence. . . .

Denying Gays Their Fundamental Civil Rights

While roughly three in four Americans believe homosexuality is always wrong, far fewer say they'd actually infringe on the civil liberties of homosexuals, especially if the liberties in question were those explicitly set forth in the Bill of Rights. Heterosexuals are more fond of those legal rights, and of their self-image as good Americans, than they are of queerbashing.

That's the good news. Now, the bad: many straights feel that homosexuals should receive the minimal rights bestowed on all citizens by the Bill of Rights, *and nothing more*. This is a problem, for two reasons. First, the Bill of Rights has done little to protect gays against other Jim Crow laws or policies at state and local levels, which serve to promote discrimination against gays in housing, employment, parental rights, and so forth. Second, the equal treatment of citizens is regulated only in small part by the nation's laws, still less by the Constitution; the rest is left up to each citizen's sense of fairness. Yet it is within this unregulated domain of private and semiprivate action that the sharp teeth of bigotry clamp down most tightly on gays.

So long as there's no law against it—and Americans generally resist the enactment of special laws to protect bedeviled minorities—our citizens think it their right to abuse and discriminate against others, as an act of self-expression. A bare majority may feel bound to let gays have their own say and (in some states, at least) their own sex, but this doesn't mean that they have to pretend they like what's going on. . . .

Workplace Discrimination

The rights of gays to work as they please, live where they wish, and enjoy equal access to public accommodations all concern an underlying right of association, the freedom to rub shoulders with whomever one must in order to get along in life. But this right of association flies in the face of straights' desire to distance themselves from homosexuals as much as possible. . . .

While employed during the mid-'80s in a large corporate office in New York, one of the authors met a somewhat effeminate middle-aged bachelor and a fortyish spinster (who clearly had been a beauty in her maiden days). Both were respected for their expertise and dedication; the woman, in fact, had been with the company for nearly twenty years. But recently, behind their backs, a homohater in top management had begun to call them "the Fudgepacker" and "Lisa Lesbo." When a decline in business led to layoffs, Lisa and the Fudgepacker were among the few to be fired from middle management. Had the homohater's name-calling stuck? Had his malevolence influenced the firing decisions?

Indeed, job discrimination against gays is harder to confirm than that against any other disadvantaged group. At least with female, black, or disabled applicants, there are objective physical characteristics to cite, quantify, and track—essential in building a legal case against systematic discrimination. But when it comes to sexual orientation, there are no valid external markers, just a passel of informal stereotypes, applied indiscriminately to both gays and those who merely 'look gay.'

There exist, therefore, no hard numbers on the exact extent of job discrimination against gays. (This lack of firm data, incidentally, gives our enemies room to protest—as a Maine gubernatorial candidate did in 1986—that "I'm not convinced [homophobia] translates directly into housing and employment discrimination. Therefore, I do not support the 'gay rights' bill.") . . .

Straights have been trying for decades to put their feet down against gay public-school teachers, and for [illogical] reasons. According to a 1987 Gallup poll, two thirds of the public believes gays should never be hired as elementary school teachers.

Some fear that gay teachers, degenerate sex maniacs by definition, will seduce their pupils. Even if they don't, gay teachers—whether 'avowedly' or only 'apparently' homosexual—are believed to exert an unwholesome influence: presumably they will, as role models, turn their previously straight students into limp-wristed pansies and coarsened tomboys. (Never mind that this presumptive role-model dynamic seems to have produced no countervailing effect upon the gay pupils of straight teachers.)

Respect All People's Sexual Orientation

Governmentally-sanctioned discrimination against gay men and lesbians continues, driven by fear, misunderstanding, and intolerance for human sexual diversity. SIECUS [Sex Information and Education Council of the United States] believes that an individual's sexual orientation—whether bisexual, heterosexual, or homosexual—is an essential quality of humanness and strongly supports the right of each individual to accept, acknowledge, and live in accordance with his/her orientation. SIECUS supports civil rights law protection to all people regardless of their sexual orientation and deplores all forms of prejudice and discrimination against people based on their sexual orientation.

SIECUS Report, December 1992/January 1993.

At the very least, straights fear, 'respectable' gay teachers will contradict one of the key social lessons of American schooling—reinforced with fists during lunch recess—about the value of conformity, of looking and acting like everyone else. (In social studies classes, America the Great Melting Pot is extolled, but the metaphor's subtext depicts the melting down of human diversity into a single all-American alloy.) In particular, straights are afraid that gay teachers will stand as living refutations of society's worst myths about homosexuals; this might soften homo-hatred in the next generation and enable gay children to come out earlier and better adjusted, with less shame and self-hatred. Wouldn't that be awful?

These fears in mind, Oklahoma attempted to enforce a law authorizing dismissal of any teachers "advocating, soliciting, imposing, encouraging or promoting public or private homosexual activity in a manner that creates a substantial risk that such conduct will come to the attention of school children *or school*

186

employees." [Stress added.] (Fortunately, the U.S. Supreme Court declared that law unconstitutional in 1985, thanks partly to the law's artlessly blatant oppressiveness, and partly to a well-argued brief from the National Gay and Lesbian Task Force.)

Such witch hunts are futile and cruel. The hunt is futile because it would—as with the clergy—turn up such an astonishingly high proportion of homosexuals among schoolteachers that we think the persecutors would regret ever having got themselves into such a mess; the Big Lie would be undermined. Although we have no firm statistics on the number of gays in lower education, that number is probably high; not because gays are out to seduce little boys or girls, but because the loving, nurturing—dare we say 'parental'?—side of adult gays seeks an outlet and is not infrequently channeled into teaching. Only now do the authors recognize that many of their best and most widely admired elementary- and secondary-school teachers were probably gay. . . .

Avoiding a "Bad" Reputation

Gays, like women, are unwelcome in many miserable occupations that depend upon macho esprit to make them attractive. As the fire chief of San Jose declared testily in 1986, "If some guy comes prancing into my office in a pink leisure suit saying, 'I just *love* truck men,' I'm not going to hire him"; one gets the impression that an openly gay applicant would fare poorly, no matter what his apparel. "I don't have anything against gays personally," explained a New York police sergeant to the *Boston Globe* in 1987, "I just don't want to work with one." What the sergeant, and many other straights, have something against, is association with homosexuals, and how this association might rub off on their reputations and job status.

The same motives can be seen behind denial of housing and public accommodations to gays. The landlord and hotel manager advise apparently gay couples that they have no more vacancies, when what they really mean is that they do not welcome gays, lest their establishments develop a 'bad' reputation. . . .

Deceptions of Homosexuality

Society, of course, suggests a solution to all this discrimination against homosexuals, young and old, in work and shelter: there can be no discrimination if there are no gays, so stay in the closet and keep the door tightly shut. Let the Big Lie beget little lies. If you're a gay male teen, keep your hands to yourself and take a nice girl to the senior prom; or, if lesbian, get a boyfriend who won't paw you too much. At your job interview, wear a gold wedding band. Once employed, get an opposite-sex stand-in for social functions; or fake a spouse, then announce a divorce. When you and your lover go hunting for a condominium, split up and apply for adjoining suites, one at a time. When you move in together, get separate telephone lines to avoid suspicion. Hotel accommodations can easily be had for your vacation together: simply settle for a room with twin beds, or let one of you hide in the car while the other rents a full-sized. And so on.

As a cure, deception of this sort is as bad as the disease, for both patient and society; worse, in fact, since it obscures the symptoms and darkens the prognosis. But for gays who cannot bear to jeopardize career, home, and mobility for gay liberation, deception seems the only option. Gays are permitted to embrace the American Dream only by entering into an endless social nightmare.

"'Sexual orientation' does not constitute a quality comparable to race, ethnic background, etc., in respect to nondiscrimination."

Homosexuals Should Not Have Increased Legal Protection

Vatican Congregation for the Doctrine of the Faith

The Catholic Church has long considered homosexual behavior to be immoral. In the following viewpoint, the Vatican Congregation for the Doctrine of the Faith (CDF) argues that legislation to reduce discrimination against homosexuals should not be enacted because such laws would promote homosexuality. The Congregation contends that homosexual behavior threatens society and the family by eroding Christian values. Because homosexual behavior is unlike race, gender, or other attributes against which people are discriminated, the CDF maintains that society may justly limit homosexuals' rights to work and housing. The Congregation, part of the Vatican in Rome, promotes and safeguards the church's doctrine on faith and morals.

As you read, consider the following questions:

1. What does the CDF believe will be the result of accepting homosexual relationships as equivalent to husband/wife relationships?
2. In the authors' opinion, how could the legal protection of homosexuals cause violent reactions against them?
3. How can homosexuals avoid employment and housing discrimination, according to the Congregation?

From "Some Considerations Concerning the Catholic Response to Legislative Proposals on the Nondiscrimination of Homosexual Persons," a letter from the Vatican Congregation for the Doctrine of the Faith, to the bishops of the Roman Catholic church, 1992.

Legislation has been proposed in various places which would make discrimination on the basis of sexual orientation illegal. In some cities, municipal authorities have made public housing, otherwise reserved for families, available to homosexual (and unmarried heterosexual) couples. Such initiatives, even where they seem more directed toward support of basic civil rights than the condoning of homosexual activity or a homosexual lifestyle, may in fact have a negative impact on the family and society. Such things as the adoption of children, the employment of teachers, the housing needs of genuine families, landlords' legitimate concerns in screening potential tenants, for example, are often implicated.

While it would be impossible to anticipate every eventuality in respect to legislative proposals in this area, these observations will try to identify some principles and distinctions of a general nature which should be taken into consideration by the conscientious Catholic legislator, voter, or Church authority who is confronted with such issues.

The first section will recall relevant passages from the Congregation for the Doctrine of the Faith's *Letter to the Bishops of the Catholic Church on the Pastoral Care of Homosexual Persons* of 1986. The second section will deal with their applications.

Passages from the Vatican Letter

1) The letter recalls that the CDF's *Declaration on Certain Questions Concerning Sexual Ethics* of 1975 "took note of the distinction commonly drawn between the homosexual condition or tendency and individual homosexual actions," the latter of which are "intrinsically disordered" and "in no case to be approved of."

2) Since "in the discussion which followed the publication of the (above-mentioned) declaration . . ., an overly benign interpretation was given to the homosexual condition itself, some going so far as to call it neutral, or even good," the letter goes on to clarify: "Although the particular inclination of the homosexual person is not a sin, it is a more or less strong tendency ordered toward an intrinsic moral evil; and thus the inclination itself must be seen as an objective disorder. Therefore special concern and pastoral attention should be directed toward those who have this condition, lest they be led to believe that the living out of this orientation in homosexual activity is a morally acceptable option. It is not."

3) "As in every moral disorder, homosexual activity prevents one's own fulfillment and happiness by acting contrary to the creative wisdom of God. The Church, in rejecting erroneous opinions regarding homosexuality, does not limit but rather defends personal freedom and dignity realistically and authenti-

cally understood."

4) In reference to the homosexual movement, the letter states: "One tactic used is to protest that any and all criticism of or reservations about homosexual people, their activity and lifestyle, are simply diverse forms of unjust discrimination."

5) "There is an effort in some countries to manipulate the Church by gaining the often well-intentioned support of her pastors with a view to changing civil statutes and laws. This is done in order to conform to these pressure groups' concept that homosexuality is at least a completely harmless, if not an entirely good, thing. Even when the practice of homosexuality may seriously threaten the lives and well-being of a large number of people, its advocates remain undeterred and refuse to consider the magnitude of the risks involved."

Homosexuality Should Not Be Condoned

6) "She (the Church) is also aware that the view that homosexual activity is equivalent to, or as acceptable as, the sexual expression of conjugal love has a direct impact on society's understanding of the nature and rights of the family and puts them in jeopardy."

7) "It is deplorable that homosexual persons have been and are the object of violent malice in speech or in action. Such treatment deserves condemnation from the Church's pastors wherever it occurs. It reveals a kind of disregard for others which endangers the most fundamental principles of a healthy society. The intrinsic dignity of each person must always be respected in word, in action and in law.

"But the proper reaction to crimes committed against homosexual persons should not be to claim that the homosexual condition is not disordered. When such a claim is made and when homosexual activity is consequently condoned, or when civil legislation is introduced to protect behavior to which no one has any conceivable right, neither the Church nor society at large should be surprised when other distorted notions and practices gain ground, and irrational and violent reactions increase."

8) "What is at all cost to be avoided is the unfounded and demeaning assumption that the sexual behavior of homosexual persons is always and totally compulsive and therefore inculpable. What is essential is that the fundamental liberty which characterizes the human person and gives him his dignity be recognized as belonging to the homosexual person as well."

9) "In assessing proposed legislation, the bishops should keep as their uppermost concern the responsibility to defend and promote family life."

10) "Sexual orientation" does not constitute a quality comparable to race, ethnic background, etc., in respect to nondiscrimi-

nation. Unlike these, homosexual orientation is an objective disorder and evokes moral concern.

Chuck Asay, by permission of the *Colorado Springs Gazette Telegraph.*

11) There are areas in which it is not unjust discrimination to take sexual orientation into account, for example, in the consignment of children to adoption or foster care, in employment of teachers or coaches, and in military recruitment.

12) Homosexual persons, as human persons, have the same rights as all persons including that of not being treated in a manner which offends their personal dignity. Among other rights, all persons have the right to work, to housing, etc. Nevertheless, these rights are not absolute. They can be legitimately limited for objectively disordered external conduct. This is sometimes not only licit but obligatory. This would obtain moreover not only in the case of culpable behavior but even in the case of actions of the physically or mentally ill. Thus it is accepted that the state may restrict the exercise of rights, for example, in the case of contagious or mentally ill persons, in order to protect the common good.

13) Including "homosexual orientation" among the considerations on the basis of which it is illegal to discriminate can easily lead to regarding homosexuality as a positive source of human

rights, for example, in respect to so-called affirmative action or preferential treatment in hiring practices. This is all the more deleterious since there is no right to homosexuality which therefore should not form the basis for judicial claims. The passage from the recognition of homosexuality as a factor on which basis it is illegal to discriminate can easily lead, if not automatically, to the legislative protection and promotion of homosexuality. A person's homosexuality would be invoked in opposition to alleged discrimination and thus the exercise of rights would be defended precisely via the affirmation of the homosexual condition instead of in terms of a violation of basic human rights.

The Problem of Discrimination

14) The "sexual orientation" of a person is not comparable to race, sex, age, etc., also for another reason than that given above which warrants attention. An individual's sexual orientation is generally not known to others unless he publicly identifies himself as having this orientation or unless some overt behavior manifest it. As a rule, the majority of homosexually oriented persons who seek to lead chaste lives do not publicize their sexual orientation. Hence the problem of discrimination in terms of employment, housing, etc., does not usually arise.

Homosexual persons who assert their homosexuality tend to be precisely those who judge homosexual behavior or life-style to be "either completely harmless, if not an entirely good thing" and hence worthy of public approval. It is from this quarter that one is more likely to find those who seek to "manipulate the Church by gaining the often well-intentioned support of her pastors with a view to changing civil statutes and laws," those who use the tactic of protesting that "any and all criticism of or reservations about homosexual people . . . are simply diverse forms of unjust discrimination."

In addition, there is a danger that legislation which would make homosexuality a basis for entitlements could actually encourage a person with a homosexual orientation to declare his homosexuality or even to seek a partner in order to exploit the provisions of the law.

Promoting Family Life

15) Since in the assessment of proposed legislation uppermost concern should be given to the responsibility to defend and promote family life, strict attention should be paid to the single provisions of proposed measures. How would they affect adoption or foster care? Would they protect homosexual acts, public or private? Do they confer equivalent family status on homosexual unions, for example, in respect to public housing or by entitling the homosexual partner to the privileges of employment which

193

could include such things as "family" participation in the health benefits given to employees?

16) Finally, where a matter of the common good is concerned, it is inappropriate for Church authorities to endorse or remain neutral toward adverse legislation even if it grants exceptions to Church organizations and institutions. The Church has the responsibility to promote family life and the public morality of the entire civil society on the basis of fundamental moral values, not simply to protect herself from the application of harmful laws.

"We cannot abandon minority-preference programs that have worked."

Promoting Affirmative Action Would Protect the Civil Liberties of Minorities

Eric Neisser

Affirmative action programs legally protect the rights of members of minority groups to equal opportunity in such areas as employment and education. In the following viewpoint, Eric Neisser argues that these minority preference programs have increased the proportion of minorities in, for instance, better-paying jobs and law school admissions. Neisser asserts, however, that since minorities still have far fewer occupational and educational opportunities than whites, affirmative action programs will remain necessary to protect minorities' rights. The author, a former legal director of the New Jersey affiliate of the American Civil Liberties Union, is a law professor at Rutgers University Law School in Newark, New Jersey.

As you read, consider the following questions:

1. According to Neisser, why is it difficult for minority-owned companies to compete against those owned by nonminorities?
2. Why does Neisser believe it is fair to give preference to minorities who score slightly lower than whites on an exam?
3. Do you agree with the author that past discrimination is to blame for minorities' lower test scores today? Why or why not?

From Eric Neisser, *Recapturing the Spirit: Essays on the Bill of Rights at Two Hundred*. Madison, WI: Madison House Publishers, 1991. Reprinted with permission.

Deeply ingrained social problems require persistent and creative solutions. Racial and ethnic prejudice is as old as humankind and particularly virulent in this country because of our slaveholding past. It was thought by some and hoped by many that removal of the formal legal barriers would lead to true racial equality. It didn't happen—either after emancipation or after the civil rights legislation of the 1960's. Much more was needed—in education, housing, and employment. Various forms of so-called "affirmative action" were developed to insure that opportunities were available to minority groups long denied access to higher education and better-paying jobs. Those programs have often provoked strong reactions by those who feel that "better qualified" whites who may themselves have never discriminated have been wrongfully denied positions or promotions in favor of individuals who may never have personally suffered discrimination. Recent events in numerous areas compel us to re-examine the situation and reassess the relative social costs and benefits. I conclude that we should re-affirm the need for continued direct and innovative action to ensure that some day we fulfill the dream that our children will be evaluated not by the color of their skin but by the quality of their characters.

The Unsolved Problem

• In January 1989 the United States Supreme Court, in its now famous decision in *Richmond v. J.A. Croson, Co.*, struck down a program in Richmond, Virginia, the former capital of the Confederacy, that required that 30 percent of city construction contracts be awarded to minority-owned businesses. Nine years earlier, the Court had upheld a law passed by Congress requiring that 10 percent of all grants from a federal appropriation of $4 billion for state and local public works projects be awarded to minority-owned businesses. The Court there relied upon the special constitutional powers of Congress, including its power to provide for the general welfare and to enforce the equal protection guarantees of the Fourteenth Amendment. In *Croson*, the Court held that, unlike Congress, states and cities must show in detail the prior discrimination that prompted such "set-aside" programs and establish that no alternative to a racially defined preference would succeed in remedying the situation.

• In the spring of 1990 Professor Derrick Bell of Harvard Law School announced that he would go on unpaid leave from his $120,000 a year job until his school, which has three African American men and five white women out of sixty-two tenured professors, grants tenure to an African American woman.

• In June 1990 the Supreme Court upheld policies of the Federal Communications Commission that give "preference points" to applications by minority-owned businesses for broadcasting licenses and that permit only such businesses to bid at "distress sales" of television or radio stations whose licenses have been called into question.

• In September 1990 a federal judge ruled for the first time that a residency requirement for municipal workers in a nearly all-white community has a racially discriminatory impact and therefore violates Title VII of the 1964 Civil Rights Act.

What do these differing events tell us? First, of course, they tell us that "the problem" is not solved. If the problem is racial prejudice, my knowledge of human nature suggests that we may never find the solution. If, however, we define the task as equalizing opportunities for persons of all origins in all facets of public life, there is hope, though much is yet to be done.

Some background facts from the four cases mentioned highlight the problem. In Richmond in the five years prior to the set-aside program, only 0.67 percent of the $24.6 million in city construction contracts went to minority-owned businesses and there were virtually no minorities in any of the major trade associations in town. Despite admissions and faculty recruitment efforts of many law schools over the past twenty years, minorities still constitute only 8.67 percent of all law faculty. By 1986, despite eighteen years of efforts at that point by the Minority Student Program at my school, Rutgers Law School in Newark, minority lawyers constituted only 4.7 percent of the New Jersey bar. In 1971, before the various efforts of Congress and the FCC, minorities owned only 10 of the 7,500 radio stations in this country and none of the more than 1,000 television stations. By 1978 minorities owned less than 1 percent of broadcast stations, and by 1986 only 2.1 percent of the by-then more than 11,000 radio and television stations. Perhaps most tragically, twenty-two years after passage of the federal Fair Housing Act barring discrimination in residential housing, the residents of the town of Harrison, New Jersey, whose residency requirement for public employment was struck down, are still 99.8 percent white and, because of the residency rule, its municipal workforce is 100 percent white.

More Work Is Needed

Second, it is now painfully obvious that removing technical barriers to racial discrimination is not enough. That should not come as a surprise. If one ties up an athlete with ropes throughout the weeks that her colleagues are practicing and then, on the day of the meet, releases her and walks her over to the starting block at the same time as the others, one would hardly expect her to come in first, or even to keep up with her practiced competitors. The same holds true for groups that have been denied adequate education, housing, and employment for decades and are suddenly asked to compete for college or law school seats or skilled job openings.

The Litmus Test of Civil Rights

In recent years, virtually every civil rights enforcement effort was cut back, every new civil rights bill opposed, every federal civil rights agency badly weakened. The U.S. Commission on Civil Rights became the longest-running vaudeville act in Washington's history. And the Department of Justice was turned into a strike force against affirmative action

Affirmative action is the litmus test of civil rights.

Affirmative action is opposed because affirmative action works. It works for states and cities that complied with court orders to hire minorities and women for jobs in city services, in police stations, in fire houses.

It works for companies that hired blacks to have respectable numbers to show, and then concluded that affirmative action is just good business.

John E. Jacob, speech delivered at a National Urban League conference, Washington, D.C., July 21, 1985.

Third, further efforts are essential. We cannot abandon minority-preference programs that have worked in broadcast ownership or law school admissions contexts because "now everything is equal." Few minorities have an investor base large enough to be serious competitors with CBS or even with other local station applicants. Few have the resources or established track record to compete for municipal contracts in Richmond or elsewhere. And, as the state supreme courts in Texas, Montana, Kentucky, and New Jersey have so poignantly and courageously catalogued in their rulings on school finances, the educational opportunities for urban minority students in this country are still far less than those for suburban whites, thirty-six years after the Supreme Court mandated integration of schools because separate is inherently unequal.

The hard issue is not whether towns such as Harrison should now have to hire African American or Hispanic clerk-typists, janitors, or firefighters who do not happen to live within the town. There can be little non-racist objection because the residency requirement is clearly not related to qualification for any job; we know that there are many minority candidates from out of town who will be at least as qualified as the persons who have been hired in the past for those positions from the artificially narrowed applicant pool of local residents. Most significantly, removing the residence rule does not create preferential treatment for minority applicants and is thus not affirmative action in the most frequently used sense of that term.

Sense of Injustice

But when it comes to admitting students or picking teachers, many hesitate because they feel it is unfair to give preference to qualified minorities over "more qualified" whites. The sense of injustice is palpable and understandable. But we must consider whether it is justified by asking what we mean by "more qualified." Does an 87 rather than an 82 on a civil service exam, a 600 rather than a 550 on the college Scholastic Aptitude Test, or a 35 rather than a 30 on the Law School Admission Test make one "more qualified" to be trained to be a competent firefighter, teacher, or lawyer? So many of the quantitative tests used to speed decision-making are in fact shortcuts that ignore or distort meaningful measurement of ability or quality. In many cases the pass mark is a meaningful cut-off, and the differences in ability between those who just barely pass and those who score the highest grades are real. But amid the great mass of scores in between, sharp differences in ability are either not measurable or have not been substantiated by evaluations conducted on the job after training.

Sharing the Burden

Even assuming that the measures used reflect actual differences in levels of qualification, the ultimate policy question in any minority preference scheme is whether it is proper to favor those who because of earlier discrimination and inequality have not yet been able to reach the same levels of experience, education, or skill as those not so disfavored. Chief Justice Warren Burger, in approving the federal minority contractor set-aside program mentioned above, explained that "It is not a constitutional defect in this program that it may disappoint the expectations of nonminority firms. When effectuating a limited and properly tailored remedy to cure the effects of prior discrimination, such 'a sharing of the burden' by innocent parties is not impermissible." One of the reasons supporting such a view is that, without the centuries of discrimination, many of the innocent whites who are "victimized" by affirmative action would probably not have ranked higher than the minorities who are admitted or hired under preference programs. That is, had we had all these years an unbiased system of education and employment, minorities would appear at all levels of measurement in the same proportion as they do in the population at large.

What we will need to focus on in the coming years is not

whether dismantling affirmative action programs is unreasonable and harmful to the social fabric, for we already know that it is. Rather we will need to analyze closely, among other matters, what kinds of disappointed expectations can reasonably be imposed on innocent bystanders in our search for open opportunity for all. As Justice David Souter warned us in his confirmation hearing in 1990, we will be at this tough question for a lot longer than we had first hoped.

*"It is better to see integration as the inclusion of
all citizens into the same sphere of rights . . .
that our Founding Fathers themselves enjoyed."*

Promoting Integration Would Protect the Civil Liberties of Minorities

Shelby Steele

Shelby Steele is the author of the book *The Content of Our Character* and many articles on race. In the following viewpoint, Steele argues that integration is the ideal way to protect the civil liberties of disadvantaged groups such as blacks and women. Steele opposes affirmative action and other government programs aimed at helping the oppressed. Only integration, he believes, can remove race and gender as barriers to freedom. Steele is an English professor at San Jose State University in California.

As you read, consider the following questions:

1. How does the civil rights movement compare to the American Revolution, according to Steele?
2. In Steele's opinion, why did America's government and institutions grant collective entitlements to women and minorities?
3. Why does the author believe that entitlements do not aid those women and minorities who need the most help?

From the beginning America has been a pluralistic society, and one drawn to a radical form of democracy—emphasizing the freedom and equality of *individuals*—that could meld such diversity into a coherent nation. In this new nation no group would lord it over any other. But, of course, beneath this America of its ideals there was from the start a much meaner reality, one whose very existence mocked the notion of a nation made singular by the equality of its individuals. By limiting democracy to their own kind—white, male landowners—the Founding Fathers collectively entitled themselves and banished all others to the edges and underside of American life. There, individual entitlement was either curtailed or—in the case of slavery—extinguished.

Collective Entitlement

The genius of the civil rights movement that changed the fabric of American life in the late 1950s and early 1960s was its profound understanding that the enemy of black Americans was not the ideal America but the unspoken principle of collective entitlement that had always put the lie to true democracy. This movement, which came to center stage from America's underside and margins, had as its single, overriding goal the eradication of white entitlement. And, correspondingly, it exhibited a belief in democratic principles at least as strong as that of the Founding Fathers, who themselves had emerged from the (less harsh) margins of English society. In this sense the civil rights movement re-enacted the American Revolution, and its paramount leader, Martin Luther King, spoke as twentieth-century America's greatest democratic voice.

All of this was made clear to me for the umpteenth time by my father on a very cold Saturday afternoon in 1959. There was a national campaign under way to integrate the lunch counters at Woolworth stores, and my father, who was more a persuader than an intimidator, had made it a point of honor that I join him on the picket line, civil rights being nothing less than the religion of our household. By this time, age twelve or so, I was sick of it. I'd had enough of watching my parents heading off to still another meeting or march; I'd heard too many tedious discussions on everything from the philosophy of passive resistance to the symbolism of going to jail. Added to this, my own experience of picket lines and peace marches had impressed upon me what so many people who've partaken of these activities know: that in themselves they can be crushingly boring—around and around and around holding a sign, watching one's own feet fall, feeling the minutes like hours. All that Saturday morning I hid from my father and tried to convince myself of what I longed for—that he would get so busy that if he didn't forget the march he would at least forget me.

He forgot nothing. I did my time on the picket line, but not without building up enough resentment to start a fight on the way home. What was so important about integration? We had never even wanted to eat at Woolworth's. I told him the truth, that he never took us to *any* restaurants anyway, claiming always that they charged too much money for bad food. But he said calmly that he was proud of me for marching and that he knew *I* knew food wasn't the point.

My father—forty years a truck driver, with the urges of an intellectual—went on to use my little rebellion as the occasion for a discourse, in this case on the concept of integration. Integration had little to do with merely rubbing shoulders with white people, eating bad food beside them. It was about the right to go absolutely anywhere white people could go being the test of freedom and equality. To be anywhere they could be and do anything they could do was the point. Like it or not, white people defined the horizon of freedom in America, and if you couldn't touch their shoulder you weren't free. For him integration was the *evidence* of freedom and equality.

My father was a product of America's margins, as were all the blacks in the early civil rights movement, leaders and foot soldiers alike. For them integration was a way of moving from the margins into the mainstream. Today there is considerable ambivalence about integration, but in that day it was nothing less than democracy itself. Integration is also certainly about racial harmony, but it is more fundamentally about the ultimate extension of democracy—beyond the racial entitlements that contradict it. The idea of racial integration is quite simply the most democratic principle America has evolved, since all other such principles depend on its reality and are diminished by its absence.

White Guilt and Black Anger

But the civil rights movement did not account for one thing: the tremendous release of black anger that would follow its victories. The 1964 Civil Rights Act and the 1965 Voting Rights Act were, on one level, admissions of guilt by American society that it had practiced white entitlement at the expense of all others. When the oppressors admit their crimes, the oppressed can give full vent to their long repressed rage because now there is a moral consensus between oppressor and oppressed that a wrong was done. This consensus gave blacks the license to release a rage that was three centuries deep, a rage that is still today everywhere visible, a rage that—in the wake of the Rodney King verdict, a verdict a vast majority of all Americans thought unfair—fueled the worst rioting in recent American history.

By the mid-Sixties, the democratic goal of integration was no longer enough to appease black anger. Suddenly for blacks there was a sense that far more was owed, that a huge bill was due. And for many whites there was also the feeling that some kind of repayment was truly in order. This was the moral logic that followed inevitably from the new consensus. But it led to an even simpler logic: if blacks had been oppressed collectively, that oppression would now be redressed by entitling them collectively. So here we were again, in the name of a thousand good intentions, falling away from the hard challenge of a democracy of individuals and embracing the principle of collective entitlement that had so corrupted the American ideal in the first place. Now this old sin would be applied in the name of uplift. And this made an easy sort of sense. If it was good enough for whites for three hundred years, why not let blacks have a little of it to get ahead? In the context of the Sixties— black outrage and white guilt—a principle we had just decided was evil for whites was redefined as a social good for blacks. And once the formula was in place for blacks, it could be applied to other groups with similar grievances. By the 1970s more than 60 percent of the American population—not only blacks but Hispanics, women, Asians—would come under the collective entitlement of affirmative action.

Integration: The Only Goal

Serious talk of integration ended when "black power" began to flourish and *equal rights* was supplanted by *affirmative action* as the rallying cry of the movement. Aggrievement—the notion that blacks deserved special compensatory treatment—replaced assimilation at the top of the activists' agenda. Integration withered as a goal. . . .

A new model is needed, one that returns to the original movement goals of integration and equal rights while addressing the deterioration that has taken place in black family structure and community institutions over the past twenty years. Integration— that is, *assimilation* into the middle-class economy—can be the only possible goal.

Joe Klein, *New York*, May 29, 1989.

In the early days of the civil rights movement, the concept of solidarity was essentially a moral one. That is, all people who believed in human freedom, fairness, and equality were asked to form a solid front against white entitlement. But after the collaboration of black rage and white guilt made collective entitlement a social remedy, the nature of solidarity changed. It was no longer the rallying of diverse peoples to breach an oppressive group entitlement. It was the very opposite: a rallying of people within a grievance group to pursue their own group entitlement. As early as the mid-Sixties, whites were made unwelcome in the civil rights movement, just as, by the mid-Seventies, men were no longer welcome in the women's movement. Eventually, collective entitlement *always* requires separatism. And the irony is obvious: those who once had been the victims of separatism, who had sacrificed so dearly to overcome their being at the margins, would later create an ethos of their own separatism. After the Sixties, solidarity became essentially a separatist concept, an exclusionary principle. One no longer heard words like "integration" or "harmony"; one heard about "anger" and "power." Integration is anathema to grievance groups for precisely the same reason it was anathema to racist whites in the civil rights era: because it threatens their collective entitlement by insisting that no group be entitled over another. Power is where it's at today—power to set up the organization, attract the following, run the fiefdom.

But it must also be said that this could not have come to pass without the cooperation of the society at large and its institutions. Why did the government, the public and private institutions, the corporations and foundations, end up supporting principles that had the effect of turning causes into sovereign fiefdoms? I think the answer is that those in charge of America's institutions saw the institutionalization and bureaucratization of the protest movements as ultimately desirable, at least in the short term, and the funding of group entitlements as ultimately a less costly way to redress grievances. The leaders of the newly sovereign fiefdoms were backing off from earlier demands that America live up to its ideals. Gone was the moral indictment. Gone was the call for difficult, soulful transformation. The language of entitlements is essentially the old, comforting language of power politics, and in the halls of power it went down easily enough.

Cheaper than Real Change

With regard to civil rights, the moral voice of Dr. King gave way to the demands and cajolings of poverty-program moguls, class-action lawyers, and community organizers. The compromise that satisfied both political parties was to shift the focus from democracy, integration, and developmental uplift to collective entitlements. This satisfied the institutions because entitlements were cheaper in every way than real change. Better to set up black-studies and women's-studies departments than to have wrenching debates within existing departments. Better to fund these new institutions clamoring for money because who knows what kind of fuss they'll make if we turn down their proposals. Better to pass laws permitting Hispanic students to get preferred treatment in college admission—it costs less than improving kindergartens in East Los Angeles.

And this way to uplift satisfied the grievance-group "experts" because it laid the ground for their sovereignty and permanency: You negotiated with *us*. You funded *us*. You shared power, at least a bit of it, with *us*.

This negotiation was carried out in a kind of quasi-secrecy. Quotas, set-asides, and other entitlements were not debated in Congress or on the campaign trail. They were implemented by executive orders and Equal Employment Opportunity Commission guidelines without much public scrutiny. Also the courts played a quiet but persistent role in supporting these orders and guidelines and in further spelling out their application. Universities, corporations, and foundations implemented their own grievance entitlements, the workings of which are often kept from the public.

Now, it should surprise no one that all this entitlement has most helped those who least need it—white middle-class women and the black middle class. Poor blacks do not guide the black grievance groups. Working-class women do not set NOW's [National Organization for Women] agenda. Poor Hispanics do not clamor for bilingualism. Perhaps there is nothing wrong with middle-class people being helped, but their demands for entitlements are most often in the name of those less well off than themselves. The negotiations that settled on entitlements as the primary form of redress after the Sixties have generated a legalistic grievance industry that argues the interstices of entitlements and does very little to help those truly in need.

Integration Eliminates Barriers

In a liberal democracy, collective entitlements based upon race, gender, ethnicity, or some other group grievance are always undemocratic expedients. Integration, on the other hand, is the most difficult and inexpedient expansion of the democratic ideal; for in opting for integration, a citizen denies his or her impulse to use our most arbitrary characteristics—race, ethnicity, gender, sexual preference—as the basis for identity, as a key to status, or for claims to entitlement. Integration is twentieth-century America's elaboration of democracy. It eliminates such things as race and gender as oppressive barriers to freedom, and democrats of an earlier epoch eliminated religion and property. Our mistake has been to think of integration only as a utopian vision of perfect racial harmony. I think it is better to see integration as the inclusion of all citizens into the same sphere of rights, the same range of opportunities and possibilities that our Founding Fathers themselves enjoyed. Integration is not social engineering or group entitlements; it is a fundamental *absence* of arbitrary barriers to freedom.

If we can understand integration as an absence of barriers that has the effect of integrating all citizens into the same sphere of rights, then it can serve as a principle of democratic conduct. Anything that pushes anybody out of this sphere is undemocratic and must be checked, no matter the good intentions that seem to justify it. Understood in this light, collective entitlements are as undemocratic as racial and gender discrimination, and a group grievance is no more a justification for entitlement than the notion of white supremacy was at an earlier time. We are wrong to think of democracy as a gift of freedom; it is really a kind of discipline that avails freedom. Sometimes its enemy is racism and sexism; other times the enemy is our expedient attempts to correct these ills.

I think it is time for those who seek identity and power through grievance groups to fashion identities apart from grievance, to grant themselves the widest range of freedom, and to assume responsibility for that freedom. Victimhood lasts only as long as it is accepted, and to exploit it for an empty sovereignty is to accept it. The New Sovereignty is ultimately about vanity. It is the narcissism of victims, and it brings only a negligible power at the exorbitant price of continued victimhood. And all the while integration remains the real work.

"Federal and state governmental units, including the [Supreme] Court . . . [can] undertake the battles for civil liberties that remain to be won."

Government Should Strive to Protect Civil Liberties

Thurgood Marshall

Thurgood Marshall (1908-1993) served as an associate justice of the U.S. Supreme Court from 1967 to 1992. In the following viewpoint, Marshall argues that the Supreme Court has been the government leader for the advancement of minorities' civil rights. However, Marshall contends, recent Court decisions in areas such as abortion and unjustified searches have put at risk the civil rights of not just minorities, but all Americans. Marshall asserts that all branches of government can work to regain lost ground in civil rights progress and win further civil liberties.

As you read, consider the following questions:

1. According to Marshall, how have minorities' civil rights been scaled back?
2. In Marshall's opinion, why should minorities avoid complacency over civil rights victories?
3. How can Congress instantly regain civil liberties limited by the Supreme Court?

Thurgood Marshall, "The Supreme Court and Civil Rights: Has the Tide Turned?" reprinted, with permission, from *USA Today*, March 1990. Copyright © 1990 by The Society for the Advancement of Education.

For many years, no institution of American government has been as close a friend to civil rights as the United States Supreme Court. Make no mistake, I do not mean for a moment to denigrate the considerable contributions to the enhancement of civil rights by presidents, the Congress, other Federal courts, and the legislatures and judiciaries of many states.

A Halt to Civil Rights Progress

However, we must recognize that the Court's approach to civil rights cases has changed markedly. Its recent opinions vividly illustrate this changed judicial attitude. In *Richmond v. Croson*, the Court took a broad swipe at affirmative action, making it extraordinarily hard for any state or city to fashion a race-conscious remedial program that will survive its constitutional scrutiny. Indeed, the Court went so far as to express its doubts that the effects of past racial discrimination still are felt in the city of Richmond, Va., and in society as a whole.

Further, in a series of cases interpreting Federal civil rights statutes—*Price Waterhouse v. Hopkins; Martin v. Wilks; Lorance v. AT&T Technologies, Inc.; Will v. Michigan Department of State Police;* and *Jett v. Dallas Independent School District*—the Court imposed new and stringent procedural requirements that make it more and more difficult for the civil rights plaintiff to gain vindication.

The most striking feature of these opinions was the expansiveness of their holdings, often addressing broad issues, wholly unnecessary to the decisions. To strike down the set-aside plan in *Richmond*, for example, there was no need to decide anything other than that the plan was too imprecisely tailored. Instead, the Court chose to deliver a discourse on the narrow limits within which the states and localities may engage in affirmative action and on the special infirmities of plans passed by cities with minority leaders.

The Court was even more aggressive in revisiting settled statutory issues under Section 1981 and Title VII. In *Patterson v. McLean Credit Union*, it took the extraordinary step of calling for rebriefing on a question that no party had raised—whether the Court, in the 1976 case of *Runyon v. McCrary*, wrongly had held Section 1981 to apply to private acts of racial discrimination. In *Ward's Cove v. Antonio*, the Court implicitly overruled *Griggs v. Duke Power Co.*, another established precedent which had required employers to bear the burden of justifying employment practices with a disparate impact on groups protected by Title VII. Henceforth, the burden will be on the employees to prove that these practices are justified.

Stare decisis [the doctrine that principles of law established by judicial decision will be accepted as authoritative in cases similar to those from which such principles were derived] has special force on questions of statutory interpretation, and Congress had expressed no dissatisfaction with either the *Runyon* or *Griggs* decisions. Thus, it is difficult to characterize these decisions as a product of anything other than a retrenching of the civil rights agenda. In the past 35 years, we truly have come full circle.

Future of the Civil Rights Struggle

We must do more than dwell on past battles, however. The important question now is where the civil rights struggle should go from here.

One answer, I suppose, is nowhere at all—to stay put. With the school desegregation and voting rights cases and the passage of Federal anti-discrimination statutes, the argument goes, the principal civil rights battles already have been won, the structural protections necessary to assure racial equality over the long run are in place, and we can trust the Supreme Court to ensure that they remain so.

This argument is unpersuasive for several reasons. Affirmative action, no less than the active effort to alleviate concrete economic hardship, hastens relief efforts while the victims are still around to be helped. To those who claim that present statutes already afford enough relief to victims of ongoing discrimination, I say, look to the case of Brenda Patterson. She alleged that she had been victimized by a pattern of systematic racial harassment at work, but was told by the Supreme Court that, even accepting her allegations as true, Federal statutory relief was unavailable.

We must avoid complacency for another reason. The Court's decisions during the 1988-89 term put at risk not only the civil rights of minorities, but of all citizens. History teaches that, when the Supreme Court has been willing to shortchange the equality rights of minority groups, other basic personal civil liberties like the rights to free speech and personal security against unreasonable searches and seizures also are threatened.

We forget at our peril that, less than a generation after the Supreme Court held separate to be equal in *Plessy v. Ferguson*, it held in the *Schenck* and *Debs* decisions that the First Amendment allowed the U.S. to convict under the Espionage Act persons who distributed anti-war pamphlets and delivered anti-war speeches. It was less than a decade after the Supreme Court upheld the internment of Japanese citizens that, in *Dennis v. United States*, it affirmed the conviction of Communist Party agitators under the Smith Act. On the other side of the ledger, it is no coincidence that, during the three decades beginning with *Brown v. Board of Education*, the Court was taking its most expansive view not only of the equal protection clause, but also of the liberties safeguarded by the Bill of Rights.

Equal Rights and Civil Liberties

That the fates of equal rights and liberty rights are intertwined inexorably was never more apparent than in the opinions handed down during the 1988-89 term. The right to be free from searches which are not justified by probable cause was dealt yet another heavy blow in two drug testing cases, *National Treasury Employees Union v. Von Raab* and *Skinner v. Railway Labor Executives' Association*. The scope of the right to reproductive liberty was called into considerable question by the *Webster* decision. Although the right to free expression was preserved in several celebrated cases, it lost ground, too, most particularly in *Ward v. Rock Against Racism*, which greatly broadened the government's power to impose "time, place and manner" restrictions on speech.

Looming on the horizon are attacks on the right to be free from the state establishment of religion. In a separate opinion in the creche-and-menorah case, *Allegheny Co. v. American Civil Liberties Union*, four members of the Court served notice that they are ready to replace today's establishment clause inquiry with a test that those who seek to break down the wall between church and state will find far easier to satisfy. We dare not forget that these, too, are civil rights, and that they apparently are in grave danger.

Guardians of Rights and Freedom

To a great extent, the intellectual framework and the professional ethos of the entire current population of American lawyers have been infused with the romance of rights. In legal education, an intense preoccupation with the Bill of Rights and the courts tends to obscure the important roles that federalism, legislation, and the separation of powers still can and must play in safeguarding rights and freedom.

Mary Ann Glendon, *Rights Talk*, 1991.

The response to the Court's decisions is not inaction. The Supreme Court remains the institution charged with protecting constitutionally guaranteed rights and liberties. Those seeking to vindicate civil or equality rights must continue to press the Court for the enforcement of constitutional and statutory mandates. Moreover, recent decisions suggest alternate methods to further the goals of equality in contexts other than judicial forums.

For example, state legislatures can act to strengthen the hands of those seeking judicial redress. A lesson of the *Richmond* case is that detailed legislative fact-finding is critical. Civil rights lawyers will stand a far better chance in Federal constitutional litigation over affirmative action if they are armed with a state legislature's documented findings of past discrimination in a particular area. Thus, persons interested in the cause of racial equality can ensure that legislators have access to empirical studies and historical facts that will form the bedrock of acceptable factual findings.

Congress Is the Key

Most importantly, there is Congress. With the mere passage of corrective legislation, Congress can regain in an instant the ground which was lost in the realm of statutory civil rights. By prevailing upon Congress to do so, we can send a message to the Court—that the hypertechnical language games played by the Court in its interpretations of civil rights enactments are simply not accurate ways to read Congress' broad intent in the civil rights area.

Let me emphasize that, while we need not and should not give up on the Supreme Court and while Federal litigation on civil rights issues still can succeed, in the 1990's, we must broaden our perspective and target other governmental bodies as well as the traditional protector of our liberties. Paraphrasing Pres. Kennedy, those who wish to assure the continued protection of important civil rights should "ask not what the Supreme Court alone can do for civil rights; ask what you can do to help the cause of civil rights." Today, the answer to that question lies in bringing pressure to bear on all branches of Federal and state governmental units, including the Court, and urging them to undertake the battles for civil liberties that remain to be won. With that goal as our guide, we can go forward together to advance civil rights and liberty rights with the fervor we have shown in the past.

"The best mechanism for creating new rights is for people to become mobilized and amend the Constitution."

People Should Act to Protect Civil Liberties

Akhil Reed Amar, interviewed by Vicki Quade

In the following viewpoint, Akhil Reed Amar argues that Americans have the power to create new rights for themselves. Amar contends that people can win new rights, such as equal rights for women, by amending the Constitution through national referendums. Citizens should take control of the Constitution and their lives by actively pursuing more constitutional rights, rather than relying on judges or legislatures, the author concludes. Amar is a law professor at Yale University in New Haven, Connecticut. Quade is the editor of *Human Rights* magazine.

As you read, consider the following questions:

1. In Amar's opinion, how would women have achieved more rights much sooner had abortion not been legalized?
2. How have lawyers crusaded for more civil rights, according to the author?
3. Why does Amar believe the proposed Equal Rights Amendment failed?

From "Who Governs America?" an interview with Akhil Reed Amar by Vicki Quade, *Human Rights*, Summer 1991, © 1991 American Bar Association. Reprinted with permission.

Quade: Do you think we need any additional amendments to the Constitution?

Amar: Yeah, sure. Some things are implicit, but haven't been well developed.

For example, the Constitution contains the idea that if we really are going to have a robust democracy, we need an educated citizenry.

From the First Amendment, you could deduce some requirement to a right to education. You could even get it from the Thirteenth Amendment, which gets rid of slavery. What that amendment is really about is not just getting rid of slavery, but promoting freedom.

And in a democracy what does freedom mean? I'm not sure you can be a true, free citizen in America and a voter under the Fifteenth Amendment if you don't have a minimal, basic education.

Thaddeus Stevens was a radical Republican who promoted the Thirteenth Amendment, but thought it was about 40 acres and a mule for all blacks, and public education for the former slaves.

That's how you would eliminate the vestiges of slavery, by giving them property, sort of a stake in society, and education. That's what made people citizens and made them free.

But the courts haven't followed up on that. And so maybe a new amendment is needed to guarantee to every citizen those minimal entitlements of education. . . .

Judicial Creation of Rights

You may wonder why I am so insistent that we should look at the constitutional text rather than just evolve new rights to fit society.

Judicial creation of new rights based on how judges read the social fabric is dangerous and democratically disempowering.

Let me be very concrete. *Roe v. Wade* came down in 1973. It created a right to abortion based on privacy, not on due process. Somewhat hard to derive from the Constitution.

Had *Roe* not been decided the way it was, you would have had the women's rights movement energized in the 1970s the way it has been in the late '80s and early '90s after *Webster.*

You would have had women mobilized 15 years earlier. They let the Supreme Court do it for them; they didn't do it themselves. They didn't get involved in politics.

Suppose *Roe* had come down the other way. Women would have been much more involved in trying to win the debate in legislatures.

There would have been more women involved in politics, more women running for office in the 1970s, more women elected for office.

I believe the ERA [Equal Rights Amendment] would have passed because more women would have been mobilized about this issue.

But instead, by coming down the way it did, *Roe* mobilized the religious right, which joined the Reagan coalition.

Roe, in large part, is responsible for the election of Ronald Reagan, if not George Bush.

So there's an example about how having judges do it for you rather than doing it yourself the democratic way—the "it" being creating new rights—can really backfire.

The people should be the ones creating the new rights as they recognize that society has changed.

What judges should do is look back and reflect on what "We the people" really decided when we abolished slavery in 1866. Or adopted the Fourteenth Amendment and provided for equal protection in the Reconstruction. Or when "We the people" provided for equal political participation for women in the Nineteenth Amendment.

It's a lot more democratic and more empowering of the people.

Masters of the Constitution

Quade: You've argued that the people are the masters and not the servants of the Constitution. Are you saying that the Constitution exists as a document out of which rights can be interpreted by the people, not the courts?

Amar: The best mechanism for creating new rights is for people to become mobilized and amend the Constitution, rather than relying on judges to update the Constitution for them.

They should be the ones creating the new rights.

Quade: How would the people amend the Constitution?

Amar: By referendum. One of the provisions I've tried to resurrect involves amending the Constitution. You can look at the Ninth and Tenth amendments and find that.

Let's take the Ninth Amendment, which talks about rights retained by the people. You will hear a lot of discussion by advocates of privacy that the Ninth Amendment is about privacy.

This is historically false. When they say "the people," they don't say the rights of the person. They're talking about the same "We the people" who ordained and established the Constitution.

And the most important Ninth Amendment right is the right of "We the people" to alter or abolish our Constitution, to amend it at will if we're not satisfied with the existing rules.

What that means is the people could amend the Constitution not by going through the Congress and legislatures, but something similar to a national referendum, on say ERA.

215

What was done 200 years ago by the people ratifying the Constitution could be done today, if people don't like provisions that are now in it.

© Sidney Harris. Reprinted with permission.

Our Constitution is much more democratic, much more majoritarian in its essence. All of these rights are derivable from majorities of the people than most folks think.

Risks in Democracy

Quade: Don't you run the risk of having the Constitution change too much?

Amar: It depends on what people want. You run risks in a democracy, but democracy is always a leap of faith that the people will govern wisely.

Quade: In the 1980s, you would have had the far right running the country by amending the Constitution.

Amar: If the conservatives are a majority, and if they are dissatisfied with the existing constitutional rules, then they're entitled to amend the Constitution, just as liberals are entitled.

Quade: Aren't you placing another layer of politics on our country? Our country seems so politicized already.

Amar: There's no escape from politics in a democracy. What's the alternative? Having judges make things up?

I don't want William Rehnquist to make things up, okay?

The justices on the Supreme Court are actually far more conservative than the country as a whole. . . .

Quade: What you want is for people to take control of the Constitution and control of their lives?

Amar: It's their Constitution. Yeah.

Quade: Do we care enough about the Constitution?

Amar: We don't, in part because we've been told over and over that it's the business for judges and lawyers, and not for ordinary Americans.

Quade: So some people are frightened away.

Amar: And muscles atrophy if you don't flex them.

The only way for the people to become responsible is to give them responsibility.

They may make a few mistakes, then they learn from their mistakes, you know.

It's a little bit like a teenager. At some point, you've got to give the teenager some responsibility. He or she is going to make a few mistakes but, hopefully, he or she will learn from those mistakes, will mature, will become an adult.

Quade: The American public is really like a kid?

Amar: At this point, yeah. In part because they've been told over and over that they should just leave this to lawyers and judges.

Lawyers: Servants of the People

Quade: You became a lawyer even though you have a basic distrust for what lawyers and judges have done to this country.

Amar: Well, lawyers and judges have also been among the great crusaders and educators. Lawyers and judges are at the forefront of various progressive crusades to amend the Constitution.

Abraham Lincoln was a lawyer and he went around educating people about what Dred Scott really meant.

Lawyers like John Bingham, Thaddeus Stevens and William Sumner helped bring about Reconstruction, the emancipation of African-Americans and the adoption of the Fourteenth Amendment.

Lawyers—both men and women—were very prominent in the

217

Nineteenth Amendment crusade for women's rights.

I think lawyers serve their highest calling when they act as servants of the people, rather than masters. And so, too, with government officials.

Quade: How likely is that to happen?

Amar: Well, it's always a risk. Many of the greatest triumphs in America have come about with the encouragement of the people.

The Bill of Rights was supported by the people in the 1790s.

The idea of free speech was reaffirmed by the people in the election of 1800 when they voted for Thomas Jefferson and voted John Adams out of office because he supported the Alien Sedition Acts, which was very repressive towards foreigners and political dissenters.

During the Reconstruction, the people ratified the Fourteenth Amendment. And they ratified the Nineteenth Amendment.

I do think that if it were put to a vote of the people today, ERA would pass. And that would be a good thing.

The folks who voted against the ERA tended to be male legislators who had been elected many years ago when women weren't as politically active, and who were able to keep themselves in power by using the advantages of incumbency.

The ERA was ratified by more than half the states. Far more. If we had instead put it to a vote of the people of America, they would have done the right thing.

Periodical Bibliography

The following articles have been selected to supplement the diverse views presented in this chapter.

Aaron Brenner	"The Politics of Affirmative Action," *Against the Current*, May/June 1992.
Robert F. Drinan	"The United Nations' New Institute for Children's Rights," *America*, May 16, 1992.
Bruce Fein	"Children's Rights Ignores Reality," *Human Events*, October 31, 1992. Available from 422 First St. SE, Washington, DC 20003.
James C. Harrington	"Court Majority Cuts Back Our Rights," *Guardian*, February 26, 1992.
International Journal of Law and the Family	Special issue on children's rights, April 1992. Available from Oxford University Press, Pinkhill House, Southfield Rd., Eynsham, Oxford OX8 1JJ UK.
George A. Kendall	"Spurious Rights and the Growth of Tyranny," *The Wanderer*, January 14, 1993. Available from 201 Ohio St., St. Paul, MN 55107.
Catharine A. MacKinnon	"Reflections on Sex Equality Under Law," *The Yale Law Journal*, March 1991. Available from 127 Wall St., New Haven, CT 06520-7397.
Tony Marco	"Oppressed Minority, or Counterfeits?" *St. Croix Review*, February 1993. Available from PO Box 244, Stillwater, MN 55082.
Donna Minkowitz	"Outlawing Gays," *The Nation*, October 19, 1992.
Robert F. Nagel	"The Supreme Court's Bad Language," *The New York Times*, February 17, 1993.
National Forum	Special issue on individual rights, Winter 1992. Available from PO Box 16000, Louisiana State University, Baton Rouge, LA 70893.
E.L. Pattullo	"Straight Talk About Gays," *Commentary*, December 1992.
ArLynn Leiber Presser	"Thinking Positive: Do We Need More Rights?" *ABA Journal*, August 1991. Available from the American Bar Association, 750 N. Lake Shore Dr., Chicago, IL 60611.
Vicki Quade	"The Politics of Race," *Human Rights*, Summer 1992.
Paul Craig Roberts	"Takings by the Bureaucracy," *Vital Speeches of the Day*, October 1, 1992.

For Further Discussion

Chapter 1

1. The U.S. Supreme Court has declared that the right to privacy protects a pregnant woman's decision to have an abortion. Should that right protect from prosecution a pregnant woman who abuses alcohol or cocaine? Why or why not?

2. The names of most victims who report crimes are public record and available to the media. However, many rape victims do not want to be publicly identified. The viewpoint by Sarah Henderson Hutt, and the viewpoint by Paul Marcus and Tara L. McMahon, address this issue. Which viewpoint is more persuasive? Why?

3. In his viewpoint, Morton A. Kaplan refers to the philosophies of John Stuart Mill. What is Mill's primary philosophy, and how does Kaplan use it to convince readers of his point?

4. Why does Cindia Cameron believe that many workers are powerless to prevent invasions of privacy by their employers? Do you agree with Cameron that government regulations can protect employee privacy? Why or why not?

Chapter 2

1. Richard Behling argues that certain published material could facilitate illegal acts or endanger the public's safety. List some of the examples he gives. Do you agree with Behling that such material should be restricted? Why or why not? How harmful is such expression compared to libel or slander?

2. What type of obscenity standard does H. Robert Showers propose to limit hard-core pornography? Do you think such a standard is reasonable? Explain your answer. How would matters such as consent and personal choice affect this strategy?

3. Why does Gara LaMarche believe that it is not for government to decide which types of speech are more offensive than others? Are there circumstances in which freedom of expression must be limited for the good of society? If so, what are they?

Chapter 3

1. Rob Boston mentions Thomas Jefferson's metaphor of "a wall of separation between church and state." Is "wall of

separation" a proper metaphor for the First Amendment's religion clauses? Why or why not? What evidence does Boston present to show that the Constitution's framers intended complete separation?

2. Why does Edd Doerr oppose any government assistance to religion? Do you agree with Doerr that school-sponsored prayer amounts to coercion of students to participate? Why or why not? How does Doerr propose to resolve the school prayer issue?

3. Robert L. Cord argues that some of the constitutional amendments proposed by the original thirteen states had nothing to do with separation of church and state. According to these proposals, what did the states fear most from the federal government? Do you believe that such fears were justified? Why or why not?

Chapter 4

1. Civil rights acts have conferred citizenship upon ex-slaves and barred sex discrimination in the workplace. Why haven't these laws adequately protected the rights of blacks and women? How could their rights have been better protected, according to the authors in the chapter?

2. The Bill of Rights does not specifically mention the right to marry or the right to travel, yet all Americans consider these fundamental rights. Make a list of other rights not mentioned in the Bill of Rights that you believe are fundamental. Why do you think these rights were not included in the Constitution? Do you think the Constitution should be amended to include any of these rights? If so, which ones?

3. Children and homosexuals possess fewer legal rights than other groups. Why do you believe this is so? What obstacles prevent them from winning more rights?

4. Charles D. Gill and Laura M. Purdy differ on the issue of granting children more legal rights. Do you agree with Gill or Purdy? Explain your answer.

5. Marshall Kirk and Hunter Madsen cite several examples of job discrimination against gays. List some of their examples. Why do you think such discrimination is difficult to confirm? If you were the president of a small company, would you hire an openly gay or lesbian job applicant? Why or why not? If not, what reason would you give that person?

221

General Questions

1. Thurgood Marshall argues that recent court decisions have eroded the rights of minorities. How do these rulings affect the civil liberties of all people? Should people depend on the federal government, as Marshall suggests, to protect civil liberties? Why or why not?

2. Universities are a forum for all types of speech. Consider one university where the student body and administration have voted to punish speech that homosexuals and ethnic groups find offensive. What do the authors in the free expression chapter believe about such policies? Do you consider such policies democratic, or oppressive? Explain your reasoning.

3. How would Akhil Reed Amar use the principle of majority rule to change the U.S. Constitution? Do you believe Amar's proposal would strengthen or weaken the Constitution? Why or why not?

Organizations to Contact

The editors have compiled the following list of organizations that are concerned with the issues debated in this book. All have publications or information available for interested readers. For best results, allow as much time as possible for the organizations to respond. The descriptions below are derived from materials provided by the organizations. This list was compiled upon the date of publication. Names, addresses, and phone numbers of organizations are subject to change.

American Alliance for Rights and Responsibilities (AARR)
1725 K St. NW, Suite 1112
Washington, DC 20006
(202) 785-7844

AARR believes that democracy can work only if the defense of individual rights is matched by a commitment to individual and social responsibility. It is dedicated to restoring the balance between rights and responsibilities in American life. It publishes the bimonthly newsletter *Re: Rights and Responsibilities.*

American Civil Liberties Union (ACLU)
132 W. 43d St.
New York, NY 10036
(212) 944-9800

The ACLU, a national organization with many local chapters, champions human rights as guaranteed in the Declaration of Independence and the Constitution. To protect rights such as freedom of inquiry and expression, due process of law and fair trials, and equality before the law, the ACLU opposes repressive legislation and protests attacks on constitutional and human rights. It publishes a wealth of materials on civil liberties, including the report *Restoring Civil Liberties: A Blueprint for Action for the Clinton Administration,* the triannual newsletter *Civil Liberties,* and a set of handbooks on individual rights.

Americans for Religious Liberty (ARL)
PO Box 6656
Silver Spring, MD 20906
(301) 598-2447

ARL is an educational organization that works to preserve religious, intellectual, and personal freedom in a secular democracy. It advocates a strict separation of church and state. ARL publishes numerous pamphlets on church/state issues and the quarterly newsletter *Voice of Reason.*

Americans United for Separation of Church and State (AUSCS)
8120 Fenton St.
Silver Spring, MD 20910
(301) 589-3707

AUSCS's purpose is to protect the right of Americans to religious freedom. Its principal means of action are litigation, education, and advocacy. It opposes the passing of either federal or state laws that threaten the separation of church and state. Its many publications include brochures, pamphlets, and the monthly newsletter *Church and State.*

Center for Democratic Renewal (CDR)
PO Box 50469
Atlanta, GA 30302-0469
(404) 221-0025

CDR is a national clearinghouse for information about the white supremacist movement in general and the Ku Klux Klan in particular. It works to end hate violence and bigotry and has participated in many First Amendment debates about the rights of hate groups versus the rights of groups targeted by them. It offers programs of education, research, victim assistance, community organizing, leadership training, and public policy advocacy. Its publications include the bimonthly newsletter *The Monitor* and the manual *When Hate Groups Come to Town: A Handbook of Community Responses.*

Children's Legal Foundation (CLF)
2845 E. Camelback Rd., Suite 740
Phoenix, AZ 85016
(602) 381-1322

The foundation assists law enforcement agencies and legislatures to enact and enforce constitutional statutes, ordinances, and regulations controlling obscenity and pornography and other materials the foundation believes harm children. It works to educate the public about the harm done by pornography in literature, television, and movies. It publishes various brochures and the quarterly *CLF Reporter.*

Citizens' Commission on Civil Rights
2000 M St. NW, Suite 400
Washington, DC 20036
(202) 659-5565

The commission is a bipartisan group of former government officials who held positions in which they were responsible for ensuring equal opportunity. It monitors the federal government's civil rights policies and practices and seeks ways to accelerate progress in the area of civil rights. It publishes periodic reports, including *Civil Rights at the Crossroads.*

Eagle Forum
PO Box 618
Alton, IL 62002
(618) 462-5415

A political action group, Eagle Forum advocates traditional, biblical values. It opposes an equal rights amendment, gay rights legislation, and children's rights. It fights political forces it sees as antifamily, antireligion, antilife, or against traditional morality. It publishes the monthly *Phyllis Schlafly Report* and the Eagle Forum *Newsletter.*

The Heritage Foundation
214 Massachusetts Ave. NE
Washington, DC 20002
(202) 546-4400

The foundation is a conservative public policy organization dedicated to free-market principles, individual liberty, and limited government. It favors limiting freedom of the press when that freedom threatens national security. Its resident scholars publish position papers on a wide range of issues through publications such as the weekly *Backgrounder* and the quarterly *Policy Review.*

Lambda Legal Defense and Education Fund
666 Broadway
New York, NY 10012
(212) 995-8585

Through test-case litigation and public education, Lambda works to defend the rights of lesbians, gay men, and people infected with HIV. It publishes the quarterly *Lambda Update.*

National Alliance Against Racist and Political Repression
11 John St., Suite 702
New York, NY 10038
(212) 406-3330

This coalition of political, labor, church, civic, and student organizations is dedicated to protecting people's right to organize. It opposes government persecution of groups and individuals seeking social or political change, including illegal immigrants, prison inmates, draft resisters, and militant students. It supports legislative attempts to limit hate speech. The alliance produces audiovisual programs and publishes pamphlets and the quarterly newsletter *The Organizer.*

National Coalition Against Censorship (NCAC)
2 W. 64th St.
New York, NY 10023
(212) 724-1500

NCAC is an alliance of organizations committed to defending freedom of thought, inquiry, and expression by engaging in public education and advocacy on national and local levels. It publishes periodic reports and the monthly *Censorship News.*

National Coalition Against Pornography (N-CAP)
800 Compton Rd., Suite 9224
Cincinnati, OH 45231-9964
(513) 521-6227

N-CAP is an organization of business, religious, and civic leaders who work to eliminate pornography. Because it believes a link exists between pornography and violence, N-CAP encourages citizens to support the enforcement of obscenity laws and to close down pornography outlets in their neighborhoods. Publications include the books *Final Report of the Attorney General's Commission on Pornography*, *The Mind Polluters*, and *Pornography: A Human Tragedy*.

National Committee for Sexual Civil Liberties
98 Olden Ln.
Princeton, NJ 08540
(609) 924-1950

The committee, comprised of lawyers and scholars experienced in civil liberties issues, works to increase acceptance of private sexual conduct between consenting adults. It calls for the repeal of all laws punishing fornication, sodomy, adultery, and pornography involving adults. It publishes the quarterly *Sexual Law Reporter.*

National Conference of Catholic Bishops (NCCB)
3211 Fourth St. NE
Washington, DC 20017-1194
(202) 541-3000

The NCCB is the national governing body of the Roman Catholic church in the United States. It opposes abortion and civil rights specifically proposed for gays and lesbians. It publishes *Respect Life* annually and the *NCCB/USCC Report* eleven times a year.

National Council on Religion and Public Education (NCRPE)
E262 Lagomarcino Hall
Iowa State University
Ames, IA 50011
(515) 294-7003

The council believes religion should be studied in public schools in ways that do not promote the values or beliefs of one religion over another, but that expose students to such beliefs. It publishes the triannual magazine *Religion and Public Education* and resource materials for teachers and administrators.

National Gay and Lesbian Task Force (NGLTF)
1734 14th St. NW
Washington, DC 20009-4309
(202) 332-6483

NGLTF is a civil rights advocacy group that lobbies Congress and the White House on a wide range of civil rights issues. It works to eliminate prejudice, discrimination, and violence against gay men and lesbians. Its numerous publications include the fact sheet *Gay and Lesbian Rights Protections in the U.S.* and the quarterly newsletter *Task Force Report.*

National Lawyers Guild (NLG)
55 Sixth Ave.
New York, NY 10013
(212) 966-5000

NLG is an organization of lawyers, legal workers, and law students who seek economic justice, social equality, and the right to political dissent. It has separate committees involved with civil liberties, affirmative action, and antidiscrimination; a subcommittee on gay rights; and antirepression and antisexism task forces. NLG publishes the monthly *Bulletin* newsletter and the national bimonthly newspaper *Guild Notes.*

National Organization for Women (NOW)
1000 16th St. NW, Suite 700
Washington, DC 20004
(202) 331-0066

NOW, the largest women's rights group in the United States, supports women's right to privacy, which includes the right to abortion. It also supports passage of an equal rights amendment. Its magazine, *NOW Times*, is published triannually.

National Urban League
500 E. 62d St.
New York, NY 10021
(212) 310-9000

The Urban League is a large organization of community service volunteers. It seeks to uphold the civil liberties of all citizens by eliminating racism in government, education, employment, and other institutions. Its publications include the quarterly *Urban League News* and the semiannual *Urban League Review.*

Oregon Citizens Alliance (OCA)
PO Box 407
Wilsonville, OR 97070
(503) 682-0653

OCA is a political organization that opposes minority-status "special rights" for gay men and lesbians because it believes same-sex behavior is wrong and injurious to public health. OCA distributes brochures and information packets on this subject.

People for the American Way (PAW)
2000 M St. NW, Suite 400
Washington, DC 20036
(202) 467-4999

PAW works to increase tolerance and respect for America's diverse cultures, religions, and values. It distributes educational materials, leaflets, and brochures. It also publishes the quarterly *Press Clips*, a collection of newspaper articles concerning censorship.

Rockford Institute Center on Religion and Society
934 N. Main St.
Rockford, IL 61103
(815) 964-5811

The center is a research and educational organization that advocates a more public role for religion and religious values in American life. It publishes the quarterly *This World: A Journal of Religion and Public Life* and the monthly *Religion and Society Report.*

United States Commission on Civil Rights
1121 Vermont Ave. NW
Washington, DC 20425
(202) 376-8177

The commission is a fact-finding body that evaluates the effectiveness of equal opportunity programs and the impact of federal laws on civil rights. It makes recommendations based on its findings to the president and Congress. The commission also serves as a national clearinghouse for civil rights information. A catalog of its publications is available from the commission's publications management division.

Bibliography of Books

Ellen Alderman and Caroline Kennedy — *In Our Defense: The Bill of Rights in Action.* New York: William Morrow, 1990.

Robert S. Alley, ed. — *The Supreme Court on Church and State.* New York: Oxford University Press, 1988.

Raymond Arsenault — *Crucible of Liberty: Two Hundred Years of the Bill of Rights.* New York: Free Press, 1991.

David Barton — *The Myth of Separation: What Is the Correct Relationship Between Church and State?* Aledo, TX: Wallbuilder Press, 1989.

Paul Berman, ed. — *Debating P.C.: The Controversy over Political Correctness on College Campuses.* New York: Dell, 1992.

Jon D. Bible and Darien A. McWhirter — *Privacy in the Workplace: A Guide for Human Resource Managers.* New York: Quorum Books, 1990.

Lee C. Bollinger — *Images of a Free Press.* Chicago: University of Chicago Press, 1992.

Alida Brill — *Nobody's Business: Paradoxes of Privacy.* Reading, MA: Addison-Wesley, 1990.

James MacGregor Burns and Stewart Burns — *A People's Charter: The Pursuit of Rights in America.* New York: Alfred A. Knopf, 1991.

Steve Clark, ed. — *Malcolm X Talks to Young People: Speeches in the U.S., Britain, and Africa.* New York: Pathfinder, 1991.

Susan D. Clayton and Faye J. Crosby — *Justice, Gender, and Affirmative Action.* Ann Arbor: University of Michigan Press, 1992.

Derek Davis — *Original Intent: Chief Justice Rehnquist and the Course of American Church/State Relations.* Buffalo: Prometheus Books, 1991.

Alan M. Dershowitz — *Contrary to Popular Opinion.* New York: Pharos Books, 1992.

Donald L. Drakeman — *Church-State Constitutional Issues: Making Sense of the Establishment Clause.* Westport, CT: Greenwood Press, 1991.

Gertrude Ezorsky — *Racism and Justice: The Case for Affirmative Action.* Ithaca, NY: Cornell University Press, 1991.

Jerry Falwell — *The New American Family.* Waco, TX: Word Publishing, 1992.

Lois Forer — *Unequal Protection: Women, Children, and the Elderly in Court.* New York: W.W. Norton & Co., 1991.

Leon Friedman, ed.   *The Civil Rights Reader: Basic Documents of the Civil Rights Movement*. New York: Walker and Co., 1968.

Ira Glasser   *Visions of Liberty: The Bill of Rights for All Americans*. New York: Arcade, 1993.

Mary Ann Glendon   *Rights Talk: The Impoverishment of Political Discourse*. New York: Free Press, 1991.

Robert A. Goldwin   *Why Blacks, Women, and Jews Are Not Mentioned in the Constitution, and Other Unorthodox Views*. Washington, DC: AEI Press, 1990.

Mark A. Graber   *Transforming Free Speech: The Ambiguous Legacy of Civil Libertarianism*. Berkeley: University of California Press, 1991.

Claudia A. Haskel   *A Time for Choices*. Denver: First Amendment
and Jean H. Otto   Congress, 1991.

Joseph M. Hawes   *The Children's Rights Movement in the United States: A History of Advocacy and Protection*. Boston: Twayne Publishers, 1991.

Evan Hendricks   *Your Right to Privacy: A Basic Guide to Legal Rights in an Information Society*. Carbondale: Southern Illinois University Press, 1990.

Nat Hentoff   *Free Speech for Me—But Not for Thee: How the American Left and Right Relentlessly Censor Each Other*. New York: HarperCollins, 1992.

Joan Hoff   *Law, Gender, and Injustice: A Legal History of U.S. Women*. New York: New York University Press, 1991.

Thomas A. Hopkins,   *Rights for Americans: The Speeches of Robert F.
ed.   Kennedy*. Indianapolis: Howard W. Sams & Co., 1964.

James Davison   *Articles of Faith, Articles of Peace*. Washington,
Hunter and Os   DC: Brookings Institution, 1990.
Guiness, eds.

Nan D. Hunter,   *The Rights of Lesbians and Gay Men*. 3d ed. Med-
Sherryl E. Michaelson,   ford, NY: ACLU Publications, 1992.
and Thomas B.
Stoddard

Gregg Ivers   *Redefining the First Freedom: The Supreme Court and the Consolidation of State, 1980-1990*. New Brunswick, NJ: Transaction Publishers, 1993.

Donald W. Jackson   *Even the Children of Strangers: Equality Under the U.S. Constitution*. Lawrence: University Press of Kansas, 1992.

Wendy Kaminer   *A Fearful Freedom: Women's Flight from Equality*. Reading, MA: Addison-Wesley, 1990.

Russell Kirk   *The Conservative Constitution*. Washington, DC: Regnery Gateway, 1990.

Andrew Kull	*The Color-Blind Constitution.* Cambridge, MA: Harvard University Press, 1992.
Theodore R. Kupferman, ed.	*Censorship, Secrecy, Access, and Obscenity.* Westport, CT: Meckler, 1990.
Michael J. Lacey and Knud Haakonssen, eds.	*A Culture of Rights: The Bill of Rights in Philosophy, Politics, and Law—1791 and 1991.* Cambridge, MA: Cambridge University Press, 1991.
David F. Linowes	*Privacy in America.* Champaign: University of Illinois Press, 1989.
Arthur C. Littleton and Mary W. Burger, eds.	*Black Viewpoints.* New York: New American Library, 1971.
Donald E. Lively	*The Constitution and Race.* New York: Praeger, 1992.
Robert Emmet Long, ed.	*Censorship.* New York: H.W. Wilson Co., 1990.
Frederick R. Lynch	*Invisible Victims: White Males and the Crisis of Affirmative Action.* New York: Praeger, 1991.
Darien A. McWhirter and Jon D. Bible	*Privacy as a Constitutional Right: Sex, Drugs, and the Right to Life.* New York: Quorum Books, 1992.
Eric Marcus	*Making History: The Struggle for Gay and Lesbian Equal Rights, 1945-1990: An Oral History.* New York: HarperCollins, 1992.
Dave Marsh	*Fifty Ways to Fight Censorship and Important Facts to Know About the Censors.* New York: Thunder's Mouth Press, 1991.
Martin E. Marty	*Religion and Republic.* Boston: Beacon Press, 1987.
Michael J. Meyer and William A. Parent	*The Constitution of Rights: Human Dignity and American Values.* Ithaca, NY: Cornell University Press, 1992.
Susan Gluck Mezey	*In Pursuit of Equality: Woman, Public Policy, and the Federal Courts.* New York: St. Martin's Press, 1992.
Richard D. Mohr	*Gays/Justice: A Study of Ethics, Society, and Law.* New York: Columbia University Press, 1988.
Art Must Jr., ed.	*Why We Still Need Public Schools: Church/State Relations, and Visions of Democracy.* Buffalo: Prometheus Books, 1992.
Ruthann Robson	*Lesbian (Out)Law: Survival Under the Rule of Law.* Ithaca, NY: Firebrand Books, 1992.
Vincent J. Samar	*The Right to Privacy: Gays, Lesbians, and the Constitution.* Philadelphia: Temple University Press, 1991.
David Savage	*Turning Right: The Making of the Rehnquist Supreme Court.* New York: John Wiley & Sons, 1992.

Garrett Ward Sheldon, ed.	*Religion and Politics: Major Thinkers on the Relation of Church and State.* New York: Peter Lang, 1990.
Rodney A. Smolla	*Free Speech in an Open Society.* New York: Alfred A. Knopf, 1992.
Bron Raymond Taylor	*Affirmative Action at Work: Law, Politics, and Ethics.* Pittsburgh: University of Pittsburgh Press, 1991.
Claire Sherman Thomas	*Sex Discrimination in a Nutshell.* 2d ed. St. Paul, MN: West Publishing, 1991.
Philip E. Veerman	*The Rights of the Child and the Changing Image of Childhood.* Boston: Martinus Nijhoff Publishers, 1992.
James Melvin Washington, ed.	*A Testament of Hope: The Essential Writings of Martin Luther King Jr.* San Francisco: Harper & Row, 1986.
Peter S. Wenz	*Abortion Rights as Religious Freedom.* Philadelphia: Temple University Press, 1992.
Jack C. Westman, ed.	*Who Speaks for the Children? The Handbook of Individual and Class Child Advocacy.* Sarasota, FL: Professional Resource Exchange, 1991.
Garry Wills	*Under God: Religion and American Politics.* New York: Simon & Schuster, 1990.

Index

217
Reitman v. Mulkey (1967), 111
religion
    art offensive to, 111, 112, 113, 115,
        117, 118
    discrimination against, 149-156
    during colonial period, 125-126,
        158-159
    freedom of, 137-138
        also means freedom from, 157-163
        court has not protected, 154
        reasons for establishing, 155-156,
            159
    Jefferson's views of, 124, 125,
        127-128, 132-133
    opposes personal liberty, 140-141
    promotes democracy, 144, 145, 147
    social problems and, 146-147
    U.S. founders favored, 132-133,
        134, 147
    con, 137
    see also church-state separation
Renton v. Playtime Theatres (1986),
    100-101
reproductive rights
    censorship and, 80
    importance of, 28, 30, 31
    right to life outweighs, 34-36
Reynolds v. U.S. (1879), 125
Richmond Newspapers, Inc. v. Virginia,
    48-49
Richmond v. J.A. Croson Co. (1989),
    196, 197, 209, 212
right to be left alone. *See* autonomy,
    individual; privacy, right to
Roe v. Wade (1973), 29, 33, 214, 215
Ruckdaschel-Haley, Kim, 44
Runyon v. McCrary (1976), 209, 210
Rutledge, Wiley, 132, 133

St. Paul, Minnesota, hate-speech
    ordinance, 94
Salholz, Eloise, 173
Samar, Vincent J., 17
Scalia, Antonin, 94, 134
schools
    affirmative action needed in, 95,
        196, 197, 198, 199
    censorship in, 77, 80-81
    desegregation of, 210, 211
    dropping out of, 176, 180
    gay teachers in, 186-187, 192
    integration needed in, 205-206
    prayer in, 130, 136, 150, 158, 161,
        162-163
    religion in, 152, 153, 160, 162
Serrano, Andres, 117
sex

among teenagers, 29, 146, 180-181
    social prudishness about, 105, 107
sex education, 30, 31, 155
sexual freedom, 28, 30, 31
sexual harassment, 95
Showers, H. Robert, 96
Sidis v. F-R Publishing Corp., 42
SIECUS Report, 186
*Skinner v. Railway Labor Executives
    Association,* 211
slander, 98, 99
slaves, 168, 202, 214, 215
Sommerville, John, 177
songs, censorship of, 93
Souter, David, 200
speech, freedom of
    is not absolute, 99-102
    is threatened, 83
    public opinion of, 82, 218
    restriction of
        denying subsidies to art
            con, 114-119
            pro, 109-113
        hate speech
            con, 90-95
            pro, 85-89
        St. Paul ordinance, 94
        state laws on, 94-95
        threatens other speech, 93
            con, 88-89
        pornography
            con, 103-108
            pro, 96-102
        reasons against, 79-84
        reasons for, 71-78
            criminal ideas, 74-75
            media's obstruction of justice,
                74
            prurient violence, 75-77
            threatens democracy, 81, 84
        types not protected, 97, 98
Sproul, R.C., 32
State v. Evjue, 42
Steele, Shelby, 201
Stevens, John Paul, 110-111
Stevens, Thaddeus, 214, 217
*Stories of Mistrust and Manipulation:
    The Electronic Monitoring of the
    American Workforce*, 56
Sumner, William, 217
Supreme Court, U.S., 34
    balancing test for conflicting rights,
        41-42
    defined privacy right too broadly,
        24
    rulings of
        censoring student newspapers,
            80-81